Persian Postcards

Persian Postcards

Iran After Khomeini

Fred A. Reed

Talonbooks   Vancouver   1994

Copyright © 1994 Fred A. Reed

Published with the assistance of the Canada Council.

Talonbooks
201 - 1019 East Cordova
Vancouver, British Columbia
Canada V6A 1M8

Typeset in Goudy and printed and bound in Canada by Hignell Printing Ltd.

First Printing: August 1994

Canadian Cataloguing in Publication Data

Reed, Fred A., 1939-
Persian postcards

ISBN 0-88922-351-3

1. Iran—Social conditions—1979- 2. Iran—Politics and government—1979- I. Title.
HN670.2.A8R43 1994   955'.54   C94-910660-7

Contents

Acknowledgements

Many have contributed to the publication of this book over these, the first nine years of my fascination with and affection for Iran and the Iranians. Mohammad Moghadam, David Sherman, Julian Samuel and Thierry Hentsch had the kindness to read sections of the manuscript. Their comments and criticism were invaluable, though I assume full responsibility for any inaccuracies.

Zafar Bangash, Ron Hallis and Hussein Taylor helped bring about my first trip to the Islamic Republic. In Iran, I owe particular and heart-felt thanks to Dr. Ali Arabmazar, Seyyed Mohammad Hosseini, Reza Seppas, Hassan Abdulrahman, and Fereydoun Saffarnia, as well as to many Iranians in all walks of life, several of whom appear in these pages. Others, given the sensitivity of the issues involved or of their positions, cannot be named.

Bernard Hourcade, Director of the Institut français d'études irani-ennes, was unfailingly generous with his time and his insight, both in Paris and Tehran. In Montréal, David Homel, Jacques Bouchard, André Patry, Victor El-Kik and Gilles Gougeon provided support that was as timely as it was crucial. It is a pleasure to be associated in print with Michael Coyne, a photographer who combines high talent with rare understanding of a misunderstood country.

Thanks to the University of Chicago Press for permission to quote from Said Amir Arjomand's *The Shadow of God and the Hidden Imam*, and to the State University of New York Press for permission to quote from Mr. Arjomand's *Authority and Political Culture in Shi'ism*; to the Center for Middle Eastern Studies of the University of Texas at Austin for permission to quote from *Stories by Iranian Women Since the Revolution*, compiled and translated by Soraya Paknazar Sullivan; to the University Press of America, for permission to quote from M. R. Ghanoonparvar's *Prophets of Doom: Literature as a Socio-Political Phenomenon in Modern Iran*; to Weidenfield and Nicholson, for permission to quote from Bernard Lewis' *The Assassins: A Radical Sect in Islam*; to Yale University Press, for permission to quote from James F. Bill's *The Eagle and the Lion*; to Librairie Arthème Fayard, for permission to quote, in compressed form, from Yann Richard's *L'Islam chi'ite*; and to to Black Rose Books, for permission to quote from Thierry Hentsch's *Imagining the Middle East*, a book whose spirit informs these pages.

Acknowledgements are also due to the authors and publishers of other books quoted directly or indirectly, paraphrased or mentioned:

Téhéran: au dessous du volcan (Paris: *Autrement*, hors-série no. 27, 1987); Ruthven, Malise, *Islam in the World* (New York: Oxford UP, 1984); Rypka, Jan, *History of Persian Literature* (Dordrecht: D. Reidel, 1968); Burman, Edward, *The Assassins: Holy Killers of Islam* (London: Crucible, 1988); Dashti, Ali, *In Search of Omar Khayyam* (London: George Allen & Unwin); Bartol, Vladimir, *Alamut* (Paris: Phébus, 1988); Shariati, Ali, *Shahadat* (Tehran: n.d.), *Fatima is Fatima* (Tehran: The Shariati Foundation); *Religious Inspiration in Iranian Art* (Tehran: Negarestan Museum, 1978); Algar, Hamid, *The Roots of the Islamic Revolution* (The Open Press, 1984); Rahnema, Ali and Farhad Nomani, *The Secular Miracle* (London: Zed Books); Adelkhah, Farida, *La révolution sous le voile: Femmes islamiques d'Iran* (Paris: Éditions Karthala, 1988); Mohtahhari, Mortada, *The Rights of Women in Islam* (Tehran: 1981); Frye, Richard N., *The Golden Age of Persia* (London: Weidenfeld and Nicholson, 1975); Al-e Ahmad, Jalal, *Occidentosis* (Berkeley: Mizan Press, 1984); Grabar, Oleg, *The Formation of Islamic Art* (New Haven: Yale UP, 1973); Allen Terry, *Five Essays on Islamic Art* (Solipsis Press); Morgan, David, *Medieval Persia: 1040-1797* (London: Longman, 1988); Pope, Arthur Upham, *Introducing Persian Architecture* (Tehran: Soroush Press, 1969).

I am especially grateful to the Akhbar News Agency in Tehran for having put its archives at my disposal.

Portions of this book first appeared in a different form in *Le Devoir* and *La Presse*, *The Globe and Mail*, and on CBC Radio's *Ideas*, as part of a three-hour program on the Islamic Revolution, elegantly produced — as is her custom — by Jane Lewis. I am grateful to Dinos Siotis, whose Athenian literary periodical, *Revmata*, published a shorter, Greek-language version of Chapter 1, *Tehran Blues*, in its June, 1992 issue.

A portion of the research, as well as of the writing of *Persian Postcards*, was made possible by a grant from the Canada Council. And in Talonbooks, I believe this book has found, through the vagaries of what James Joyce called the commodius vicus of recirculation, the publisher for which it was destined.

Finally, I owe a special debt of gratitude to my children, Eleni and Anthony, for their often wryly critical, but unfailingly intelligent, inquiring and faithful support. But the task of marshalling the scattered notes, tapes and memories of nine years, and of investing them with the critical mass necessary to write these *Persian Postcards* would have been unthinkable without the vital sustenance — and the graceful forebearance — of my wife Ingeborg. This book is for her.

On completion of an enterprise, its faults will be revealed, and when it is said that an affair is concluded, anticipate its deterioration and dissipation.

— Imam Ali

Lime mine, Northern Iran. Photo © Michael Coyne / The Image Bank.

Foreword

The eye cannot see the eye.
— Roberto Calasso, *The Marriage of Cadmus and Harmony*

I WENT TO IRAN for the simplest of reasons: to see for myself. The reasons that led to this book are only slightly less simple: to bear witness, to uphold the multifaceted complexity of real events, and to submit our prejudices as Westerners to the same scrutiny I proposed to bring to bear on Iran's Islamic revolutionaries.

WHEN THE REGIME of the defunct former Shah, Mohammad Reza Pahlavi — he of Richard Nixon's "island of stability" — collapsed in February, 1979, friends of liberty everywhere rejoiced. The tyrant's admirers were, after all, as few as his enemies were many. Those were the best of times: Montréal's premier Persian restaurant served free meals. Tehran, in the throes of revolutionary ferment, was a focal point of world media attention, a city fecund with potentialities. Western experts and authorities proffered unsolicited advice; editorialists handed down ringing pronouncements.

But reality quickly — and powerfully — reasserted itself. As the revolution unfolded, driven by an impetus uniquely its own, forces that seemed dark and obscure overwhelmed those of what we are wont to call, in the oddly naïve shorthand of Western public discourse, "democracy and freedom."

In December of that same year, unarmed university students loyal to none but Ayatollah Ruhollah Khomeini stormed the American Embassy, disarmed the terrified Marine guards, took the embassy personnel hostage, and proceeded to publish the hitherto secret information they found there, implicating the United States in damaging espionage activities. The secular provisional government fell, to be replaced by a Shi'ite Muslim theocracy. Antipathy for the Iranian revolution in the West began to grow, with overt hostility not far behind. When Iraqi troops, undissuaded by the West, crossed the border into Iranian territory in September, 1980, few voices were raised in protest against this act of aggression.

As the Shi'ite Muslim clerical class strengthened its grip on power, formerly well-disposed commentators and experts in our latitudes began to depict the Islamic regime as an obscurantist throwback to the dark ages. In a few short years the demonization of Iran, and of its animating force, Islam, was complete. "These people," the subtext read, "are not like us." Iran had become a baleful, malevolent Other, the focus of our repressed fears. A mirror in which our own unavowed myths were confirmed over and over, to the drone of some forgotten, incomprehensible, but still powerful western European liturgy.

AS A JOURNALIST, I had acquired some understanding of the malleability of human consciousness that allowed practitioners of our trade to be swept along by prevailing political winds, or to be seduced — as the rabbit by the python — by *raison d'État*. As a former employee of a Canadian press conglomerate, I had gained insight into the way news is structured: not in the service of truth, but in the cause of increased revenue and its attendant socio-political considerations, or vice versa. As an ex-American, I had developed particular sensitivity to the dedication of the United States government to the promotion and protection of its imperial project, however fulsome the vocabulary in which that project is framed.

Common sense kept whispering in my ear. If the ruling establishment in the West so loathed Iran's new rulers, might these mysterious men of the cloth have a positive aspect? Might their invocation of revealed religion in response to a secular ideology provide answers to Muslims — or even to us — by asking questions which we had learned to avoid politely, or to dismiss haughtily? Might the fiasco of the failed hostage rescue mission in the Iranian desert near Tabas have been due to divine intervention? Less speculatively, how serious were American attempts to organize a military *coup* to kill Khomeini and thwart the Islamic revolutionaries? How respectful of Iran's national sovereignty were these efforts? Questions, questions. The *mollahs*, I concluded, had reason to be suspicious. Their hostility could be understood. Whatever the case, their side of the story was not being told.

I was curious. Curious about the power and the roots of these peculiar, category-defying insurrectionists who had founded a modern parliamentary theocracy. About their ability to marshall a powerful majority; to outmanoeuvre and politically defeat their secular foes; to revive a retrograde — so the linear ideology of progress assures us — code of social behaviour and public morals. I set out to learn more. This book is a chronicle of that process.

MY FIRST VISIT to Iran took place in the summer of 1985. Visa clearance came while my wife and I were vacationing in the Greek island of Chios, within hailing distance of Asia Minor. The Islamic Republic, locked in bitter combat with Iraq, was understandably reluctant to admit journalists in general, let alone Canadian free lancers. More than eighteen months after my first application, after recommendations by colleagues sympathetic to Iran, assurances, reassurances and bouts of despair at ever setting foot in Tehran, the door had finally cracked open. When I stepped off the Iran Air flight from Athens onto the tarmac at Mehrabad airport, the hot night air enveloped me like a velvet glove.

Once there, and on subsequent trips, I set myself the task of trying to understand how a frail, elderly man with a soft, intense and sorrowful voice, could move millions of men and women to tears, to action, to self-abnegation, and ultimately, to face death without apparent fear. Was Islamic Iran a nation gone mad, in the grip of mass psychosis? Was it a country reaching out for a lost identity?

The sense of obligation to ask these questions has brought me back to Islamic Iran eleven times over the last nine years. And though most of my visits have been brief, each has been intense and fruitful: in glimpses into the character of a society, and in the richness of the sights, sounds, smells and textures of everyday life. Finally, in the winter of 1992-93, I lived for two months in Tehran, with brief forays afield to glorious turquoise and ochre Isfahan, to dour, dusty Qom, to Kashan and Shiraz.

In the course of these visits I attended plays and concerts, wandered the streets, strolled in parks, visited museums, waited for interviews in the anterooms of government officials or in the corridors of hospitals, took tea with villagers, inspected dirt-poor agricultural projects and grandiose irrigation schemes, rode in Toyota Land Cruisers, Cadillacs and Paykans, overflew the enormous crowds at Imam Khomeini's funeral in an Iranian Air Force Chinook helicopter, suffered heat exhaustion and dysentery, endured body searches by diligent young revolutionary guards, met remarkable men and women, encountered a far lesser portion of scoundrels and knaves masquerading as pious believers.

Though I saw many armed men, I met no terrorists. Though I heard the stories of many common people who had every reason to be emotional, I met few fanatics. I ate at the tables of ordinary Iranians, shared with them hearty, simple fare or sophisticated many-course banquets, all served in an atmosphere of warmth and hospitality unique to the Islamic world. I made fast friendships, lasting acquaintances, met religious leaders and dissidents, supporters of the regime and opponents. To each of them I attempted to listen with an open mind.

The argument of this book is a simple one: there are at least two sides to every story. But it is also complex. North Americans have access to a wealth of accounts of the Islamic revolution. Most of these accounts are written from the point of view of the vanquished, or examined from the standpoint of what the United States might have done to avoid "losing" Iran, as the tongue always returns to the aching tooth. We have suffered through *Not Without My Daughter* — book and film — and assumed its unique, and sententious, case history to be the general truth about Iranian society.

Bluntly put, these accounts and interpretations of events are of little help in putting into a clearer perspective the distorted image of Iran that we ourselves have helped create. They reveal, too, a deeper, historical constant: "More than in any other region of the globe, the political incoherence of the Western powers in the Middle East clearly shows that policy is shaped not only by material or strategic imperatives, but also by passions to which the leaders and the peoples of the Occident are largely oblivious," writes Thierry Hentsch.[1] Perhaps over-optimistically, I hoped my approach to Iran was, if not free of these passions, at least informed by awareness of their pervasiveness in shaping our way of looking at the world.

ONE OF THE BEDROCK certainties of Islamic Iran is its unpredictability. The ruling establishment of *mollahs*, the Shi'ite Muslim equivalent of clergymen (though we must speak cautiously of a "clergy" in Islam, where no formal intermediary stands between God and the believer) may well be staunchly conservative. Its technocrat allies, however, are young, aggressive and intelligent modernizers. Not the least of the country's self-enfolding paradoxes — a recurring theme in these pages — is the dovetailing of Islamic orthodoxy with modernity.

Efforts to convince us that the end of history is at hand must, of course, be dismissed with the scorn that they deserve. The future resists our attempts to force it into the straightjacket of inevitability, to lead it through the flaming hoops of an economic determinism no more sophisticated than now-moribund Marxism. Examined in the context of Iran, this unpredictability makes the task of suggesting the future a particularly challenging one. What yesterday seemed carved from the most time-resistant stone may, tomorrow, prove suddenly friable. Ask the Shah's men.

In the Islamic Republic, as elsewhere, institutions are the creation of men. Only the Qur'an, the fulcrum, is the work of God. Already the constitution has been amended once, to establish a strong presidency tailored to Ali Akbar Hashemi Rafsanjani, variously described as a politician in a cleric's robe, as "Akbar Shah," and as the King of Pistachios. (The president's family, from the pistachio-growing town of Rafsanjan, controls the lucrative nut export trade, Iran's second largest source, after carpets, of non-oil revenue.) It may be changed again, if the religious establishment, through Rafsanjani, cannot solidly establish not only its capacity to overthrow a regime, but its ability to create a new one.

I RETURNED TO IRAN in early June, 1994, for the ceremony marking the fifth anniversary of the death of Imam Khomeini. It took place in the mausoleum which marks his grave. But where millions had converged on a hot day in June, 1989, today a select crowd of only a few tens of thousands was present. What has become, over these five years, a place of pilgrimage had been transformed for a day into a political forum designed to illustrate the continuity of the religious leadership. As if it were sufficient to appear beside the Imam's grave to be touched by his charisma.

Uptown, in every office and public space in Tehran, large portraits of the late Imam hang side by side with those of Seyyed Ali Khamene'i, the current Spiritual Guide. Where President Rafsanjani's portrait is present, it is placed a notch lower on the wall. But perhaps the most striking change in hierarchical standing is on display in the arrival hall at Mehrabad airport. There, on the wall facing the ranked portraits, glares a huge illuminated billboard advertising Coca-Cola.

The symbolism is lost on no one. Coca-Cola is the designated vehicle for *rapprochement* with the erstwhile Great Satan. While Iran's inveterate cola drinkers, fed up with poor quality domestic products, rushed to Coke, its introduction also touched off sharp public criticism, even student demonstrations. And as Iran's national currency, the rial, continues to fall in relation to the country's real currency of reference, the American dollar, economic discontent threatenes to boil over into political and social unrest.

Once hailed as Iran's saviour, President Rafsanjani now looks on in apparent helplessness at his eroding power. His ambitious economic plans, designed to hasten post-war reconstruction, are seen by most

Iranians to have failed. However, some commentators argue — accurately, in my view — that the president's economic policy is, in fact, succeeding. It has further concentrated wealth, produced several rial multi-trillionaires ("Everybody's a millionaire now," scoffed a friend), reduced the civil service, made Iran's work-force more "productive," and run up a substantial foreign debt: all necessary preliminaries to admission into the New World Order.

The country's radical faction, though out of power, has tried to play on concerns that Iran is moving too rapidly to embrace the very ideas — and the source of those ideas, the United States — that it rejected *en masse* in 1979. Ayatollah Khamene'i, who under the constitution holds supreme spiritual as well as temporal power (the Guide commands the armed forces, and may ratify the dismissal of the president), is said to favour a more cautious, balanced approach, playing the United States against its European economic and political adversaries, led by a resurgent Germany whose historic interest in Iran remains constant. But others describe the tug-of-war between the two religious dignitaries as a struggle between the two conservative factions who had earlier joined forces to push aside the "radicals."

SINCE THIS BOOK was written, Iran's grass-roots revolutionary institutions, the neighbourhood-based *Komiteh* and the revolutionary guards, have been merged into a single, country-wide corps amusingly, though accurately, referred to as the "disciplinary forces." Public security may have been rationalized, but surveillance of citizens, while capricious, remains a fact of life. The intellectual climate in 1994, several dissidents told me, was more oppressive than at any time since the first, tumultuous years of the revolution. Newspaper editors have been arrested and held without charges; writers are unable to publish; leading intellectuals have been deprived of a public platform and isolated from their friends and students.

Still, one dissident confided that he had chosen to remain in Iran. "I'm fascinated by what's happening here. The future is far from sealed," he said. "Today's situation is cause for great concern, but I still believe there's hope for Iran."

IN AN AGE when visual images have become infinitely manipulable, and have thus forfeited their credibility, words alone can convey the multifaceted, fleeting, elastic yet intractable truth of memory and events. In *Persian Postcards*, I have attempted to describe — mobilizing the only forces at my disposal, the twenty-six toy soldiers of the alphabet — the depth and the complexity, the tragedy and raw beauty of this truth. Chronologically discontinuous, this book seeks to draw a deeper thematic unity from places and events: the funeral of Imam Khomeini at Behesht-e Zahra cemetery, the Assassin castle at Alamut, the great mosques of Isfahan, the shady sidewalks of Vali-ye Asr Avenue in downtown Tehran, rural reconstruction projects in the mountains of Rudbar.

Persian Postcards is not a journalistic report, an academic treatise, or a travel book, although it enfolds elements of all three. It explores an unknown quarter, a territory inhabited by people of culture, dignity and poetic genius, moved for an instant by forces which escape the omnipresent classification mania-theology of Reason and Technique. This is a book, finally, which aspires to raise many more questions than it answers. Such, I believe, is the author's duty to his readers.

TEHRAN - MONTRÉAL
JUNE, 1994

Tehran. Photo © Michael Coyne / The Image Bank.

1

Tehran Blues

ON SUMMER EVENINGS AFTER SUNDOWN when the air was hot and still, I could hear the sound of a clarinet floating above the clash of traffic on Vali-ye Asr Avenue. I walked toward it, and came upon a street musician half crouched against a crumbling ochre brick wall. Like many passersby — adolescent militiamen with close-cropped heads, women with *chadors* held tight at the chin, or ill-shaven middle-aged men carrying scuffed briefcases — I paused to enjoy the music. And as I listened, the subtlest of syncopations progressively infiltrated its Persian theme, transforming it inexorably into a tight-knit purling, an unmistakably Oriental blues. Now the contralto warble of the instrument blended with the rush of water in the *joub*, now it soared off on its own, to chirp or mock the ambient cacophony of car horns.

I returned often to the corner where the blind musician, a slight man with round dark glasses, was a nightly fixture. On Thursday, at the end of the week, I convinced my friend Ali to ask him for permission to record one of his sidewalk recitals. Ali was skeptical but finally agreed. We strolled up to the musician, waited for a pause. People were gathering, there was a hum of tension in the air. Ali spoke to him in a low voice. Then, suddenly, the clarinet player swept the handful of tattered bills and coins into his pocket, broke down his instrument, fitted it hurriedly into its case, and darted off into the darkness. I last caught sight of him as he scrambled aboard a southbound bus.

Summer, 1986. Iran was winning the desert war against Iraq. Saddam Hussein, the strongman of Baghdad and then great friend of the West in his battle against militant fundamentalism, was on the ropes. Iran's Islamic combatants, as they were called in the Tehran press, had fought their way to the outskirts of Basra, Iraq's second city and only port with access to the sea. Any day now, any week, would come Iran's Final Offensive. The Iranian capital seemed to be holding its breath. In shops, in *kebabi* houses, in cars trapped in the city's perpetual traffic tie-ups, radios were tuned to hourly battle bulletins broadcast in the sonorous, apocalyptically strident tones of Radio Tehran.

Basra would fall, went the popular semi-official scenario stimulated by Iranian war propaganda. The Iraqis would crack, Saddam would be overthrown and the Imam's revolutionary guards and young volunteers would march victoriously through Baghdad and on to liberate al-Quds — Jerusalem in Arabic. Certainly we will end the war, declared Iranian foreign ministry spokesman Hossein Sheikholeslam speaking for the record. But first, he added, Saddam — "worse than Hitler" — must go.

It looked as though the infant Islamic Republic might succeed; the dynamics of revolution have a way of quickly stepping beyond internal consolidation to active, armed propagation of the Good News. Anxiety tinged with panic flared from Baghdad to Amman to Cairo, and shortly among Saddam's patrons, creditors and arms brokers in Washington, London, Paris and Moscow. From the inside, I picked up the sense of guarded euphoria. Prices were high, of course, and walls were plastered with small posters noting the martyrdom of young men: workmates, classmates, sons and brothers and husbands. And on the sidewalks and in narrow, high-walled alleys, small impromptu altars strung with coloured lights advertised martyrs' funerals. But Iran seemed to be drawing strength from adversity, from its gritty determination to punish the invaders.

Had not Imam Khomeini warned that Iran, with its citizens' army of twenty million, would fight on for another twenty years if need be? With 60% of the country's population under age fifteen, the threat was plausible. I could feel the mood on the street. Every day, Radio Tehran signed off with *Jang, jang, ta pirouzi*, a martial song (the only kind of music permitted in public, with the barely tolerated exception of itinerant accordionists or blind clarinet players) which chanted war, war, until victory.

Foreign journalists were few, carefully chosen and closely watched. Wherever they went, spontaneous demonstrations seemed to materialize, particularly when the video cameras began to roll. Suddenly, fast-expanding nuclei of angry, bearded young men would form, brandishing their fists and chanting the litany of down withs and death tos: America, USSR, Israel.

Only a handful of Iranian officials and the inner circle of Ronald Reagan's National Security Council knew that Iran's military success had been accomplished in part with war material supplied by the arch-devil himself — Washington. The same men also knew it had been secured through an Israeli connection. What was soon to become the Iran-Contra scandal in the United States would also sow the seeds of demoralization in the country's front-line forces, prepare the ground for the dismissal of Ayatollah Hossein Ali Montazeri as appointed successor to Imam Khomeini, and sound the death knell of Iran's revolutionary experience.

SAME STREET; one year later.

Gone was the euphoria, the confidence evaporated. Capricious as a vengeful God, Iraqi missile strikes had crosshatched the urban sprawl of Tehran with piles of smouldering rubble. Windows were taped, storefronts sandbagged, bomb shelter signs had been posted at every intersection. The damage to morale was more devastating still. Iraqi chemical attacks — the tangible result of Western panic at the possibility of Saddam's collapse — had shattered the resolve of Iran's ragtag volunteer army at the front. Accustomed to surprise operations and sharp offensive thrusts, not positional, defensive warfare — nerve gas least of all — the Iranian forces were retreating. Even the Revolutionary Guards, the Pasdaran, recruited from the country's most dedicated young revolutionaries, seemed to have lost the will to die for Islam. Were they bargaining chips instead of martyrs?, they had begun to ask themselves. And on the home front, grumbling about the war became widespread and virulent. If Saddam was prepared to use chemical weapons at the front, reasoned the skeptical Tehranis, could he not also use them against Iran's cities? People began to leave town. The once-massive flow of youthful volunteers for the sacred war dropped to a trickle.

THE TEHRAN MUSEUM of modern art lies several blocks west of Vali-ye Asr Avenue in a corner of Laleh (Tulip) Park, formerly named for Farah, the ex-Shah's last wife, now for the flower emblematic of martyrdom. The museum's permanent collection, which included several French impressionists, cubists and surrealists, was removed during the war; for ideological reasons, some whispered. Now the space was used for exhibitions of photography, children's book illustrations or political cartoons.

At the annual photography show intense, bearded Islamists rub shoulders with intellectuals, still affecting the glasses-and-well-trimmed-mustache look, and with sleekly dressed women from north Tehran, wearing colourful headscarves and well-cut, broad-shouldered manteaux instead of the black *chadors* of Tehran-the-militant.

Three groups of photographs mounted in the museum's descending spiral halls are drawing large knots of people, and admiring whispers: one is a large colour print depicting the traditional domed roofs of the city of Kashan in such a way that they could be seen as a woman's bare breasts. Further on, a stark series of flash-lit black and white prints follows the last moments of a gang of rapists from the prison gates until they hang dangling from an impromptu gallows in a Tehran public square before dawn. But most people are gathered around a vertical triptych repeating the same photo of an open railway carriage window crowded with four or five young volunteers on their way to the front. In the top panel the young men are smiling, the image is clear and sharp. In the second panel, the same image, but clouds of steam from the undercarriage have begun to float upward. In the bottom panel, smoke and steam have entirely obliterated the soldiers.

The war was over, even before the shooting stopped.

AS MAIN STREETS GO, Vali-ye Asr is a masterpiece: a broad, panoramic avenue fifteen kilometres long, bordered by double rows of plane trees growing in the midst of the fast-flowing water rushing south in the *joubs*. These runoff channels-cum-gutters which line most major Tehran streets form a complex parallel network which distributes runoff water from the melting snows of the Alborz mountains throughout the city.

It was, and is, a street of shoe shops, clothing, jewelry and bookstores, movie theatres — featuring Japanese martial arts films mixed with the more refined products of the new Iranian cinema — florists and sweets shops offering glistening dates in winter, domestic iced delicacies like saffron-flavoured *bastani* or *faludé shirazi* in summer, and tea in any season. And it is a street where the political history of the proximate past is almost palpable.

Monarchist diehards were wont, in the early post-revolutionary years, to hang out in lobbies of the big international hotels and pass their idle hours buttonholing foreign journalists. How wonderful was the Shah and how great his works, they hissed. When the imperial family would return in triumph, they boasted ominously, an Islamic man of religion, a *mollah*, would be hanged from each of the thousands of plane trees. The *joubs* — now full of the flotsam and jetsam of a city without a modern sewer system — would flow red with fundamentalist gore.

But even these bloodthirsty predictions had a poetic resonance about them, a high declamatory falsity that almost, but not quite, provoked the requisite suspension of disbelief. My monarchist "sources" knew, deep down, that a return of the Pahlavi dynasty was not in the cards, and they knew I knew. Still, the fiction was diverting, agreeable in a macabre way, titillating. A sub-sub-genre of Persian poetry.

"Before," as those of a certain generation still say, it used to be called Pahlavi Avenue. "Before," when Tehran had cabarets with stunningly beautiful dancing girls, a chemistry professor whom I'll call Mr. A. told me in a fractured mixture of German and English as, from the balcony of his apartment, we surveyed the snow-capped peaks looming above Tehran turning from peach to crimson in the sunset.

Mr. A. has approached me on the street in the course of one of my leisurely evening strolls (one strolls a lot in Tehran of a summer evening). His battered Mercedes is parked outside; the apartment is spacious if Spartan, his bookshelves crammed with textbooks and the works of Iran's great poets: Ferdowsi, Sa'di and Ha'fez. His wife will be arriving any minute, he says. You are our guest. After a crippling automobile accident, Mr. A can no longer teach full-time; his wife is the main breadwinner, her earnings supplementing part-time teaching and a modest pension which is, itself, being continuously undermined by inflation. There are rationing coupons of course, so the couple can still afford modest quantities of imported frozen meat and chicken. Luxury is as remote a memory as the dancing girls.

Mrs. Professor bursts into the house, the fabric of her *chador* rustling. But within seconds the *chador* is gone, and the woman, who could well have been a cabaret dancer "before," holds out her hand in welcome. Two things had just happened which, in Islamic Iran, would now be unthinkable in public. For a woman to appear bare-headed and bare-armed in front of a total stranger, a male stranger, and to offer him her hand, would have touched off a minor disturbance, complete with the quick appearance of unmarked cars filled with the stern bearded youths and austere ladies of the *Komiteh* — the Islamic morality enforcement squad.

However this is not happening in public, but in the privacy of the professor's home. And in Islamic Iran, the privacy of a man's home is proverbial, providing his public demeanour does not draw undue attention to himself, and providing neighbours, whose motivation might range from the desire to appear holier than thou to jealousy, do not talk. A bowl of fruit, accompanied by dishes of nuts and raisins, appears on the table; Mr. A's wife brings tea, and he launches into a long recitation of poetry, rich with the rounded vowels and melodic gutturals of classical Farsi.

Mohammad Mossadeq is his favourite politician, he tells me. Mossadeq was the patrician prime minister who nationalized Iranian oil in 1951 with the support of a section of the Shi'ite clerical establishment led by Ayatollah Kashani. Two years later, deserted by his clerical allies, he was overthrown by the CIA-sponsored coup d'état of 1953. The coup, plotted by Kermit Roosevelt and General Norman Schwartzkopf, father of the victor of Kuwait, was aided and abetted by a coterie of American "Iran hands," including a *New York Times'* journalist purchased for the occasion to depict the Mossadeq government as a virtual captive of the Soviet Union. Mossadeq's movement was defeated, fractured when Kashani — as well as the Communist Tudeh party — withdrew support; but his defeat helped spawn the upheaval of 1979.

Immediately after the fall of the Shah, as religious, leftist and traditional nationalist forces contended for power, the government of the first revolutionary prime minister, Mehdi Bazargan, baptized Pahlavi Avenue "Mossadeq" Avenue. Even the most obdurate Islamists had to accord the wily old politician some credit for having dared, back then, what the mainstream clergy could or would not do until almost thirty years later: take on Uncle Sam. But as Khomeini's followers gradually consolidated their positions, street names followed suit, marking the symbolic progression from imperial to nationalist to religious. Pahlavi, which had become Mossadeq, now became Vali-ye Asr. The name means "Lord of the Age" and stands for al-Mahdi, the Twelfth and ultimate Imam of Shi'ite theology, the Messiah whose reappearance after centuries in occultation will signal the birth of a new world of justice.

24

The significance of the progression was lost on no one. Pseudo-dynastic Iran, then liberal nationalism, were consigned to the trash-bin of history. Henceforth, all wishing to travel back and forth between the depths and the heights of Tehran would travel along the path of the Twelfth Imam or they would not travel at all.

During the heroic years of the revolution, Vali-ye Asr was the street through which demonstrations flowed. I recall one such march, organized by the Tehran University Islamic students' association to support the volunteers at the war front, and to bolster flagging morale on the home front. At the head of the procession marched a compact group of particularly intense young men, each wearing a white shroud signifying their willingness to die a martyr's death. At the middle of the procession, directly behind the sound truck, came a large contingent of young women in *chadors*, clutching schoolbooks in one hand, their voices shrill and hard with defiance, yet sweet and poignant.

As the marchers surged up the street in the dusty dappled shade of the plane trees, a flying squad of two-wheelers preceded them, sweeping the pavement clear of pedestrians. Meanwhile, on the sidewalks, shoppers went studiously about their business without so much as a passing glance, perhaps even inwardly cursing the sputtering phalanx of motorbikes.

Men on motorbikes — young men, husbands with wives riding postillion, grizzled older men — were one of the constant dangers to be faced when crossing the broad avenues. Traffic laws in Tehran seemed designed to be mocked, but the two-wheelers, in their tens of thousands, raised this mockery to a high science. Bus lanes, one-way streets, sidewalks...nowhere seemed safe from their high speed manoeuvring and the insouciant stares of their riders. Later I learned why. One of the most successful innovations of Iran's outgunned Revolutionary Guard forces in the early days of the desert war was the use of irregular motorcycle-mounted cavalry. Riding powerful Honda, Kawasaki or Suzuki motocross bikes purchased by contributions from mosques in villages and towns, teams of two daredevils — a driver and an RPG (rocket propelled grenade) launcher operator — would engage Iraq's Soviet-built main battle tanks, often in broad daylight. Too quick for the cumbersome tanks to draw a bead on, the motorcycles would close to short range, fire, and then dart away across the hard-packed desert terrain at break-neck speed.

Iranian friends' eyes lit up as they described how adolescent Tehranis took pride in practising their moves in city traffic, as if to say: if we can survive this, the Iraqi tanks are a piece of cake.

MEYDAN VALI-YE ASR — Vali-ye Asr Square — with its fountain, its demonic traffic, its layabouts, beggars and Islamic committeemen, marks the midpoint of the long ascent from the dust and poverty of the south to the cool, tree shaded suburbs of the north. The street is Tehran's geographic and social backbone. Until the consolidation of the Islamic regime, the capital's highly stratified divisions of class and wealth correlated almost exactly with altitude. South Tehran was for the poor; the city centre, just slightly to the north, for the government employees and the well-established middle class; the north was for the rich. And while the rich might travel south, the poor would never go north. In 1925, Iran's first constitutional government was overthrown by Reza Khan, the semi-literate but cunning commander of the Cossack brigade. A year later, under the benevolent eye of Great Britain, then the protecting power, Reza Khan crowned himself Reza Shah, founded the ersatz dynasty of the Pahlavis, and proceeded to drag Iran, kicking and screaming, into what he fancied was the European twentieth century.

Modelled on the reforms of Kemal Attatürk in neighbouring Turkey — but without the benefit of Attatürk's credentials as a revolutionary leader — Reza Shah's urban planning (and social engineering) program was carried out at bayonet point. When he laid out the avenue which he had ordained would bear his name in perpetuity, he meant it to symbolize his own ascent from the facelessness of poverty in the south to power and affirmation of identity in the north. As a usurper, he well grasped the mortal danger surrounding him. As a military man, he needed rapid lines of communication, a way of getting troops into position to protect his hated regime from the cauldron of mass discontent bubbling in the southern slums.

The Islamic Revolution would reverse all that. The upsurge of the *mostazafin*, the disinherited, the urban villagers, the dispossessed, the lumpenproletariat, the millions who poured into the streets at the call of an elderly cleric who offered them only sacrifice as a certainty, would turn Tehran — and Iran — upside down.

South Tehran, south of the bazaar, in the crowded quarters around the railway station, was, and still is, a country within a country, a bottomless manpower reserve, an urban mob, a riot waiting to happen, a maelstrom of revolutionary energy and political resentment. During the war with Iraq, foreign journalists bold enough to venture into these dust-clogged narrow streets where the mosques are built of the same ochre brick as the dilapidated apartment buildings and shops, where the water runs turbid brown in the *joubs* and sheep are sacrificially slaughtered on the sidewalks, were met with wild-eyed chanting: *Allah-o Akbar, Khomeini rahbar!* (God is great! Khomeini is our leader!)

They meant it. This was to be their revolution. They were the foot soldiers of the Imam, the men and women who offered their chests to the Shah's machine guns. When the urban guerillas — the *mujahidin* and the *fedayin* — along with Islamic committees, distributed arms captured from the Imperial Guard or the police to the populace, they took them up. When the religious authorities called back the arms, they returned them. And when Imam called for more sacrifice, they marched off to war and death. Before they had nothing; now, they were as water mingling with a great torrent. Before they had been less than dirt; now they *were* the revolution; they had respect, self-esteem. Hope. Ambition.

> *Rain shall destroy the southern part of the city*
> *Rain*
> > *shall destroy*
> > > *the southern part of the city.*
> *And I, astonishingly, will not be sad.*
> *[...]*
> *The southern part of the city shall be destroyed*
> *And there is no room at all for sorrow,*
> > *no room at all for sorrow:*
> *The southern part of the city MUST be destroyed.*
> *[...]*
> *Who says that destruction is not a sight to see?*
> *Who says that destruction is sorrowful?*
> *The southern part of the city shall be destroyed*
> *And there is no room at all for sorrow:*
> *The southern part of the city shall be*
> > *destroyed by the water's debris*
> *And the northern part of the city*
> *By the destruction of the south.*[2]

SPRING 1991. On a long stroll down Kargar Street which runs parallel to Vali-ye Asr from north to south, my friend Hassan and I encounter little of that early revolutionary fervour. Hassan has just returned to Tehran after eleven years studying and working in Canada. He knows the city, and yet he cannot recognize it. The streets are the same, the names different. His city map is in tatters from constant folding and unfolding, he seems almost lost in a once-familiar world that has become unutterably foreign.

Young men dressed in dirty military uniforms, shoes with broken-down heels, grease-stained service caps, congregate at the main intersections. The uniform, says Hassan, is probably all they have to wear. They wait patiently, under the burning sun, for the hope of a construction job or a day's work on a municipal clean-up crew. Or perhaps they will spend their last *tomans* on smuggled cigarettes, to be resold individually. Buy wholesale, sell retail: the fibre of commerce, as any merchant knows. In butcher shops just below Enqelab (Revolution) Square customers who can afford it purchase several kilos of meat, usually thawed imported frozen beef or lamb. Then they walk several hundred metres south and sell the meat along the sidewalk in smaller servings. Poor Tehran families come here to buy a lump of bone, fat and gristle for the week's *ab-gusht*, a slow-simmering stew of chick-peas and fatty meat pounded with a pestle and eaten with torn bread.

Hassan had not expected this. A man who endured physical and social abuse in Canada for his support of Khomeini — a tough position to take, especially in the sharply divided Iranian exile community — he anticipated a new social order, a sense of justice, a will to redress the evils of the *ancien régime*. Now, he whispers to me where no one might possible overhear, things are as bad, or worse. "What has happened to the Islamic revolution?"

As we walk further south, the crowds grow more dense; commercial activity has spilled out onto the sidewalks. Whole blocks have been taken over by open-air machine shops, where everything from small electric motors to diesel truck engines are torn down, rebuilt and replacement parts are machined on the spot. A choking bluish haze of exhaust fumes — omnipresent component of the smellscape of Tehran — hangs in the air; the sidewalk is black and slippery with motor-oil; the mechanics and their apprentice boys look like archetypal grease monkeys, like the stokers on a Travenesque death ship, like survivors of a refinery disaster.

To our right is the former "New Town," Tehran's once notorious red-light district. Up until 1979, the area drew crowds every night of the week; traffic congestion was as endemic as venereal disease. Now nothing remains of the "zone" — the houses of ill-repute have been bulldozed, the prostitutes rounded up for "rehabilitation." A medical clinic has been built, and parks — more accurately, open fields planted with scraggly trees — established among the poor brick houses and tiny shops.

But the destruction of the whorehouse quarter, coupled with the advent of Shi'ite orthodoxy, has not meant the end of prostitution. In a country where an entire generation of once and future husbands now lies buried at Behesht-e Zahra cemetery or languishes in the wards of military hospitals, a corresponding generation of women must face the rigours of Iran's free-fall free market economy and strict family-oriented social code on their own.

Finally we reach the railway station, where the tracks demarcate the southern limits of the old city. We wander down the concourse, checking the schedules. You can catch an express to Istanbul or to Mashhad; a local to Qazvin or Qom, although most Iranians travel by bus or air these days. Rolling stock has not recovered from the war, when the railroad carried troops and supplies south to the front. But Hassan swears by the railway. Sure it may take a bit longer, but anything is safer than Iran's notorious Cooperative bus lines, whose coaches can often be encountered racing one another nose-to-nose down two-lane highways. And with less-than-cost-price tickets for domestic flights, Iran Air is virtually always booked solid weeks in advance.

My eyes wander over the echoing arrival hall. The building is monumental, overbearing, with a distinctly non-Iranian feel. To my surprise, I notice swastika motifs set in plaster relief on the ceiling. Later I learn that the structure was designed and built by German experts in the late '30s, at the height of Shah Reza's enduring infatuation for fellow Aryan Adolf Hitler. It was precisely this infatuation that convinced the anti-Axis powers — Britain, the Soviet Union and the United States — to dismiss the Shah, and to replace him with his feckless, vainglorious and malleable son Mohammad Reza. Loathsome though the Iranian Nazi sympathizers were, however, the communists were even more so in the prescient eyes of the Allies. Among the lesser-of-two-evils later to be granted new life in anti-communist garb was Fazlollah Zahedi, who became CIA-supported prime minister in the aftermath of the 1953 *coup*.

Examples of the proto-Nuremburg brutalism which gave symbolic weight to official Iranian sympathy for the Third Reich can still be seen in the downtown area, particularly in a former barracks west of Imam Khomeini Square, but these remains are slowly giving way to the wrecker's ball and urban renewal projects. The reasons are more economic than aesthetic: most Tehranis are unlikely to weep at their passing — although the philosopher Martin Heidegger still has his admirers at the Tehran University philosophy faculty. And Bahram Shahrokh, the unrepentant acolyte of Joseph Goebbels, who once flourished as the Shah's minister of propaganda, may well have secreted a residue of crypto master-race theory among the now-dormant but not extinct Pahlavi faction.[3] But other survivals of the Pahlavi era's great sympathy for the Nazis — including many of the massive German-designed buildings which today house much of the state and military bureaucracy — still continue to stand, sullen reminders of the ambiguity of relations between Germany and Iran.

Not far from the station, Hassan and I ease into a coffeehouse for a breather and some refreshment. Coffeehouses in Iran serve no coffee, only small glass tumblers of tea, along with tomato omelets cooked in tiny skillets, and fragrant fresh-baked Persian bread. The presence of a foreigner sets tongues wagging. And the tongues speak about inflation, economic hardship, unemployment. But wait. One of the tea drinkers is a demobilized non-commissioned officer and government supporter. "Sure, life is tough," he admits. "But we're managing. What do you expect after eight years of war?"

The fifty-six-year-old father of six, and grandfather of four, quickly strays across the official line and into slippery terrain. Tehran (still one of the safest of the ex-Third World's exponentially expanding mega-cities) is facing an upsurge of criminality, he complains. The coffeehouse is perched on the outer edge of the city's Shush and Molavi district, notorious even among Tehranis for the gangs of indolent young men who roam its narrow, winding streets in search of excitement. "It's because people are poor; people are hungry; what are they supposed to do? Look, this is capitalist society, and that makes life difficult. My army pension won't even pay my rent."

What kind of people live in the neighbourhood?

"Manual workers, small traders, refugees, peasants from the villages looking for work, unemployed people." And, from the back of the tiny café, another, louder voice, from a younger man, his eyes glazed by a combination of despair and narcotics: "Many unemployed. Why don't you tell the truth about how things are? We're starving! Me, I studied for fifteen years, and now I have to sell cigarettes in the street."

IN A COUNTRY AS OLD as civilization Tehran is a new town, a boom town, a town built on oil revenue, real estate and currency speculation, public administration, and of course, corruption: an exponentially expanding megalopolis. The architectural glories of traditional Iran are elsewhere — in Isfahan and Kashan. The religious roots of Islamic revolution are elsewhere — in Qom and Mashhad and Tabriz.

But the Islamic revolution had to conquer Tehran; had to unhorse the emperor, as Mao Zedong the poet used to put it. Pahlavi Avenue traced a curving route from the dust and poverty of south Tehran, where rural migrants set up housekeeping in the *gowds* — shallow pits excavated to supply the stinking brick works that line the city's industrial perimeter. The emperor, however, lived at the other extremity, in Shemiran, among the verdant foothills of the Alborz range, whose snow-capped peaks float above the city on a clear day.

When Tehran became the capital of Iran in 1789, the city centre lay halfway between the bazaar and the royal palace of the ruling Qajar dynasty. And there it remained, until the arrival of Reza Shah. The population of the city then stood at 210,000. During the years preceding World War II, the centre gradually shifted north as the capital's population continued to expand. The embassies of Great Britain, Germany, France, Turkey and the USSR all gravitated around Istanbul crossroads south of Ferdowsi Square. Meanwhile, the Americans built their embassy — in a compound covering an entire immense Tehran city block — to the north. Did they know, as Bernard Hourcade suggests, "that their time would come when the city center finally came to them?"[4]

Come it did — in more ways than one — in the early '60s, when Washington supplanted London as Iran's "protecting power." In October, 1964, the Majlis (Iran's parliament, which was then controlled by the Shah's hand-picked yes-men) approved a law that provided full diplomatic immunity to all American military personnel and their dependents stationed in Iran. The United States, caught up in the obsession of its holy war against communism, had been pushing hard for the legislation. Finally, Iranian government reluctance, fuelled by the knowledge of the widespread condemnation the agreement would provoke, was overcome by a $200 million loan which was to be used for the purchase of American military hardware. One day later — on the Shah's forty-fifth birthday — a religious leader little known to Western-oriented Iranians and totally unknown to Western Iran experts took the pulpit at the great Fazieh theological seminary in Qom, on the edge of the salt desert, to issue a ringing condemnation of the immunity agreement.

> They have reduced the Iranian people to a level
> lower than that of an American dog. If someone runs

over a dog belonging to an American, he will be prosecuted. Even if the shah himself were to run over a dog belonging to an American, he would be prosecuted. But if an American cook runs over the shah, the head of state, no one will have the right to interfere with him.[5]

The speaker was Ayatollah Ruhollah Khomeini: the only public figure in Iran to take such an intransigent stand against the Shah and his powerful backers, to say aloud what millions of Iranians were thinking. Sixteen years later, the Light of the Aryans, the Shah of Shahs was gone and the old, bearded man in the black turban returned to Tehran on an Air France 747 from Paris to institute the Islamic Republic.

TODAY MOHAMMAD REZA PAHLAVI is little more than a fading memory, but Tehran's verdant northern suburbs are still dominated by the palaces he and his father built. Some have been transformed into Revolutionary Guard barracks, others set aside as museums. These monumental and grotesque structures are painstakingly maintained, in contrast to almost everything else in the Islamic Republic, where public buildings and spaces tend to be dusty, weed-grown and ill-kept. Busloads of people from south Tehran and the surrounding towns are guided through, treading shoeless on the cold marble floors, gaping and whispering at the wealth and the even more prodigious bad taste of the man who sat atop the Peacock Throne. Enormous silk carpets interwoven with silver and gold thread cover the floors. Huge ceremonial halls bulge with lavish French furniture, and are hung with gold and crystal chandeliers that would have dazzled the nightly assemblies of grovelling sycophants and courtiers, diplomats, bemedalled military men, spies and Yankee hustlers. Through an open door one can glimpse the cavernous shoe closet of the then-Empress Farah, big enough to humble that of Imelda Marcos.

One gruesome legend relates that Reza Khan, unhappy with his bread one morning, ordered the offending baker baked. But his son Mohammad Reza was a weak, distrustful man, whose indecisiveness must have been in part the product of the infinite loneliness of the tyrant, of the cold, bleak isolation that still pervades this place.

Prophetically perhaps, bread was part of the younger Shah's *hubris*. Iran must be modernized, he reasoned, anticipating the New World Order. Women must not wear *chadors*, and people must eat their bread in Western-style loaves, not in the traditional large flat sheets bought hot and crisp from the tiny neighbourhood bakeries with their wood-fired clay ovens. The bakers' guild protested. The Shah began closing the bakeries. But the Tehranis refused to buy loaves. They would have their bread in sheets or not at all.

Today, the same bread provides the raw material for a home-grown, gravity-driven ecologically advanced Tehrani cottage industry: the bread-gleaning trade. Pushcart operators called namaki ("salties") begin their daily run in the high northern suburbs in the wee hours, collecting the previous day's uneaten bread from homes and shops in exchange for salt. Then they coast downhill, toward the south, stopping their carts by throwing their weight on a friction brake made from a strip of old tire carcass.

Once, late one winter's day, the taxi in which I was travelling overtook a namaki careening at breakneck speed down one of Tehran's north-south expressways, perched on the back of his cart, clutching the handles like grim death, rubber friction brake flapping crazily against the pavement. I couldn't bear to look back; looking back in Tehran traffic — as in life — can only lead to trouble. Something is bound to be overtaking you.

Come evening, carts overflowing, the namaki reach the southern districts where they are met by pickup trucks which deliver the day's haul to farms and feed lots in the region. Cows, producers of the next day's milk, and sheep, tomorrow's kebab, love the crisp, slightly salty fare.

Bread, as the Shah learned, was politics at gut level. The Islamic regime may face its stiffest test when it is forced to remove price subsidies from basic commodities — including the staff of life. Faced with the doctrinaire intransigence of the International Monetary Fund, the present government of Ali Akbar Hashemi Rafsanjani must prove its bona fides to international investment circles, even if bread prices must soar. When this happens, more than the namaki may lose their jobs.

COMMENSURATE WITH ITS STATURE as Tehran's prime thoroughfare, beggars used to flock to Vali-ye Asr Avenue. Not far from the Bostan Hotel, my residence during the exalted and fateful summer of 1986, a grimy, emaciated little boy, whose legs were covered with suppurating sores, would spend his afternoons and evenings sleeping on a scrap of cardboard in the middle of the sidewalk. Islam demands compassion in the payment of alms, but my friend Abbas was rarely in a compassionate mood, and more rarely in an alms-giving mode. "Probably makes more than I do," he grumbled as we stepped over or around the boy. Begging was one of the better trades, he said, lip curling contemptuously. The work is easy, the money is good. Why, not too long ago the authorities discovered a retired military man working as a professional beggar, and earning ten times his army pension, he expostulated.

Abbas was one of hundreds of thousands of civil servants, wretchedly paid by definition, hired to keep unemployment statistics respectable and keep the lid on social unrest. The only way to make ends meet was to take a second job. In this case it was teaching English, although Abbas' English was an approximate affair at best. Nouns and pronouns have no gender in Farsi, so his "he's" and "she's" kept getting transposed, as did "very" and "too much": clear in English, not so in Farsi. But in the realm of the blind, the one-eyed man is king.

Finally, Abbas resigned his position, and using money borrowed from his family, opened a tiny corner grocery store in one of the burgeoning suburbs. In the new Tehran recreated by the revolution, the north-south dichotomy has lost much of its old significance: Expansion has been chaotic, stretched out along broad new avenues leading south, west or east.

Here, in the flat, dusty new suburbs, a new Tehran is taking shape: an Islamic Tehran of families who rose quickly with the revolution, occupied land, threw up overnight houses, became homeowners, storekeepers, revolutionary guardsmen, workers, lower level functionaries. People with a stake in the new regime: a job, a house, social prestige, identity, each with a family or social connection — however tenuous — with a *mollah*.

COMMERCE FLOURISHES in the streets of Tehran. What economists would call entry-level entrepreneurship, what sociologists might term severe social dysfunction and what the French call "System D" (for "debrouillage," low resourcefulness combined with economic desperation), could consist of a roadside cigarette stand, or less, a perambulating purveyor of individual smokes, usually Iran-made *Tir* or contraband Winstons. (As are his dollars, the cigarettes of the Global Arrogance are esteemed, and smuggled in industrial quantities. The operation, whisper gossip-happy Tehranis, is run by the *Bonyad Mostazafin*, the powerful state-within-a-state Foundation for the Oppressed, which was originally set up to manage the assets of companies seized and nationalized when their owners fled in 1979, but rapidly transformed itself into a juggernaut for lining the pockets of its clerical advisors and their cronies.)

Those in need of pharmaceuticals need only stroll north from the bazaar on Nasr Khosrow street where, in a smaller maze of tiny shops or microscopic stalls, Tehranis come to shop for everything from prescription drugs to name-brand cosmetics. Pharmacies, including all-night affairs run by the Imam Khomeini Foundation, often do not stock all the pills, capsules, solutions and elixirs prescribed by doctors. So many citizens end up taking their prescription to Nasr Khosrow, where virtually any medicament produced in the world can be located and purchased at minimum markup. Rumour, often the only reliable source of information in Iran, insists that the drugs which find their way to Nasr Khosrow are sold to the small retailers by no less than the national ministry of health, providing the capital's hard-pressed bureaucrats with another way of keeping body and soul together and giving a typically Iranian twist to the notion of a free market.

During the work-week, nearby Lalehzar (Tulip Field) Street, running north from Imam Khomeini Square, is prosaic enough, its shops filled with electrical appliances, tools and hardware. But on Friday, it swarms with young men up from the southern districts — militiamen with shaved heads, sinister-looking layabouts, groups of urban punks with too much time and not enough money on their hands — come to try their luck in the open-air shooting galleries that materialize from nowhere, like mushrooms after a rain, only to disappear at the first hint of police or *Komiteh*. Islamic Iran's strict moral code forbids gambling, or games of chance. Chess has only recently been rehabilitated, and permanent chessboards have been set up in public parks. But the Friday denizens of Lalehzar Street probably care as little about the finer points of chess strategy as they do for the Qur'an's strictures on gambling. They want to take a shot at the target, whether it's a duck or a grimacingly evil portrait of the fiendish Saddam. As an outsider I had a sense of acute discomfort: Here the stares lacked the good-natured inquisitiveness or transient interest I had grown accustomed to on Tehran's busy sidewalks. These young men were more than curious. Better look straight ahead and walk purposefully, I said to myself as I walked quickly through the crowd. These, too, were Tehran's downtrodden — the *mostazafin* — which opponents of the Islamic regime have dismissed as a rabble, as a mob for hire. I could sense the barely repressed resentment, the volatility, the fine dusting of hostility on the shoulders of so many dark, sweat-stained shirts.

Friday is small-business day throughout the city. From dawn to dusk along the *joubs* the passerby could once find the city's open-air car washes: men with metal or plastic pails, soap and a fistful of rags who would scrub, polish and buff your Cadillac, BMW or locally-built Paykan or Saipa (Renault 5) to a lustrous sheen for a few *tomans*. Now they have been driven into the side streets in the cleansing zeal of the city's aggressive mayor Gholam-Ali Karbaschi. But one afternoon before the crackdown as I strolled down Hijab Avenue, I spotted a sleek Tehran crow perched atop a freshly washed and polished automobile, preening itself in the reflection and looking for all the world like the most self-satisfied of car washers.

CHANCE IS THE TRAVELLER'S BEST FRIEND. As I was plucking the last grains of rice from my plate in a restaurant on the Boulevard not far from Vali-ye Asr Square one cold evening, I became aware a presence hovering about my table. I looked up and saw an older man with pink cheeks and a craggy face smiling at me. In gruff, disarming and almost unaccented English he said: "I'm not disturbing you, I hope?" "Not at all," I replied, and invited him to take a seat. Though Iranian friends have warned of the possibly dire consequences of talking with strangers ("They could be spies" goes the argument, although more likely they would be from the Information Ministry, Iran's feared secret police), chance meetings have always been a source of instruction, often of pleasure, even of epiphanic insight into the country's elusive soul. Besides, as I ticked off the circumstances of the encounter — it was my first visit to this particular restaurant, and the gentleman now addressing me had been there when I walked in — I decided that my interlocutor was no police plant.

No, the impromptu guest at my table was an energetic sixty-five-year-old called Francis Aviet, the last name a contraction from the poly-syllabic Armenian: "But you can call me Frank, simpler that way," he said, breaking into a cavernous guffaw. The veteran engineer and businessman came from a huge, ramified family stretching from southern India, where it owns vast properties, through the suburbs of San Francisco, where his eldest son manages a highly-rated French restaurant, to the northern Iranian province of Mazandaran on the Caspian.

His paternal grandfather, he tells me with pride, migrated from Armenia at the turn of the century to the Isfahan suburb of New Joful, home to a large Armenian community for 400 years now. The family bible is on display at the museum there, adjacent to Vank cathedral. While most of Iran's 250,000-strong Armenian community are Gregorian Orthodox Christians, Frank is a Roman Catholic, educated by the Carmelite Order. I soon learned — how great the surprise of the ignorant — that the Carmelites had been granted a dispensation by Shah Abbas the Great to establish a mission in the imperial capital of Isfahan four centuries ago.

Frank Aviet combined the skills of the storyteller in the purest Oriental tradition with a wide streak of congenital optimism. Now, he told me, slow but sure relaxation of post-revolutionary rigidity is under-way as the regime reaches out to the West for business know-how and capital. The liberal trend is also making itself felt in religious matters. The Carmelites, banished from Iran after the revolution, may be allowed to return to Isfahan. Religious, not national, identity has tradi-tionally distinguished the region's minority groups. "We're flourishing here," he assured me, as he greeted an assistant deputy minister of indus-try who has dropped by for a late meal. "There's never been a problem for us Armenians," he added. "We've been a stable, strong and influen-tial community in Iran for hundreds of years." What Frank did not say, but what I have since learned, is that the prosperity and cohesiveness of the Armenians have induced Iran to adopt a position of relative neu-trality in the bloody conflict between the newly independent former Soviet Republics of Armenia and Azerbaijan. Iran, he noted with a grin, wants to make sure Armenia not only survives but thrives as a buffer between the Islamic Republic and Turkey, with whom relations, though cordial, can be testy. But, he concluded, what the Middle East — and by implication the world — needs now is more trade. "If you're trading, you're not likely to be fighting, now are you?"

We met often, and each time he would regale me with his accounts of adventure on Persian Gulf oil rigs or attempt to convince me, with Biblical arguments whose complexity left me breathless, that when you get right down to it, the Muslims were heretics. Or he would reminisce about things Iranian and Armenian: rugs, caviar, Armenian writers and Persian poets, elk and boar hunting in the "jungle," the thick deciduous forests of Mazandaran where Frank grew up, eyes gleam-ing with nostalgia as he talked about the orange and lemon groves, the cattle, the wildlife and the family hunting lodge. Frank's face, with its bushy eyebrows, powerful nose, prominent cheeks, wide forehead and twinkling eyes, was like a relief map of Iran in miniature: the plateau with its girdling mountains, its deserts and oases, and across it in the shifting sand, the traces of dynasties, kings and rebellions.

AS A JOURNALIST, and a visible one at that, I always assumed my movements were, if not followed, at least monitored. Discreetly or not, depending on the circumstances. One afternoon shortly after I'd sat down to chat with Monsieur Grigor, the exquisitely-mannered owner of the New Naderi Hotel, an intense bearded young man took a seat just opposite us and began to stare. Suddenly Monsieur Grigor looked down at his watch and remembered an urgent appointment elsewhere. "Please forgive me," he said as he hurried off. The man continued to stare at me with what appeared to be a mixture of hostility and curiosity. I held my ground for a few more minutes, then withdrew to my room. Next day, Islamic Guidance — the government ministry that assigns "minders" to visiting reporters — suggested I change hotels. To be closer to downtown, more convenient. Of course it's up to you, Mr. Reed. Monsieur Grigor understood, of course. I moved the following day, to the Bostan, where I began my passionate affair with Vali-ye Asr Avenue.

Up until it had been suggested that I move to the Bostan Hotel, I had made my home at the New Naderi, in the heart of Tehran's Armenian district. Monsieur Grigor and I always conversed in French, once the language of Iran's intellectual elite. Not far from the hotel stood the Café Naderi, which had been in the family for generations. The café's Turkish coffee is still the best in town, which is not saying much. And its shaded garden, once alive with lively polyglot conversation and Iranian popular music, is today overgrown with weeds; stacked outdoor furniture is rusting under a layer of soot and dust. High on the wall, beside the clock and above the photographs of Imam Khomeini and current leader Khamene'i hangs a colour photograph of Mount Ararat. Armenian intellectuals still gather here of a Sunday afternoon for coffee, a sweet, and small talk.

Like all Tehran hotels, the New Naderi emptied its swimming pool to meet new Islamic regulations. During the frequent blackouts of the war years I would sit around the empty pool after dark listening to the whisper of conversation, and catching the telltale odour of alcohol on the night breeze. The forbidden, and unmistakable, scent was coming from teacups held by the drivers of Turkish freight trucks, who augmented their already lucrative haulage rates by smuggling whisky in the undercarriages of their vehicles.

BEFORE THE GOVERNMENT decided to let the rial, Iran's national currency, fall to the semi-legal free market rate and permit unrestricted foreign exchange trading, there was only one place in this roaring metropolis of eleven or twelve million where one could cash Canadian dollar traveller's cheques: the central offices of the Melli (National) Bank, on Ferdowsi Avenue. Once, in the bank's marble-panelled hall, a young man approached me with a polite request that I undertake to "tell the truth" and refute the slanders broadcast in the West about the Islamic Revolution. But within three minutes, the bank's security guards had — speaking euphemistically — encouraged him to leave. "If the *Komiteh* shows up, then there will really be trouble," one of them whispered to me. "Besides, we are only trying to protect you from terrorists."

But who would protect Iranians from the *Komiteh*, I wondered.

The street outside the bank had none of the shaded elegance of Vali-ye Asr Avenue, but all of the raw reality of economic life in a city which had once tried to look like Los Angeles — expressways, interchanges and all — and now had the unmistakable grit of Third World poverty, more like L.A. South Central. Minus the deadly clash of heavily armed gangs, of course.

"Pssst! Dollars, marks, pounds," sidewalk money changers would hiss as I walked by. This was the Istanbul crossroads, where Jomhouri Eslami (Islamic Republic) Boulevard met Ferdowsi Avenue, unofficial financial nerve centre of Islamic Iran, where trading on the street set the real price of the rial. For most of the war years, the free market exchange rate functioned as the one true barometer of economic confidence. In the months before Iran agreed to United Nations Resolution 598 setting up a cease-fire in the war with Iraq, one US dollar bought 1,500 rials, with the official rate pegged in the low seventies.

For the government employees and labourers who form a substantial part of its population, Tehran is a backbreakingly expensive city. Inflation is high. Efforts by the mayor — supported by the central government — to bring prices of everyday goods and services into line with their real cost have led to clashes between the poor of south Tehran and the police.

Iran may have been awash in petrodollars during the Shah's regime, but it took the Islamic Republic to redefine trickle-down economics. The number of billionaires (expressed, granted, in devalued rials) has soared from 50 to more than 5,000. Land and currency speculation, along with import-export, have emerged as the prime sources of individual wealth, and that wealth has become increasingly concentrated. Unverifiable statistics shown to me by credible Iranian journalistic sources indicate that 15% of the country's population today controls more than 85% of its wealth. Who needs the Shah?

Early on, I had to face the question: Why carry traveller's cheques in wartime Iran? Streetcorner money changers, taxi drivers, hotel waiters, even Islamic Guidance Ministry operatives — all were prepared to exchange hard currency (meaning the dollars of the Great Satan) for fistfuls — for bundles — of rials, and not at the ludicrous "official" rate which made Tehran the world's most expensive great city, instead of the cheapest.

The penalties for illegal currency trading were draconian, I was told. Death by firing squad, or worse. But fortunes were being made, and prices were commonly quoted not in rials, but in dollars. At first my respect for revolutionary norms prevailed, but it soon became clear that my Iranian friends thought me a simpleton, perhaps even a buffoon. Besides, no free-lance correspondent could survive for long on $30 breakfasts. God would, I hoped, deal more harshly with the big-time traders than he would with my devout and dedicated suppliers — or with me.

DURING THE WAR basic necessities like gasoline, cooking oil, sugar, rice and meat were rationed. But the coupons allotted to individuals through the mosques could be sold or traded like any other commodity — as long as the trading was not done in public. Out for a stroll one fine spring afternoon, I passed a double lineup: the first was made up of women waiting to exchange coupons for frozen chickens at a small hole in the wall. The second was less well-defined, consisting entirely of men slouching with feigned casualness against the wall, flashing fans of ration tickets. Suddenly a white Nissan Patrol roared up and screeched to a stop; five bearded young men with AK-47s piled out, pounced on the hapless coupon sellers before they could scatter, and bundled them into the vehicle. The women in the chicken line waited, impassive. Two hours later I walked by the same intersection. There, slouched against the wall, were the same men plying the same trade.

The city, complain well-to-do Tehranis, is crowded with poor people from the provinces searching for work. Many grimace when using the words "poor people." As a set of institutions governed by the rule of divine law, the Islamic Republic may indeed be less than exemplary. Income redistribution has taken place, to the benefit of the rich. But the revolution did achieve a true democratization of urban space. No longer do people from south Tehran feel either compunction or hesitation about hopping onto a bus — if they can afford the 50 rial (2¢) fare — to window-shop and rubberneck on Vali-ye Asr, or visit relatives in Tehran Pars or Abbas-Abad, or troop to weekly Friday prayers at Tehran University, once the preserve of the country's Westernized intellectual elite, the embodiment of "West-sickness."

On Vali-ye Asr Avenue, though, as water still flows downhill, so too does power. One of the Islamic regime's most potent symbols, Evin Prison, can be seen, on a clear day, at the top of the hill. The prison was there before, of course. Prisons have a way of outlasting the regimes that build them. Abbas the civil servant become convenience store owner, who lives about a kilometre down the hill, assured me, in whispered tones, that gun shots resound from within the walls every evening, signalling executions. Is this the Iranian penchant for tragedy enveloped in a mantle of exaggeration, or is it true?

IRAN SEEMS AWASH in ambiguity, bound in the near-infinite elasticity of truth. In a country of true believers, where devout Shi'ite men of religion keep a firm hand on the tiller of public morality, everything — including even pornographic video cassettes, hard liquor and women — is available with a telephone call and sufficient hard currency. Iran is fascinated by industrial development, Western-style, while it simultaneously abominates the evils of the West. The country's religious leaders pay fulsome lip service to the austerity preached and practised by Imam Khomeini, yet relish the newfound luxuries and lavish lifestyles of north Tehran villas. Its skilled professional diplomats are more at home in the chanceries of Europe than at the mass Friday prayers at Tehran University. Its profound sense of religious identity has not destroyed an equally deep sense of national and cultural distinctiveness which long antedates Islam. Here is a country which produces immense quantities of oil, yet draws its greatest pride from its glorious poetic tradition and its equally glorious carpets — both superfluous, moan Iranians, in the bright new age of the global marketplace.

Iranians take grim pleasure in boasting that their capital is, after Mexico, the world's second-worst polluted city. But on a clear, warm evening, when the stinking cloud of pollution has been wafted off into the desert and the stars are blinking, the city comes alive to the nose of the unhurried stroller.

The late-day sun-evoked perfumes of rose and jasmine linger in the air, while the smell of freshly moistened earth blends with the grassy, damp odours of the *joubs*. Along Vali-ye Asr Avenue, the night breeze brings, along with the choking stench of diesel fumes from a passing Iran-built Fiat minibus, the fragrance of ripe fruit — melons, bananas, mandarins — from sidewalk juice bars, or the acrid pungency of pickles fermenting on a nearby window sill. Further on, even before you notice the restaurant entrance, you will have picked up the unmistakable aroma of Persian rice steaming, soon to be spooned onto your plate, topped with a dollop of melting butter, a bed for sizzling chicken or lamb *kebab* dusted with *samak*, or mounded and sprinkled with sweet-sour red jewels of *zereshk*. Through the open doors of brightly-lighted sweets shops waft the heady smells of saffron, lemon, rosewater and pistachio. There, just down the *koucheh*, the alley way, a hole-in-the-wall bakery is about to close, but the scent of the last sheets of fresh-baked bread still lingers in the air. And late at night, in a side street just a few yards north of Vali-ye Asr Square, a Paykan is parked, its open trunk displaying wicker baskets of bright slithering fresh Caspian white fish redolent with salt water and iodine.

MY FRIEND ABBAS' tiny grocery store, in the long shadow of Evin Prison, is one of my favourite places in Tehran. Far from the hustle and bustle of the international hotels and the musty foreign correspondents' room at the Islamic Guidance office, the store smells of mothballs, strong soap and yogurt. Outside, in the street, neighbourhood kids play soccer; people go quietly about their business. Here in the new, Islamic suburbs modest homes shelter behind high brick walls and metal gates. Step through the gates and you find yourself in flowering gardens, with fruit trees and small reflecting pools. Iran: the country of the inner garden, protected from the hostility of the surrounding environment by high walls. People from the neighbourhood — office workers, retired military men, Afghan refugees with wary, cat-like eyes and baggy pantaloons, wide-eyed kids with a 10-rial coin to spend — wander in and out from early morning until late at night. They buy sugar, packages of noodles, milk, eggs, curds, and Abbas weighs it out on an ancient, clanking balance, accompanied by a salutation.

Abbas is a typical modern-day Iranian, caught in the throes of social schizophrenia. As the revolutionary tide has ebbed, he sees himself, a penurious, devout Muslim, stranded by the new credo of economic productivity, while still clinging to his faith. "Ah, the *mollahs*," Abbas grumbled one day between customers, as he scratched his stubbly beard. "They tell the poor what is bad and what is sinful, but they do all these sinful things themselves. The people are too angry that such a regime which claims to respect an ideal as noble as Islam can be so corrupt."

The Assassins' Castle at Alamut. Photo by Fred A. Reed.

2

My Day with the Assassins

IMPATIENT, I PACE back and forth in the hotel parking lot, breath frosting in the crisp, cool December air. Unerring heralds of dawn, the birds in the trees around the waterless swimming pool have begun to chirp. Through the glass doorway I can see the night manager slumbering behind the dimly lighted reception desk. Tehran, an early riser as cities go, is still half asleep.

Suddenly the glare of headlights flashes across the blank wall of the hotel compound as an automobile turns into the driveway. In the reflected light I glance at my watch: six o'clock sharp, right on time. The battered blue Mazda pickup comes to a stop, I clamber in and we rumble off, heading northwestward into the lingering night. Behind the wheel is a slightly built man in his mid-thirties: Majid, my guide/driver/interpreter/boon companion. Majid sports a discreet mustache and, depending on the circumstances, a few days' growth of stubble on his cheeks and chin. Today he is clean-shaven, meaning that we are unlikely to encounter any *mollahs*. "I didn't tell you?" he says, catching my surprised reaction to the pickup. "I use this for my gardening business, in between jobs, you know."

Raking leaves and pruning trees did seem an unlikely pastime. The Majid I'd known for the last five years was an adventurer and facilitator, a man who lived and prospered by his wits. But demand for adventurers was not what it used to be, even in Islamic Iran. After more than a decade of war and revolutionary turmoil, the country is now enjoying a period of fragile stability. His business, escorting American network television crews on daring, hell-for-leather incursions into rebel-held Iraqi Kurdistan or the southern marshes, had evaporated and along with it, the steady inflow of hard currency. Along the Iran-Iraq border the massacre of the innocent continued, but that was old news. The blood was fresher, the carrion plumper in Bosnia or Somalia. Still, for the expedition I had in mind, Majid had the right stuff: the latent energy of a tightly-coiled spring, a ready laugh, a lively intelligence, a wide streak of bravado, an insatiable curiosity and an excellent command of English. An action addict. A man who could not sit still. He would be interested, I was certain. In fact, he'd leaped at my suggestion for a day trip. "Alamut? The Assassins? I'll pick you up at six."

Alamut! For nearly two hundred years the name struck mortal terror into the hearts of the World Order of the twelfth and thirteenth centuries, when the House of Islam still stood at the pinnacle of world civilization. Today a dot on the maps of historical atlases, the Alamut fortress was notorious as the headquarters of a shadowy Muslim sect which advocated and practised selective murder in support of its religious convictions. From Damascus and Baghdad to Isfahan and Samarqand, political and doctrinal adversaries trembled or raged impotently at this handful of seemingly untouchable malefactors. For the great powers of the day the Assassins were the living expression of evil incarnate. For their sympathizers they were enlightened avengers, men of the highest virtue. For the common people, who lived or died at the mercy of caliphs and sultans, tyrants and conquerors, their insurrectionary message must have compelled widespread admiration.

I had my own reasons for making the trip. The fortress at Alamut stands at the antipodes of pack journalism, far from the self-feeding loop of the world media circus. I've long believed that the dry-land shipwrecks, the abandoned or ruined monuments to the faith of the true believers or the folly of the powerful can, in their stark testimony to the past, tell more about the present than an infinity of set-piece interviews with self-important and profoundly ephemeral decision makers, the talking heads of this world. Only by visiting the mountain aerie of

Hassan Sabbah, founder and mastermind of the Assassins, could I hope to reconstruct the myth-charged story of their archetypal "terrorist" movement. But I have another motive. I first read of the Assassins in my early teens, as part of a fleeting fascination with the Crusaders and their Muslim adversaries; since then, they have been lurking like sleepers in my subconscious, awaiting their moment to be activated. On a trip into the countryside west of Tehran several years before, I had spotted a signpost to Alamut: I knew then that the Assassins had called. Today I was answering that call.

At the entrance to the westbound Karaj expressway the Mazda comes to a shuddering halt. A traffic cop has waved us over. "Only cars and buses allowed on this part of the road," Majid mutters. "But don't worry, I'll fix it." Pointing first to me, then down the road, Majid tells the cop, a wide-eyed recruit, to call his superior. As traffic backs up behind us the officer ambles over. After a quick conversation, a smile and an exchange of salutations, he waves us through.

"I told him you were an Englishman going to visit the horses," he chortles. "Did you know John Simpson has an interest in, what do you call it, a horse-growing farm along the Karaj road? Well, I told the policeman you had to inspect some horses there and get back to Tehran to catch a flight." I knew nothing of John Simpson's horse ranch, if indeed he had such a ranch. The BBC's chief international correspondent, an old Iran hand, moved in loftier circles than I, and information in Iran often had a way being more poetic than accurate. But I was glad I'd asked Majid to join me. The trip would not be a dull one.

THE SUN HAS CLEARED the mountains to the east by the time we reach Qazvin, one-time capital of Iran under Tahmasp I, the Turkish-speaking Safavid shah who ruled from 1524 to 1576. On the way into town, we pass through an exurban purgatory of dusty fruit stalls, greasy open-air garages, impromptu dumps of oil drums, and semi-derelict cars, trucks and buses drawn up seemingly at random. Iranian towns are a city planner's hell rarely balanced, except in historic centres of cities like Isfahan or Mashhad, by the urban equivalent of heaven: the main mosque or the sanctuary. This landscape of disarray I came to appreciate, perhaps too hastily, as a pervasive lack of regard for public space, consistent with the regime's policy of restricting social intercourse to bazaar, mosque and family. But it strikes deeper roots, too, in the structure of traditional Islamic society which sees no anomaly in the use of public spaces for private purposes. Ultimately, in Islamic law, individuals are answerable only to God for their actions, not to disincarnate public interest as manifested in something like a municipal corporation charged to advance the common good.[6] What I take for Islamic disarray and disorder is really a different kind of order, proceeding from different cultural premises.

As we turn down a boulevard lined with scruffy evergreens Majid's chipper voice suddenly jars me out of my meditation on how societies give shape to cities. Our entry into Qazvin has touched off a rapid-fire series of scabrous anecdotes about the town's citizens. No matter where you go in Iran, you will find the town's male residents being ridiculed on account of their reputed proclivities for buggery, pederasty and dull-wittedness, explains my walking encyclopedia of Iranian apocrypha. (I later asked friends in Tehran about the Qazvinis, and inevitably got in return an amused rolling of eyes.) Yes, it is true, Majid assures me with theatrical sincerity — the rhetorician lurking in every second Iranian — ladies refuse excellent marriage offers from men of the town. Visitors dare not pick up loose change should it fall to the sidewalk. Appropriate advice for those coming to Qazvin for the first time, then, would be: keep your back to the wall and under no circumstances bend at the waist, I venture. Majid laughs: "Here, you must be careful all the time." But the city appears calm enough this cool morning; men and women seem to be hurrying normally enough about their tasks. My untrained, admittedly naïve eye can detect no sign of unnatural practices. In fact, I spot several groups of children on their way to school, raw evidence that procreation must indeed take place here.

During the early days of the revolution Iran's Islamic justice system gained international notoriety for its draconian expeditiousness. Along with thousands of real or alleged counter-revolutionaries judged by the tribunals to be "corrupt on earth," the kind of catch-all charge that allowed the regime to cast a very wide net indeed, an unknown number of homosexuals were executed. But while homosexuality remains official-ly a capital offense, Qazvin's reputation, let alone its population, seem hardly to have been affected by the homophobic wrath of the *mollahs*.

Human nature being what is is, argues Majid, the more sternly for-bidden a subject — sex, for example — the greater its secret fascination. In Iran, pornographic videos, including recent US-made products featuring Iranian girls which he describes as "very dirty" are readily, if not widely available. It is said (the ever-recurring cautionary phrase I must employ to denote absolutely unverifiable, though plausible, information) that the *mollahs'* obsession with the flesh is exceeded only by their fondness for money.

But I digress.... Majid parks the Mazda near the Darb-é Kushk, the arched gateway to the old city where the inlay of gold and turquoise faience is still visible beneath a layer of dust. Before proceeding up-country to Alamut, we must check in at the Qazvin Islamic Guidance office and present our credentials. A few days earlier, officials in Tehran had threatened to "stop us" if I insisted on making the trip without approved escort. Majid, I was given to understand, was somehow unsuitable, perhaps even out of favour. Though the disagreement was smoothed over before we left and I obtained the necessary official pass, I later had cause to regret my lack of sensitivity, for what Islamic Guidance gives, it can also take away. Hadi Tavakoli, the Qazvin bureau chief looks up from the sheaf of papers on his desk when we state our destination, then pauses for an instant before declaring peremptorily: "Oh, you won't be able to make it. The place is completely cut off by snow."

Aware that this is but an opening position, Majid and I confer briefly, then reply that we'll go as far as we can before turning back. Mr. Tavakoli, with a flexibility uncharacteristic of a bureaucrat, accepts our compromise proposal.

IBN HASSAN AL-SABBAH, the charismatic organizational genius who founded the Assassin Order in 1090 (493 years after Mohammad's migration from Mecca to Medina, which marks the beginning of the Islamic calendar), has become something of a local hero throughout the rugged mountains and breathtaking valleys to the north of Qazvin — although Hassan's lofty status probably owes more to the reverse influence exerted by Western fascination than to folk memories of his long-vanished brotherhood.

Hoary tradition derives the name "Assassins" from the Arabic *"hashishi"* — hashish takers — suggesting that the sect's members were little more than drugged zombies, or perhaps, to put things in a more contemporary idiom, primitive human cruise missiles. But, protests Mr. Tavakoli, the true followers of Hassan Sabbah never took hashish. How could they possibly carry out their assignments with such deadly precision and self-sacrifice under the influence of such a volition-numbing drug? No, he protests with a righteous flourish, they cultivated medicinal herbs (many of which belong to the corpus of traditional Iranian herbal medicine), and provided them, along with medical care, to the fiercely independent peasants who inhabited the rugged uplands north of Qazvin in order to gain and maintain their loyalty. The recipe for one of Hassan Sabbah's remedies has survived: a mixture of finely ground nuts, honey and coriander to be employed against aches and ill humours. Hashish was probably unknown to the sect; most sources say it was introduced into Iran from India by Sufis only in the thirteenth century. A later outgrowth of the Assassins, based in Syria, was indeed known for its use of hashish; never its Persian founders. Mr. Tavakoli is right.

Whatever pseudo-historians or dabblers in the occult were later to call them, this much is certain: The Assassins were a sect within a heresy within a schism. In the turbulent Islamic world of the early twelfth century, they were radical believers in the Ismaili creed, itself a split-off from the Twelver Shi'ism which today rules Iran. As in most doctrinal disputes, as Christians and Jews of all shadings and denominations can attest, the story is bewilderingly complex and, to outsiders, baffling. But placed in the troubled political and religious context of the times, it can be appreciated. The Islamic world had been torn by the conflict between the expanding empire of the Seljuq Turks who had arisen to power in Central Asia in the early eleventh century and extended their rule as far as the borders of the Byzantine Empire, and the remains of the once-mighty Arab dynasty of the Abbassids which exercised spiritual authority from Baghdad. Like the Abbassids, the Seljuqs were Sunnites, the majority persuasion in Islam.

In a religious age, as the politics of domination found expression in orthodoxy and hidebound scholasticism, so the politics of opposition and revolt took the shape of heresy. Traditional Shi'ism grew out of the conviction that the descendants of the prophet Mohammad, through his daughter Fatima and his son-in-law Ali, should guide the community of the faithful, not the wealthy usurpers who founded the Ommayad dynasty and established the Arab Islamic Empire. It became the major schism in Islam. After the Abbassid revolution against Omayyad corruption came to power with Shi'ite support in 750, it turned brutally, as revolutions often do, on its most fervent supporters. The Shi'ites withdrew into quietism and complacency; sectarian breakaways became more frequent. After the death in 765 of the Sixth Imam, Ja'far Sadeq, the Shi'ites split into two factions. One of these supported the claim that Ja'far's son Ismail, who had predeceased him, was in fact the legitimate descendant of the *ahl al bait*, the Prophet's household. The other followed Ja'far's younger son Musa Kazem, who was put to death by Haroun al-Rashid at Baghdad in 799. It went on to become the "orthodox" Twelver Shi'ite sect which rules Iran today — so named because it recognizes a lineage of twelve holy Imams.

The Ismailis, dissidents within dissidence, breathed new insurrectionary vitality into the Islamic World, and for the better part of two centuries mounted the main challenge to dominant, politically corrupt Sunni power wielded by the Seljuqs. The Assassins of Alamut, the most extreme form of Ismailism, provided the spearpoint.

IN THE COURSE OF pleasantries it emerges that I'm working on a book on Iran. Mr. Tavakoli hastens to add, perhaps with an eye to head office, that it is the outlawed MKO (the Iraq-based, US-funded "Peoples' Mujahidin") which has today adopted the tactics of Hassan Sabbah's sect. "Not, God forefend, the Islamic Republic." God forefend, I nod in agreement. But I cannot help reflecting that some in the Islamic Republic might well share a spiritual affinity with these twelfth-century fighters against the empire which ruled the civilized (read Islamic) world. The tactics of the Assassins, it could be argued, were perfectly in tune with the temper of the times. In an age of corruption and duplicity they were men of unbending principle, hardened by their minority status in the house of Islam, brilliant tacticians and propagandists, religious purists who had developed killing and martyrdom in the cause of God to a fine and deadly art. They were also, after their fashion, defenders of Persian cultural patriotism, warrior-heirs of the ancient Persian nobility in Islamic guise.[7]

After a cup of tea — whose heat and fragrance suddenly reminded me that I had cavalierly omitted to take breakfast before leaving the hotel at the crack of dawn — and a final, cautionary word about the weather, we are joined by a sad-eyed man called Mahmoud, who has been designated as our guide. Mahmoud, says Mr. Tavakoli, is well known in these parts for his knowledge of the craggy peaks and deep valleys that separate the uplands of the Iranian plateau from the semi-tropical Caspian littoral, a bare 100 kilometres away. This remote region, known as Daylam, was famous well before the arrival of Hassan and his followers for the fierce and warlike ways, and even fiercer independence, of its inhabitants. Daylam was also the homeland of the

Buyids, the first native Iranian, Shi'ite dynasty to rule the Abbassid caliphate from Baghdad. But for all the martial prowess of his countrymen, Mahmoud the mountaineer looks as though he would rather be at home. The impromptu winter expedition to Alamut is clearly not his idea of a good time. In fact, he doesn't even seem to know the road. We may, he warns preemptively with the kind of dramatic flourish that often artfully masks ignorance, have to drive the last five kilometres hubcap-deep in the Shahrud, the wild river which rises in the mountains above Alamut and tumbles through the Valley of the Assassins on its way to the Caspian. Majid and I exchange glances of agreement: it's a go, as far as the road will take us. The three of us bundle into the cab, and we're off for Alamut.

From Qazvin the road winds due northward up the flank of the Alborz range. Majid is peppering Mahmoud with questions — about the roads, the weather, the government — which he occasionally translates for my benefit. Bad, threatening and expletive deleted comes Mahmoud's reply. Although Majid translates, I've become familiar enough with Farsi to understand our passenger's feelings. Before long we begin to meet Paykan farm trucks and Iranian-made Fiat minibuses clanking slowly down the steep switchbacks in tire chains. Snow has fallen overnight, not only on the summits, but in the passes. But the warm sun is melting the freshly fallen snow on the asphalt. Good fortune is riding with us, I decide. Majid's Mazda is not equipped with chains. Treading cautiously, the Mazda whining in first gear, we wind our way over the icy summit and down a series of throat-clutching double bends, slowly working our way down to low altitude. Below us the Shahrud valley stretches west to east, dappled with fast-flowing cloud shadows. Situated on the extreme southern edge of the Caspian climate zone, the valley is bathed year round in warm and humid sea air. Rice paddies line the gently sloping river banks and the hollows are dotted with green-leafed citrus groves.

Just across the Shahrud bridge we pause to pick up hitchhikers — peasants on their way back to their villages. Two of them, Khairollah, a shepherd with a pencil mustache, and Fadollah, a fuzzy-cheeked young soldier on leave from Kermanshah, in Kurdistan province, are from — God be praised! exclaims Majid, half jokingly — Gazorkhan village, which providentially sits at the very foot of the Assassin fortress, our destination. "Drive through the Shahrud?" scoffs Khairollah, now wedged into the pickup cab, while his young friend squats on the truck bed. "No need for that, I'll show you the road. If there's no mud, you can make it easily." Mahmoud the mountaineer, arms braced against the dashboard staring glumly straight ahead, says not a word.

For two hours we follow the twisting roller coaster of a road, where crude paving alternates with bone-rattling washboard gravel. The conversation suddenly becomes animated: Our passengers have told Majid that the government is mining uranium up in the mountains. Always on the lookout for a story, he presses them for details. They speak of truck convoys, mysterious foreigners, hidden settlements. Could the Daylam hinterland be the site of some secret nuclear project, Majid speculates. But assuming this to be so, why has it been so easy for us to enter the area? Why have we seen no signs of activity? No revolutionary guardsmen, no roadblocks, no military vehicles, no vehicles of any kind? Why was the road so abominable, when roads leading to strategic facilities were usually broad and well-paved? Ah well, it was a tantalizing thought.

Suddenly Fadollah bangs on the cab roof and cries out: the turnoff! With a sharp pull on the steering wheel which almost sends our passenger flying, we lurch onto a steep-pitched dirt track toward the uplands of Alamut. The land is rich, the hillsides covered with a crosshatch of fallow barley and millet fields. In some smaller plots, peasants are plowing with oxen. As we climb, the fields give way to orchards and vineyards.

All at once, as we round a curve, I catch sight of the reddish-brown hulk of the citadel looming in stark majesty through a windbreak of leafless poplars. "Alamut!" shouts Majid, with an inflection of manic glee. There, high atop the craggy outcropping which commands the spur valley, I can make out the faint remains of crenellated battlements etched against a snow-pregnant sky, with the village of Gazorkhan huddled at its feet.

HASSAN SABBAH, the citadel's most famous tenant, was born in the holy city of Qom in the middle of the eleventh century. As a young man, he fell under the influence of an Ismaili itinerant preacher, a *da'i*, and converted to the new doctrine. Soon thereafter he travelled to Cairo, the capital of the Fatimids, an Ismaili dynasty then locked in a bitter struggle with the powerful Sunni caliphs of Baghdad for ideological primacy in Islam. The Fatimids, who legitimized their claim to power by asserting descent from the house of the Prophet by his daughter Fatima, had arisen in North Africa at the beginning of the Christian tenth century, founded Cairo sixty years later, and built it into a great centre of culture and learning.

After several years among the Fatimids in Egypt, Hassan returned via Syria to Persia, travelling from Isfahan southeast to the desert cities of Kerman and Yazd before turning north to the mountain fastness of Daylam. He finally took control of the citadel at Alamut without a fight in 1090, after his skilled propagandists had won over its occupants to the Ismaili preaching. Some say that Hassan acquired the fortress by stratagem. Approaching the commander, he petitioned for no more land than could be covered by the hide of an ox. Bemused at his visitor's absurd request, the commander agreed. Hassan slit the rawhide into fine thongs which he then spliced together, using the immense length of leather to circumscribe the castle.

For the next thirty-five years, he never left the rock. Rashid al-Din, a thirteenth-century Persian historian, relates that "The rest of the time until his death he passed inside the house where he lived; he was occupied by writing books, committing the words of the *da'wa* (preaching) to writing, and administering the affairs of his realm, and he lived an ascetic, abstemious and pious life."[8]

Within sight of our goal, at the outskirts of the village, the gallant Mazda finally grinds to a halt, wheels spinning aimlessly in ankle-deep mud on the steep slope. We clamber out and pick our way gingerly along the side of the path. The villagers we encounter recognize our consorts and welcome us with smiles and greetings of "salaam." The doctrinal rigours of small-town Iran have not reached places like Gazorkhan. Here, as throughout most of the countryside, women work beside men in the fields, favouring bright headcloths worn over sweaters and long skirts, with not a *chador* in sight. Boys and girls dash past us on their way to school, sloshing through the mud in high rubber boots, giggling "What ees your name meester?" before they scramble ahead up the steep muddy path like mountain goats.

The village houses are built in traditional style: walls of sun-dried ochre mud-brick with roofs made of tree trunks covered with several layers of earth. These roofs often come alive, as the fresh-cut trees continue to send green shoots down into the warmth of the room below. Gazorkhan echoes with the sounds of rushing water, crowing cocks, quacking ducks and braying donkeys. We decline several invitations for tea. Mahmoud the mountaineer is worried about snow higher up. Majid is apprehensive about clearing the pass to Qazvin before dark. The sky is ominous. We press on.

It's early afternoon by now, and fat black clouds have begun to close in as we slog uphill. Suddenly one of our escorts stumbles and cries out. He's tripped over a long, rounded whitish object protruding from the thin layer of topsoil. We pause to examine it: a human femur. The ribs and skulls can't be much farther away. This place was a cemetery, volunteers Khairollah, before the 1991 Rudbar earthquake swept it away. The bones keep turning up, emerging from the loose earth like a macabre crop.

Already lack of food and the 2,500-metre altitude have turned me lightheaded. A fine rain mixed with snow has begun to fall. As I stumble over the snow-covered rocks my pace grows steadily more deliberate. Putting one foot in front of the other has suddenly become a matter of careful planning, of reflection. Now I begin to understand what Himalayan disaster epics are made of, and feel a sudden surge of affinity for frostbitten Maurice Herzog lost on the heights of Anapurna. Visions of sizzling *chelo kebab* on a bed of steaming fluffy rice flit across my consciousness. My ears are buzzing.

Khairollah and Fadollah, who have already scrambled on ahead, come bounding down the steep slope. Each one grabs an arm and, half lifting, half dragging, they sweep me along between them like a great disarticulated crash-test dummy, limbs akimbo. Effortlessly lightfooted now, I flit nimbly across the rocks until we reach a small plateau, the doorstep of Hassan Sabbah's mountain retreat. We pause on the windswept saddle to take in the view across the valley with its ring of snow-capped peaks. On a clear day, say our escorts, you can see the "jungle" — the dense rain-forest of Gilan province which teems, even today, with elk and wild boar and perhaps, high up in the untrodden wilderness, the Caspian tiger.

Once ensconced here, atop the crag of Alamut, Hassan Sabbah directed his attention to winning converts to his revolutionary creed, and to gaining control of more castles. His charismatic teaching, carried now by skilled religious propagandists and agitators, had given him the means to perfect the ultimate offensive weapon: men of absolute devotion trained to seek a martyr's death as their only reward. For such a death, taught Hassan, was but the portal to immortality in paradise and as such was not to be feared, but aspired to. Now, the network of castles and fortresses gave him the ultimate defensive weapon: an impregnable network of base camps and training grounds, self-sufficient, isolated, yet within striking distance of the centres of power of the day, the cities of Qazvin, Rayy, Qom and Isfahan. His aim was not the defense of territory, the classic function of the medieval castle, but the establishment of an invulnerable offensive springboard. Farther westward lay the ultimate goal: treacherous Baghdad, seat of corruption and inequity, symbolic centre of the world.

Hassan and his lieutenants recruited the finest builders and engineers. Battlements were strengthened, and an ingenious system of canals and catch basins carved into the heart of the great rock to provide an unquenchable supply of water. Deep holes were filled with stores of seeds, grain and dried fruit sufficient to outlast the most determined besieging force. The fertile countryside around the fortress could sustain a garrison of thousands of fighters and their families, most drawn from the warlike Daylamites but many others recruited from among the discontented and rebellious from farther afield, young Iranians who chafed under the foreign yoke and were drawn to a religious teaching which offered them action instead of passivity, involvement in the world instead of withdrawal from it.

Hassan Sabbah's first victim was one of the world's most powerful and brilliant men, Nizam al-Molk, scion of a great Persian bureaucratic family and grand vizier of Seljuq Sultan Malikshah. To this day Iranians swear that Nizam, the Assassin leader, Hassan, and Omar Khayyam, formed an unlikely trio of school friends who had taken a vow of mutual support and assistance. Like every legend, the story may contain a kernel of truth, but the difference in the ages of the protagonists makes it unlikely. While Hassan Sabbah and Khayyam were roughly contemporaries and may well have met, Nizam al-Molk was much their senior. Still, in Iran then as now, one can never be entirely certain. Who, twenty-five years ago, expected the elderly Ayatollah Khomeini and his young associates to overturn the Pahlavi regime? The strange connection between the three men is the premise of *Samarcand*, a historical novel by the gifted Lebanese writer Amin Maalouf. Three men of outstanding qualities: Nizam al-Molk, the wealthy aristocrat who placed his skills and intellect at the service of the mighty but unrefined Seljuqs, turned on his one-time companion, and perished under an Assassin's blade; Omar Khayyam, astronomer, philosopher and minor poet (who, in Edward FitzGerald's fanciful version of his *Rubiyyat*, became a major, if exotic, poet in English), driven from his observatory in Isfahan and transformed from court favourite into a pariah on the death of his protector, the great vizier; and Hassan Sabbah, the man who sought, through the power of his will, to shape the world to match his own spiritual purity.

Of the fate of Nizam al-Molk this much is known: On October 16, 1092, an Ismaili agent called Bu Tahir Arrani, disguised as a Sufi, infiltrated the grand vizier's retinue and struck him down with a poisoned dagger — the Assassin weapon of choice. Nizam al-Molk's master Sultan Malikshah would soon follow. Before the sect was finally crushed by the invading Mongols 166 years later, it had extended its operations to central Persia and Syria. The names of hundreds of victims, along with those of their pious executioners, had been inscribed in the Alamut roll of honour.

Contrary to European myth, which many Iranians have come to believe, the Brotherhood of Alamut was only marginally interested in the Crusaders, whose powerful columns of armour-clad knights had thrust deep into the heartland of Islam from the West. The Assassins' sworn enemies — and almost exclusive victims — were their doctrinal and political opponents: the Seljuq sultans who had taken over the Abbassid Empire, including Iran, and perpetuated Sunni orthodoxy atop the caliphate. The Assassins were no mere hired knives, but designated executioners who called themselves *fida'i* — *fedayin* — those who are prepared to die for the cause of the faith. They saw themselves as loyal and devout warriors of God locked in mortal combat against oppressors and usurpers. Disdaining secret killing, the executioners would almost invariably strike in public, preferably at Friday prayer ceremonies in the mosques. They would then declaim a short speech identifying themselves and their aims before being put to death. Their audacity gained them converts, while striking ever deeper terror in the faint hearts of the mighty, some of whom became so well disposed toward the Lords of Alamut as to pay tribute. The strategy was devastatingly effective. In the Muslim Empire, authority, being invested in the individual who gained and kept power by subterfuge, by claim to hereditary right or usurpation, was particularly vulnerable to assassination as a matter of policy.[9]

Much less is known of Omar Khayyam's relations with the Assassins. The dominion of the Seljuqs hardly provided a climate in which the free-ranging philosophical inquiry of a freethinker like Khayyam could prosper. The empire had fallen into the ideological clutches of Sunni scholastics who looked on rational argument with grave suspicion, and whose influence on secular authority was enough to cause all dissent to be silenced. Sympathy for Ismaili ideas was the most serious accusation in the eyes of the orthodox princes who ruled the world of Islam. But there is no trace of such sympathy in the poet's work. Even assuming Khayyam to have been an crypto-Ismailite, or perhaps a friend of Hassan Sabbah, it is unlikely that he would have endangered his life in attempting to propagate the subversive theological politics of the Assassins.[10]

BACK ON THE MOUNTAIN slope clouds are closing in around us and the rain, sweeping out of the northwest on a biting wind, has become a fine sleet, turning the landscape even more forbidding. A Caspian storm is gathering, spilling over the mountain barrier. Majid and I stare up at the remains of the battlements that withstood two centuries of assault and siege until the Mongols, through a combination of cunning and patience, finally starved out the castle's last defenders.

Here's what happened, explains our taciturn guide Mahmoud, as I perch exhausted on a rock, gnawing scraps of dry bread and lump sugar which Fadollah has fished from the bottom of a pocket. Majid, who has been taking photos, suddenly comes over to listen. It seems Hassan Sabbah's most trusted men were eunuchs, thus able to resist sexual deprivation indefinitely. Except for one, that is, who contrived to avoid the sect's ultimate security check and, desperately craving the flesh, snuck down to the village to join his wife. When he returned, the Mongols trailed him to a secret entrance. Storming through the gap, they overwhelmed the exhausted defenders, tore down the walls and torched Hassan Sabbah's historic library. The date, early December, 1256, could well have been a day like this one, with snow flurries and low scudding clouds. Though the tale has slender historical basis (eyewitness reports tell another, inglorious tale of treachery) it does have an inner core of symbolic truth. Like empires with their dreams of 1,000-year rule, the most hermetic confraternities, despite the spiritual and physical rigours of membership and the draconian powers of their disciplinary codes, will eventually be eroded from within. Like the Barbarians at the gates of Rome, the Mongols merely hastened the inevitable decay and collapse of the Assassins.

Well before the Mongols poured out of the high Asian steppes, another Hassan, the grandson of Hassan Sabbah's chosen successor, had already begun to transform the deadly conspiratorial organization into its opposite. One day in early August, 1164, early in Ramadan, the month of fasting and abnegation, Hassan, accompanied by his unveiled wife, mounted the steps to a wooden pulpit constructed in such a way that the assembled multitude had their backs turned on Mecca. There, dressed entirely in white, he addressed "the inhabitants of the world, *jinn*, men and angels," proclaimed himself the Redeemer and announced the advent of the Millennium.

With the day of Resurrection now at hand, the Law of the *Shari'a* henceforth no longer applied, he declared. Banished were the formal codes and ritual observances that mark the life of every Muslim. The austere, puritanical code of the Assassins had, at one stroke, been turned upside down. The faithful were now enjoined to drink wine, enjoy music and revel in the delights of the flesh. The spiritual Resurrection promised and awaited in all religions and creeds had been revealed by Hassan; what had been previously forbidden now became obligatory. Founded on the law of cruel austerity, the Order had become, in a single crashing oscillation of the great pendulum suspended from the immovable point of the universe, a sect given over to what, in Islamic eyes, were nothing more than debauchery and license.

How could such a stunning, overnight reversal have been made credible to the Order's members and supporters?

The brotherhood of Alamut had been a brilliantly conceived and diabolically executed deception, an elaborate exercise in manipulation from the beginning, contends Slovenian author Vladimir Bartol in his 1939 novel *Alamut*.[11] Bartol's book depicts the sect as a paradigm of ideological absolutism gone badly awry, in thrall to the cult of personality, to the manipulative nihilism of absolute power. Bartol's Hassan Sabbah is a cynical monster who guards the ultimate secret of his creed for himself and a few chosen underlings: "Do you know what our doctrine teaches is the summit of knowledge?" exclaims his fictitious Assassin chief to one of his subalterns. "Nothing is true; all is permitted!"[12]

Mention the Assassins in polite company and the response may be barely concealed revulsion, except among fanciers of the occult who seem drawn to them, as they are to any hermetic or mystical group. This affinity probably originates with the Austrian monarchist and orientalist von Hammer-Purgstall, who used Masonic terminology in his fanciful descriptions of the brotherhood of Alamut. His aim was transparent enough: to propagate a general European conspiracy theory connecting the Assassins with the Masons whom, he claimed, were the instigators of the French revolution.[13] In *Foucault's Pendulum*, Umberto Eco's world conspiracy fabulators claim Hassan Sabbah and his disciples not only as spiritual masters of the Templars, but as heirs to the occult heritage of Egypt, by purest coincidence the seat of the first Ismaili dynasty, the Fatamids, among whom Hassan Sabbah would have perfected his mastery of secret doctrine. But while Hassan, like many learned men of the day, was certainly familiar with astronomy and with the science of zodiacal signs, no evidence of any occult connection exists. The Old Man of the Mountain and his zealots were, for better or for worse, human. Like you and like me, *hypocrite lecteur, mon semblable, mon frère.*

LITTLE HAS REMAINED of the stronghold which once contained an entire community of warriors and ascetics. Direct access to the summit remains blocked by a high masonry and rock wall which guards the only natural cleft in the rock. At the height of Hassan Sabbah's power, the fortress boasted a garrison of more than one thousand supplied by an extensive network of fields and orchards. It also concealed, in the luxuriant imagination of legend, a secret garden where young ladies trained in the voluptuous arts would, for one night, create the illusion of Qu'ranic paradise for young *fedayin* whose faculties had been dulled by wine and hashish — the ultimate degree of their initiation into the Order's nihilistic sanctum sanctorum. When they awoke, the initiates would be told that, by the grace of Hassan Sabbah, they had tasted of paradise — a paradise that they could only revisit when, after driving home the dagger, they would die a martyr's death. So devoted were these *fedayin* to their master that they would leap from the summit to the rocks below at his command to prove their fealty and their faith. This too is probably a fiction, concocted to complete the diabolical portrait of Hassan.

Standing at the foot of the fortress I struggle to visualize the paths of assault, the road to the hidden garden which most probably never existed, the pinnacle atop which the Grand Master's observatory and library were perched. But the hour is late, the weather is closing in, and the narrow path which leads across a 45° scree-strewn slope to the summit is coated with patches of ice. My running shoes, though sturdy and thick-soled enough for the worst of Tehran sidewalks, are laughably inadequate to the challenge of icy stones. One missed step would surely send an unfortunate climber hurtling hundreds of metres onto the jagged, rocky mountainside below, with no assurance of a soft landing in the heavenly garden.

The impregnable rock that defeated so many assailants has defeated me. Discretion, as my ever-cautious father never failed to remind me, is the better part of valour. Let's turn back, I suggest to Majid. There is some grumbling in the ranks. Mahmoud the mountaineer, for whom this

climb is the merest of bagatelles, glares at me with reproach and, I suspect, a barely masked measure of scorn. Khairollah and Fadollah, who
dragged me up the last few hundred metres of hillside, seem torn
between amusement and mystification at the ways of the foreigner.
Majid, an increasingly apprehensive eye on the weather, sees my point.
Now that he knows the way, he can return in summer, when the road
will be passable and the cool upland weather a relief from the heat and
pollution of Tehran.

With a pang of regret mixed with relief which I attempt, unsuc-
cessfully I fear, to conceal from my companions, I wobble rubber-legged
down the hill. Climbing the fortress of Alamut, especially in winter
weather conditions, is not for the faint of heart. Defeated by a combination of hunger, altitude and lack of that mysterious quality that makes
men climb ever higher, I am still happy to have all but touched my goal
— the Eagle's Nest — and survived to tell the tale. Now, as we stumble
down through the village and into relative warmth, I reflect how cold
and lonely Hassan Sabbah's life would have been atop the rocky crag —
its only inhabitants now a flock of goats which appear silhouetted
against the lowering sky, their bleating blending with the rush of the
wind — in the cold hard months of the Iranian winter. Our two boon
companions stride off diagonally across the hillside toward the village
with a wave and a smile. This is home, after all, and their families are
waiting, probably over a bubbling pot of chicken barley soup with sour
lemon. The thought of food brings tears to my eyes, and saliva to my
mouth.

Back at the truck Majid and I tear ravenously at the bread he'd
stashed behind the seat, and gulp down lukewarm cola so fast I slice the
tip of my nose on the sharp edges of the can opening. Mahmoud the
mountaineer seems resigned. Manoeuvring backward down the precipi-
tous track, Majid finally gets the Mazda turned around, and we roar off
in a flurry of wet gravel, waving to the crowd of village kids that have
congregated.

As the pick-up snakes back down the hill into the humidity of the
Shahrud valley, Majid snaps a cassette of Iranian pop music into the
tape deck. Forbidden stuff it is, with sensual, percussion-backed rhythms
and languid women's voices. While the music drones on, I look back
over my shoulder: Dark clouds have descended over Alamut, hiding the
fortress from view. Did the Assassins not ultimately fail? I wonder.
Certainly the Order never changed the course of history as did the

Seljuqs or the Mongols, or even the Crusaders. As champions of exemplary violence, their policy of terror brought on increased repression as often as it won concessions. The ruling religious establishment brought down anathemas on their heads: they were apostates, agents of the devil. In an era of widespread violence by the forces of established order, the Assassins never sought to channel popular resentment into a revolutionary movement. Perhaps their accomplishment was to have kept alive the flame of religious purity inextricably coupled with a sense of Iranian identity which no conqueror, in the course of 2,500 years, has been able to destroy.

TWO BONE-RATTLING HOURS out of Gazorkhan we enter Mo'allem Kellayeh, a large village on the Qazvin road beneath another of the region's Assassin fortresses. It is perhaps even wilder than Alamut, but without the craggy, isolated grandeur of Hassan Sabbah's headquarters. Exhausted, our shoes caked with mud, but mostly thirsty, we stop off at the first teahouse we encounter. One of the customers, a grizzled mountain man, suggests I'm a Muslim because I drink my tea in the Iranian country fashion: slurping from the saucer which holds the small glass tumbler, having first placed a cube of sugar between my teeth.

In the teahouse, foreigners are rare indeed. We hear vague references to some Englishmen who visited the area last year — although it may well have been John Simpson several years ago, or Dame Freya Stark sixty years earlier, when she passed through gathering material for her *Valleys of the Assassins*, a small classic of English adventure literature. The small talk turns from the Assassins to a local marvel, in the nearby village of Zarabad. There, says another local, stands an ancient plane tree which weeps real blood on every Ashura, anniversary of the martyrdom of Imam Hossein on the battlefield at Karbala. "That's where you foreigners should be going; forget the Assassins," Majid translates the man's words. "They're long dead and gone." I raise my eyebrows in faintest doubt. Yes, the teahouse patrons insist, it is so. Eye-witnesses are brought in to corroborate the story. "I've seen it myself," declares a white-bearded man. And since Iran is still — but for how long? — a culture which reveres the wisdom of the old, who were we, unbelievers and city folk at that, to doubt his word. Instead of the poverty of disbelief and the aridity of Western techno-rationalism, I feel a sudden temptation to cast my lot with the old man who has seen the ancient plane tree at Zarabad shed its bloody tears. The story is perfectly congruent with this cruel and beautiful landscape, and its exalted and bloody past.

Again I think of the Assassins. For all its remoteness in time and space, the rise and fall of Alamut holds some instruction for our age, if only as a symbol. Pockets of exemplary resistance, they seem to argue, are an inevitable by-product of the tyranny of empire, whatever the empire, no matter what its claims to mark the end point of history. For no better reason than the faithlessness of our age, we cannot dismiss the faith of another. Nor can we ascribe to others our own emptiness as we prostrate ourselves at the feet of the golden calf. Somewhere in our midst an Assassin waits, sharpened dagger at the ready.

Behesht-e Zahra, the Martyrs' Cemetery, Tehran. Photo © Michael Coyne / The Image Bank.

3

Rose Water and Zahra's Paradise

WHEN THE IRANIAN ARMY Huey helicopter landed to discharge its cargo, the shadows were long on the dusty earth. Elbows linked and bearded faces straining with exhaustion, security men fought to hold back the crowd as it rushed forward like a flood tide, ebbed then surged forward again. Working frantically, a team of revolutionary guards placed the shroud-wound body of the white-bearded ascetic who had destroyed the once-mighty Pahlavi dynasty and humbled its even mightier American sponsors into a shallow grave and covered it with the red soil of Behesht-e Zahra cemetery. Ayatollah Ruhollah al-Mousavi Khomeini had returned for good to the place where he had proclaimed the advent of the Islamic Revolution ten years before.

I'D HEARD THE NEWS in Athens, where I'd been reporting on the 1989 election campaign. This, I'm convinced, was more than happenstance. There exists a deep, obscure affinity between Greece and Iran: the Greeks share with the Iranians an affection for gesticulation — nothing like an election to prove that — as well as a musical tradition, a basic stock of Arabic words, a sense of conviviality and hospitality common to the Middle East, a taste for philosophical disputation and an ancient, glorious, intersecting past. The Greek countryside still echoes with the clash of arms at Thermopylae and Salamis, as does Iran with the war cries of Alexander's revenge-intoxicated Macedonians. Greece's infatuation with the idea of its putative European past, and fear of its arch-rival Turkey, have come between it and its ancient, much respected antagonist, and obscured its rich substratum of Oriental sensibility. But the two lands share a powerful sense of cultural perenity, and the burden of a past which may never be equalled. The Greece I knew faced East: the door through which I entered Iran. Once again, that door was creaking open.

Walking through the downtown area on my way back from a short trip to the provinces, I had paused — perhaps on a hunch, perhaps seeking respite from the empty sound and fury of the campaign — at an information booth set up by Kurds in front of the University. The Greek government tolerates, even encourages these crypto-Marxist insurrectionists, perhaps hoping to destabilize Ankara's eastern flank. I walked over to their table. "Did you know?" they said in broken English. "The Imam, he is dead." As Marxists they should have been pleased; as Sunnis, indifferent. They were neither. Khomeini left few Middle Easterners, and fewer Muslims, indifferent. When I reached my hosts' house in the suburbs a half-hour later they had a message for me from the Iranian Embassy in Ottawa. A visa was waiting for me in Tehran.

Within twelve hours I was on a flight to Frankfurt where, following a ten-hour wait, I boarded an Iran Air 747 packed with journalists and television crews bound for Iran. After a midnight landing at Mehrabad Airport and several more hours of on-the-spot visa formalities, we reached the Laleh Hotel just before sunup. Within an hour we were bundled into a waiting bus, most of us in various stages of exhaustion and anticipation.

THE DAY — JUNE 6 — DAWNS hot and clear and the air is electric with the distant yet enveloping murmur of the crowd and the throb of funereal music more felt than heard. Under normal circumstances our destination, the immense but rarely used public prayer ground called Mossallah, is only ten minutes from the hotel. But on that morning traffic has ground to a halt. The broad downtown avenues are impassable, thronged with black-clad men and women trudging not north toward the site of the public memorial ceremony, but south, toward Behesht-e Zahra cemetery: Paradise of Zahra — the Radiant, as the Shi'ites call Fatima, daughter of the Prophet Mohammad.

We clamber, muttering, out of the bus and begin walking, led along toward the prayer ground by Islamic Guidance Ministry escorts. As we go, groups of men rush past, some bearing black flags or huge sad-eyed portraits of Imam Hossein, shouting slow, rhythmic chants comparing Khomeini to the martyr of Karbala, or expressing Fatima's heavenly grief at the death of her martyred husband Ali. Soon rumours begin to circulate: the ceremony, presided over by Iran's senior cleric, the ancient Grand Ayatollah Golpayegani, has been cut short. The funeral cortege has departed for the cemetery twenty-five kilometres to the south. Wait here, we are told, helicopters will come to take you to Behesht-e Zahra; the crowd is too great, our buses cannot move.

An hour later, packed sweating into the passenger hold of a Chinook helicopter, we are flying south. Beneath us, in all directions, the morning streets are dark with people making their way toward the cemetery. Within a few minutes the helicopter touches down in a dusty, flat field. We leap to the ground where we are met by a squad of revolutionary guards, young men in dark-green fatigues with black mourning bands on their sleeves. Behesht-e Zahra is on the edge of the desert; the sun is already burning down, and the immense crowd has stirred up a cloud of fine dust which gradually coats our clothing, our faces and hands, and sifts into our noses and throats.

Now, as we reach the perimeter of the compact throng pushing forward toward the grave site, our escort forms a flying wedge to guide us through. Around me I can see an ocean of dust-covered heads; it is as if tens, hundreds of thousands, millions of black-haired Iranians have suddenly gone dark blond. Faces, staring eyes turn toward us, hands reach out to touch; we feel ourselves driven from side to side, now born along by the flow of the crowd, now veering toward the tiniest gap in the compact human mass as water seeks an opening.

There, on the near horizon, stands a low tent. We turn toward it, duck beneath the sheltering canvas and sit down on cots while our escorts bring us cold water. At the far end of the field hospital doctors are working over an old man prostrate on one of the cots. Curious eyes peep through wind holes in the walls, and from all around us comes the roar of the multitude, and the distant, sombre resonance of a dirge; or am I imagining the sounds. No, it is a day of enfolding sounds; the wailing of sirens as police vehicles and ambulances seek vainly to advance through the press of humanity, the rhythmic beating of helicopter rotors, the roaring of portable electric generators, the sombre funeral music throbbing like a gigantic pulse, the chants rising from the throats of thousands, of millions, and the fragmented choking of sobs, the high-pitched warble of women ululating, each a thread in a complex fabric of clamour.

The mass of mourners is denser now; they seem oblivious to us as our escort works its way forward. To my left, I catch sight of a mobile bakery. From its doors black-clad bakers are throwing sheets of bread as the crowd of men and women surge around them, hands upraised. And now, mingled with the acrid smoke from the field bakery and the stinging dust I catch the scent of roses. A Tehran fire engine is spraying the crowd with rosewater.

Suddenly I spy a contingent of flagellants, thrusting like a wedge through the compact mass. Led by a huge drum which echoes like the heartbeat of grief itself they come, bodies jerking rhythmically from side to side under the impact of their chain flails, their exhalation coming in sharp, unison outbursts. The men, their faces engraved with the pain they inflict on themselves in memory of Imam Hossein, prefigure the blood feast of Ashura, most solemn day of the Shi'ite calendar. For them, today is Ashura.

The revolutionary guard formation escorting us is beginning to break down in the grieving. I can only catch a glimpse of the other members of our group, an occasional hat rising above the dust-covered heads or *chadors*. For an instant I stumble; the young guardsman at my elbow quickly pulls me to my feet. To fall here would mean death by trampling: There is no panic, no rush forward — simply the inexorable flow of feet in their millions moving on toward the grave site.

A lone helicopter swoops low over the multitude, releasing a cloud of what seemed like gigantic confetti. But as the particles flutter down into the crowd I realize they are flowers the colour of dark blood floating down onto a heaving dusty sea.

> *Someone will come*
> *someone who's with us in his heart, with us*
> *in his breath, with us in his voice*
> *someone who cannot be prevented from coming,*
> *who cannot be handcuffed and thrown in jail.*[14]

AS THE EMBERS of resistance against the rule of Shah Mohammad Reza Pahlavi finally flared into a revolutionary conflagration in the late 1970s, the imperial regime's victims, whether inspired by Islam or Marxism, were reunited in the hard-packed red earth of Behesht-e Zahra. First came the students, the intellectuals and the clerics, or the members of Islamist groups who sought to kill the snake by striking at its head. These men and women met death in front of firing squads, or in the horror chambers of the Shah's homegrown but American- and Israeli-trained torturers.

As the upheavals grew in size, and spilled out into the streets, they became regularly punctuated by police, then army bullets culminating in large-scale massacres. As the composition of its residents changed, the cemetery emerged as the mirror image of a nation in turmoil. These were the people Imam Khomeini called the *mostazafin*, the poor and the disinherited who rallied behind the old man with the black turban and the blacker eyebrows, the frail man with the tremulous, hurt-filled voice with its deep echo of iron. A voice which moved grown men to tears. The people who brought down the Shah by confronting his Immortal Guards — a sententious and alienating reference to the pre-Islamic Sassanian Dynasty — with bare chests in the final battle which, Khomeini declared, would be the triumph of blood over the sword.

It was here that Khomeini first came when he returned to Tehran in mute, sober triumph on a cold February morning in 1979, driving across Tehran along flower-strewn streets lined by millions, welcomed by chants of *Shah raft, Imam amad* — the Shah has gone, the Imam has come.

When Shi'ite Muslims say "Imam," they may mean the prayer leader at the neighbourhood or village mosque, or one of the revered Twelve Imams descended from Fatima, the Prophet's daughter, and Ali, the fourth caliph. More precisely, they can mean the long-awaited one, the Twelfth Imam, the Mahdi who is now in occultation awaiting the day of resurrection and divine justice. Was Khomeini the One? His entourage did nothing to discourage the speculation — or the ambiguity. And for the common people who lined his route in their millions — profound reverberations.

"I had my daughter at that time and I was pregnant," recollects Dr. Sussan Parsa, an American-educated professor of public hygiene at Tehran's Shahid Beheshti University. "We went to my sister-in-law's home because it was very close to the road that Imam Khomeini was going to pass, and as he was passing we had a flower in our hand and everybody was throwing the flower to the little bus that was passing, where Imam Khomeini was sitting. And the thing that I remember is, I was crying a lot. All my face was wet and I was crying because we were so happy and so excited."

Another eye-witness, investment banker and publisher Sadeq Sami'i, who today sarcastically dismisses the overthrow of the Shah as the "golden revolution," remembers how happy the people of the capital were that day, as they distributed sweets and pastries and kissed one another: "They were practically washing the streets and putting flowers right in the middle of the pavement. I still remember it vividly," he told me twelve years later, in a voice caught between irony and respect.

It was a moment that revolutionary Iran's fervent supporters describe as a complete end and a new beginning. An old man of austere manner and penetrating intelligence, who spoke the language of the peasantry, the urban poor and the village *mollahs* and who articulated with masterful ease the emotionally-charged rhetoric of the 1,400-year Shi'ite tradition of resistance to illegitimate authority, was among them at last, returned from years of exile in the holy sanctuaries of Najaf, in Iraq, and a threadbare apartment in Neuphle-le-Château, a Paris suburb. Bypassing the parliament buildings — symbol of an imported democratic model with which his dream of Islamic rule had little affinity — Ayatollah Khomeini's car headed south, through Tehran's raucous commercial districts and teeming southern slums, and to the cemetery. There, his first public gesture was to weep openly over the graves of the fallen.

NOTHING COULD HAVE prepared me for what I was about to witness on this hot, windy day in June, 1989. Our small group of journalists has broken up in the seething crowd; now each of us struggles forward guided by one, perhaps two revolutionary guardsmen. Suddenly a double wall of freight containers looms up in front of us. Strong hands reach down to grasp mine while my escorts help my feet find protrusions on the side of the steel walls. Half dragged, half pushed, I heave myself atop the container and climb to my feet. There before me, as in the courtyard of a great mosque-to-be set out as a square compound demarcated by a rank of containers, a close-ranked mass of black-clad humanity surges back and forth around the grave site. Most of the containers are sagging from the weight of cameras and crews from the major American and European networks and Iranian television, along with hundreds of still photographers and dozens of newspaper reporters. Jot down a few notes. How? Journalist's reflexes paralyzed. Take notes on a tidal wave or a cyclone.

The throng within the compound whirls, now clockwise, now counter-clockwise, a viscous maelstrom, as banners and huge posters of Khomeini flare in the dusty air, then vanish, supplanted by waves of men striking their chests in the rhythmic cross-handed fashion of Shi'ite mourning rites, the slapping of open palms marking a counterpoint to the constant drone of the dirge. One group of mourners veers aside while other groups, younger men these, rush forward chanting the political slogans of the revolution: Death to America, Death to the Soviet Union, Death to Israel, *Allah ô-Akbar* (Great is God), *Khomeini is our leader, O Hossein, we are with you in Karbala*. These groups, smaller and more coherent than the others, are led by uniformed marshalls and appear to be disciplined. They wheel, counter-march and manoeuvre in near-military precision from one television camera to another, brandishing fists in the air, roaring a defiance I had come over the years to recognize as well-rehearsed, if heartfelt only for the moment when the red light of the video camera blinked on, a kind of high rhetoric of the body collective.

Like a fisher-bird skimming the surface of troubled waters, the body of a man — unconscious, perhaps dead, for dozens would die before the sun had set — floats across the heads of the crowd carried high on outstretched hands to one of the field hospitals or to the makeshift morgue. While the convulsive circling of the crowd around the grave site has the appearance of a whirlpool in the wild yet deliberate swirl of its choreography, behind us, beyond the perimeter of freight containers, lies a boundless, formless, rising and falling expanse from which, at intervals, young men, their faces engraved with intense despair, suddenly emerge and scramble up the sides of the steel-box walls with the power and agility of an epileptic seizure. Once atop the battlements they are taken aside, gently at first, by the revolutionary guardsmen who attempt to persuade them to go back. But the young men are in no mood to listen to reason; this is not a day for reason. This is a day for dying, a tearful Islamic Guidance interpreter tells me as he points skyward; a day to be reunited with the Imam in Zahra's paradise. A day of rosewater, dust and blood.

The interlopers have come from some ochre brick alleyway in south Tehran, perhaps from the satellite towns populated by jobless rural migrants, perhaps from a village in the region, but they have come to pay their last respects to their Imam, to weep for him as he wept for them. They are not to be deterred. Equally unbending, the guards first lower, then drop them back; other would-be participants are thrown back bodily into the crowd like sacks of potatoes, landing on upstretched hands. Clearly the security forces fear being overrun by the grief-crazed multitude; the mode switches from persuasion to exemplary, if summary, dissuasion.

Through the journalists atop the palisade sweeps the news: The ambulance carrying Khomeini's body cannot move through the streets. The coffin will be brought to Behesht-e Zahra by helicopter, then delivered to the grave site in a vehicle. It is early afternoon when the car, an ambulance or a hearse, inches through the crowd. But when the doors open frantic mourners rush toward the exposed, white-wrapped body, grasping for a piece of the shroud as a holy relic. Suddenly a glimpse of stark flesh as his body falls from the coffin to the earth followed by a sharp gasp of sacrilege and horror. The burial detail quickly loads the old man's frail corpse back into the vehicle. Two hours later the winged horse of death, its beating rotors whipping the dust into a choking cloud, eases to earth and the Imam's body, rewrapped in a fresh shroud, is quickly laid to earth.

I return to Tehran in the passenger seat of an army helicopter piloted by a helmet-clad, mustachioed air-force officer. Tear streaks line his dust-caked face like scars. We swing up and over the grave site, circling higher and higher as the crowd, in its millions, makes its way slowly homeward, thronging the Qom expressway and the avenues leading north toward Tehran.

How many millions? The regime settled on ten. Probably never had so many people congregated in one place with one single purpose. As I learned later, Khomeini's survivors did not know what to expect and had been prepared for the worst. But the people did not rise up against the government; the regime did not collapse in factional strife. Instead the Guardian Council quickly convened to appoint Seyyed Ali Khamene'i, the president, as new Leader and spiritual guide. Neither did the country's hard-pressed citizens turn against the *mollahs*, despite the hardships of the war and the regime's inability to solve Iran's seemingly intractable economic problems. Ultimately, I believe, the massive turnout at the funeral was also a reminder from Iranians to their leaders that, in Islamic Iran, revolutionary legitimacy still springs from the street.

§

It should never be imagined that those who are martyred on the path of God are dead, on the contrary they have eternal life, and are blessed by God.

— The Qur'an

WHENEVER I VISIT IRAN I return to Behesht-e Zahra. The cemetery has stopped growing at the boomtown pace of the early and mid-'80s, when each day would see the burial of dozens — hundreds — of war dead, becoming the epiphenomenon of an ancient culture which had been long obscured in the rush to Westernized modernity: that of martyrdom.

On a bright, windy day in December, 1992, my wife Ingeborg and I stroll among the graves. Some are marked by standing structures displaying a faded photograph of the deceased, or a document, a military decoration, a tiny bouquet of dried flowers or a tattered flag snapping in the cold wind off the desert.

At one end of the cemetery's main footpath leading from the fountain which once gushed water dyed bloodred lies the grave marker of Ayatollah Taleqani, one of the Islamic Revolution's most revered ideological and moral leaders. Further along, renovations are underway at the small mausoleum, dedicated to Ayatollah Martyr Beheshti, which houses the remains of one of revolutionary Shi'ism's most powerful thinkers and organizers, assassinated along with more than one hundred others in a bomb attack on the headquarters of the Islamic Republic party, in 1981. Although more than a hundred died, their number is always listed as seventy-two, the number of Imam Hossein's faithful supporters who perished with him in the fateful engagement at Karbala.

Tears come to our eyes when we pause to look more closely at the simple grave markers of the young men who died in the uprising that brought down the Shah, or in the Iran-Iraq war which followed, as night must follow day. A flat marble plaque with the dead man's name, birthdate and the outline of an open book with the inscription "This is the book of the life of Ahmad," or of Ali, or Reza or Mohammad, or of Hamid or Masoud or Daryoush. The books of our own comfortable lives must by now contain several chapters — whether well or badly written, whether accounts of courage or caution, we cannot — perhaps dare not — judge. The text of these young men's books hold perhaps a page or two of hope, or blind bravery. Maybe the immortal bravado of adolescence. Certain or uncertain faith in the face of unexpected terror, then death: cruel, sudden, perhaps welcome. The grave of a young *shahid* (martyr) dead at age seventeen, killed in street fighting against the police. A mother washing her son's grave. A father arranging a few stems of bloodred gladioli atop a marker. As he leaves, he pauses to offer us a handful of candies.

BEHESHT-E ZAHRA, JULY 1985. In the numbing midsummer heat people throng the necropolis. It is Thursday afternoon, the day when the Tehranis flock to the cemetery. Filmmaker Ron Hallis and I have driven here after a meeting with Abdulvahad Hosseini, who lost three of his four children in the revolution and then the war. Mr. Hosseini is a powerful man in his late fifties with the strong hands of a carpenter although, he confesses with a shy smile, he is also an amateur wrestler. Scars and broken teeth remain as mute testimony to his encounters with SAVAK, the Shah's secret police. For the occasion, he sits between two large portraits of his sons, Hossein and Hassan. His gentle, measured tone is in absolute contrast with the tragic account of their death.

"Any father or mother knows a parent's feelings toward his children. But we knowingly sent our children off to martyrdom, even though we knew they would be an asset to the revolution. But they made their decision to serve Islam, because at that moment, the very existence of Islam was in danger."

Abdulvahad Hosseini's personal tragedy and pride is a drop from the bloodred fountain that greets all visitors to the graveyard. A few hundred metres beyond the fountain workers are pouring fresh concrete atop the grave of an entire family of air-raid victims. Black-clad men offer us hard green astringent plums and glasses of cold water. The scent of rosewater hangs in the air blending with the aroma of freshly watered soil where spindly young saplings have been planted between the rows of graves. The sounds of mourning crackle in the parched air like a flames racing along the edge of a sheet of desiccated paper.

The melodious rise and fall of the dirge-like psalmody reaches our ears before we turn the corner. There, at the end of a row of expectant burial plots stands a group of mourners, mostly middle-aged men, gathered around a grave, participants in a memorial service for a young man killed at the southern front in the war against Saddam. (In Iran, where the name of the martyred third Imam is revered by all Shi'ites, the Iraqi dictator was never called Saddam Hussein, only Saddam.) The chief mourner, in a richly timbred voice, intones a rhythmic chant as the men strike their chests with the slow, measured blows of an Ashura procession: *What rains down? Blood! Who? The Eye! How? Day and Night! Why? From grief! What grief? The grief of the Monarch of Karbala! What was his name? Hossein! Of whose race? Ali's! Who was his mother? Fatima!* The narrative voice recounts the death of Imam Hossein at the hands of the usurper Yazid in the desert at Karbala, supreme moment of Shi'ite martyrology and eerily evocative, even for a lapsed Catholic, of Holy Week ritual in its sense of expiatory sacrifice.

Immersed in their grief, transported by the ritual representation of it, the group of mourners barely notices the video camera. But before we can advance more than a few steps, we are surrounded by dozens of men and women who suddenly coalesce into a demonstration around us, waving fists and shouting the litany of slogans which, over the years, insinuated themselves into the soundscape of revolutionary Iran. Iraqi aerial bombardment of Tehran has eased, but tension and feelings were still running high. Here at the burial ground women outnumber men: women from Tehran and from the border provinces come up to us, shouting abuse at Saddam and his foreign backers. *Jang jang ta pirouzi*, shout groups of adolescent girls and boys, brandishing their fists, *War, war until victory*. Curiously — or perhaps not — the sexes mingle much more freely here in the emotion-charged precincts of death than on the closely watched workaday streets, black-clad bodies often touching in holy, fleeting promiscuity.

Something about these groups of spontaneous demonstrators catches our attention: The same faces seem to appear and reappear. One of the most vocal women, who carries a blue plastic radiator anti-freeze bottle, appears to be following us around, urging on the others in a strident voice from the fringes of the crowd. Later, back in Tehran, we encountered similar groups, individuals who would emerge as if from nowhere, and gel into a fiery-eyed, fiercely chanting crowd. We never could determine whether the demonstrators were indeed indignant passersby or flying squads of trained spontaneous demonstrators made up of idle youths recruited to spread the revolutionary message. Whatever the case, no sooner had we packed away camera and microphone than the angry crowds dispersed, reverting once again to a multiform and disparate mass of shoppers, tea drinkers, small merchants, itinerants and militia men.

EVEN BEFORE HIS DEATH, the Radiant One's husband, Ali, had become the focus of dissent within the small but growing community of the faithful. Designated by his father-in-law, the Prophet Mohammad, as his successor, Ali was pushed aside by a coalition of military men and tribal chiefs who chose Abu Bakr, the leading general of the Muslim armies, to lead. However, in deference to the older military leader, Ali did not press his claim. Twenty-five years later, he was finally elected caliph following the murder of Osman, a representative of the Bani Omayyid, a wealthy Meccan merchant clan whose members were latecomers to the faith. Osman's followers quickly accused Ali of complicity when he failed to denounce the killers.

Ali's reign, for the Shi'ites, ushered in the golden age of Islam. But it was as tumultuous as it was short-lived. Mo'awiya, a Bani Ommayad chieftain, raised a rebellion against the Imam from Damascus; after an inconclusive battle, human arbitration favoured his claims to the caliphate. At the same time Ali, who ruled from the city of Kufa in the Iraqi desert, faced internal upheaval at the hands of the Kharejites, pietists who claimed that only God could decide the matter. After destroying a Kharajite army in battle, Ali was struck down by the poisoned dagger of a lone killer sent by the sect, and died in 661. Mo'awiya became caliph in Damascus soon afterward. The Shi'ites trace their origins back to this, the first scission in the house of Islam. Those who supported his claims called themselves *Shi'at 'Ali* — the party of Ali.

§

> *Every month is Moharram,*
> *Every day is Ashura,*
> *Every place is Karbala.*

AS THE RULING DYNASTY declined rapidly into absolutist corruption, the hopes of Ali's followers rested on his two sons by the Prophet's daughter Fatima, Hassan and Hossein. Hassan, the second Imam, withdrew to Medina after entering into a pact of imposed peace and non-resistance with the caliph to preserve, so argues Shi'ite exegesis, the higher interests of the community of the faithful. But his younger brother Hossein refused to make obeisance to Yazid, the son of Mo'awiya, whose impiety and taste for luxury were a matter of public notoriety. In fact, the Imam had vowed to fight. "The point is," wrote Dr. Ali Shariati in 1972, "that a criminal rules over the fate of the people, and a person who is responsible for the fate of the people must, to the point possible, eliminate the usurpation and administer justice and take over the rule. This is not only the right of the Imam; this is his certain and clear duty."[15]

In 682 AD (60 AH), warned that the new caliph was undertaking energetic counter-measures to suppress his incipient revolt, Hossein marches off toward Kufa, the city in Iraq whose citizens have promised him support. That support never materializes. Hossein's small force of some seventy men, accompanied by their wives and children, is intercepted by the forces of Yazid in the desert and forced to bivouac near Karbala, cut off from the water of the Euphrates by the surrounding troops. Yazid offers Hossein terms. Hossein does his duty. He fights. His half-brother Abbas fetches water from the river, but on his return to the encampment his hands are cut off by the attackers. Hossein's youngest son is struck by an arrow while his father holds him in his arms. On the tenth day of the Qur'anic month of Moharram, Hossein is decapitated and his followers massacred by the imperial troops amid scenes of heart-wrenching cruelty. His elder son Ali and his sister Zaynab survive, spared by Yazid, his bloodthirst now slaked.

> Had he garments for his body? Yes, the dust of the road!
> Had he a turban on his head? Yea, the staves of the wicked ones!
> Was he sick? Yes. What medicine had he? The tears of his eyes!
> What was his food after medicine? His food was his heart's blood!
> Did any bear him company? Yes, the fatherless children![16]

In military terms the engagement was insignificant. Its political and moral impact was shattering. The martyrdom of Imam Hossein galvanized the followers of Ali and, nourished by time and the rancour of powerlessness, shaped the Shi'ite dissidence into a full-fledged oppositionist movement against Sunni domination. Imam Hossein came to personify, for the Shi'ites, the fate of humanity in the face of overwhelming and tyrannical power. More, insists Ali Shariati: the responsibility of the righteous to say Yes when the voices of hopelessness and fatalism clamour No. Triumph of blood over sword; defeat as victory.

Ever since, Shi'ite religious and political culture — even more closely intertwined than in Sunni Islam — has been marked by the cult of martyrdom in which every believer may participate, through the rituals which evoke emotion and intent, in Imam Hossein's doomed yet ennobling struggle against the power of corrupt authority.

Every month is Moharram,
Every day is Ashura,
Every place is Karbala

— the Islamic revolutionaries used to say. Unlike the tragic fourth Imam, however, they were intent on defeating the oppressor Shah, and the perfidious Saddam/Yazid.

Rarely in the stormy and convoluted history of Shi'ite opposition had the cult of martyrdom found such powerful expression as it did in the hands of Imam Khomeini. What struck Westerners as an incomprehensible yet potent mix of insurrectionary zeal and death-seeking fatalism as bound in ambiguity as the historical figure of Hossein himself, had crystalized into an ideological weapon. Ali Shariati had provided a generation of young Iranian intellectuals with the conceptual tools which enabled them to respond to Khomeini's charismatic call to arms. Muslims, declared the Imam, must do what Allah bids them to do; it is then up to Allah whether to supply the results in this or a future lifetime.[17]

Allah had given His marching orders. On the streets of Iranian cities, on the road to the front and in the trenches facing Iraqi lines, the foot soldiers of the Islamic revolution were constantly confronted with slogans, sometimes displayed on huge billboards, designed to remind them of their sacred mission. *The path to Al-Qods [Jerusalem] lies through Karbala; to reach the shore of happiness we must pass through a sea of blood.*[18] The exhortations that had rallied street fighters against the Shah later became a singular reminder of the absolute particularity of Iran's armed forces, for whom the shedding of their own blood was as great a virtue as the shedding of the enemy's; to die in battle against the agents of infamy was as ennobling as to inflict death upon them. Though suicide is a grave transgression for Muslims, death as martyrdom would open the portals to paradise.

"*Shahadat*, in our culture, in our religion, is not a bloody and accidental event," wrote Shariati. "In other religions and in the histories of nations, martyrdom is the sacrificing of the heroes who are killed in battle by the enemy. It is considered to be a tragic event, full of sorrow.... But in our culture, *shahadat* is a desired death which a *mujahid* (fighter for the faith), with all of his consciousness, logic, reasoning, awareness and understanding chooses himself."[19]

Individual soldiers, particularly the ill-trained *bassijis* and the revolutionary guards who bore the brunt of the most brutal combat in the desperate early days of the war, wore red headbands bearing short inscriptions. *O Hossein, Allah ô-Akbar....* Many of these young men wrote (or had written for them) wills to be sent to their families after their death. Most were anonymous, some the clumsily initialled standard letters provided for the illiterate. Others were collected and published by the Iranian government in a slim volume entitled *In memory of our martyrs.* In one of them Ahmad Musai'e, age and place of birth unknown, writes: "I ask you all to try and understand the Imam better. He is the representative of Mahdi and the echo of God. Like Abraham and Mohammad, he is also a destroyer of idols. Never abandon his path. Remember that if you do not solve the problems of the deprived masses, you will be defeated. Tell those who still do not know the Imam to go and reflect over him and come back to their senses. He is the spirit of God, he is the destroyer of idols, and he is the man who has continued the path of Ali and Hossein."

ONE OF THE HUNDREDS OF THOUSANDS of rectangular flat marble plaques of Behesht-e Zahra bears the name of Hossein Arfati beneath the Qur'anic inscription: "We are from God and to God we return." Through a friend, I had met Hossein's parents at their home in Ektiarieh, a middle-class residential area of northeast Tehran, where they tell their story. No Islamic Guidance minder is present, and they speak directly in Farsi for my tape recorder. (Later, back in Montréal, an Iranian friend translates the tape for me.)

Ahmad Arfati: "I had three sons and two daughters. Martyr Hossein was my first. He was a fine son, with a deep faith in Islam. He wanted to become a clergyman, and a teacher. The best teachers are *rohani* (clergymen), he always used to say."

"One day he came home from theological school where he was studying and told us about Imam Khomeini's decree. Now he intended to go to the front, and he came to tell us good-bye. He left the next morning. A week after, Operation Karbala Five began, and he participated in the offensive. One of his friends was wounded; he told us that Hossein's leg was wounded and bleeding. The friend told him to wait where they were, for transfer to the rear. Hossein said "When I came to the front, I didn't do it to turn my back,' and went forward. He was martyred on December 13, 1985."

Mrs. Arfati: "It was easy for us to accept his martyrdom, because much as we miss our dear son, God is dearer to us. I do not regret his death; I know he did it for Islam. My son is no dearer than Imam

Hossein's son, or those martyrs who fought for Islam in the early days of our religion."

Ahmad Arfati: "When Islam is in danger, we are ready to sacrifice everything. My son Hossein's funeral didn't mean black. Black is the colour of death, not of martyrdom. Bloodred is the colour of martyrdom."

I could not help flinching at these recitations of a loved one's death. The Arfatis were not the first martyr family I had interviewed. The death of their son was no less tragic than that of millions of other sons, brothers, uncles, fathers. But at the same time that I attested the grip of the culture of blood and martyrdom on Iranians, I found myself unable to conceive of a power of belief so intense as to cause mothers not to mourn their sons. The Iran of the Arfatis was a country far removed from that of the glib Westernized uptown polyglots, the war profiteers and the sanctimonious *mollahs* who preached self-sacrifice and practised self-enrichment. It was a country which dipped its hands in the blood of martyrs. Exhorted its soldiers not to victory but to death. The Iran that lives at Behesht-e Zahra, city of the dead.

Iran's military strategy in the war against Iraq proclaimed the superiority of men over weapons, at the cost of an entire generation. Hundreds of thousands died or were wounded in positional warfare of a kind last seen in the trenches of World War I; in charges by raw, ill-armed recruits through withering fire against well-defended positions. Though Iran's forces held the first Iraqi thrust and fought back courageously, they were not victorious. An apologist might claim that the engagement at Karbala was over in a matter of days while the modern-day emulators of Imam Hossein had heroically fought the modern incarnation of Yazid for eight years. An Ali Shariati might have argued that the politics of the Middle East in the late twentieth century were quite congruent with the Karbala paradigm.

Certainly, without drawing on the hidden power of the cult of martyrdom, Iran could not have preserved its political or territorial integrity during the first years of the war when massive groups of poorly armed young volunteers who knew they were the country's first and last line of defense held, then repulsed, well-armed Iraqi forces. Carnage. Hardly paradoxical that the blood-drenched purity of these Islamic combatants was undermined by the influx of sophisticated US arms via Israel. The process culminated in the tragicomically botched high-level visit of President Ronald Reagan's former National Security Adviser Robert

McFarlane and Lieut. Colonel Oliver North to Tehran in May, 1986.

As US TOW anti-tank missiles neutralized previous Iraqi-armoured domination of the front lines, the military initiative had swung over to the Iranian side. But a minority segment of the country's political and religious leadership had concluded that Iran's victory party had sealed a Faustian bargain with the Great Satan himself. The word was out: Secret deals and negotiations had replaced blood fervour and sacrifice. The battlefield was no longer a sea of blood whose far shore was Jerusalem. It had become a chessboard. Deep in the entrails of the martyr culture the worms of doubt had begun to gnaw.

AT THE NORTHERN EDGE of Behesht-e Zahra, its huge gilded dome gleaming in the winter sun, its four towering minarets visible from kilometres distant, the Aramgah-e Khomeini — the Khomeini Mausoleum — rises on the precise spot where, in 1989, the Imam was buried, according to his wishes, in a poor man's grave. Atop the dome flies a crimson flag: the only other place in the Islamic world where such a flag flies is over the shrine of Imam Hossein at Karbala.

As Ingeborg and I wander about the outskirts of the sanctuary on that bright December morning, I try to search out some point of orientation to jog my memory of this once barren field. Perhaps the reflecting pool with its fountains and raw concrete ablution basins now occupy the space where the field hospitals had been hastily thrown up, or perhaps the mobile bakery. The mausoleum itself is a huge structure whose outer walls, I estimate, trace the perimeter of the cargo containers drawn up for the burial. It reminds me of nothing so much as an indoor arena, an architectural derivative of the suburban shopping mall, built to accommodate tens of thousands. In its present form, roof resting atop structural steel girders which leave light fixtures, air-conditioning and heating ducts exposed, it is much more a warehouse in a new suburban industrial park than a religious structure.

Where once the dusty field swarmed with near-frantic multitudes, a small city is now taking shape. When completed, the complex, whose chief promoter is Seyyed Ahmad Khomeini, the Imam's politically powerful son and jealous guardian of his father's legacy, will include hotels, a theological seminary and, of course, a bazaar. For Islam is a religion of townspeople, of traders and merchants, and Iran's own Islamic revolution — not to say the *mollahs* as a social group — owes its success to the financial support of wealthy and pious *bazaaris*.

We leave our shoes with the doorkeeper, as must all who enter Muslim holy places, and go inside, men and women through separate entrances. The atmosphere this Friday morning is calm, peaceful. Men and women are praying or meditating, each in separate sections, while children gambol across the expanse of polished marble floors kept spotless by a brigade of sweepers working their way between the Persian carpets. Families are already laying down plastic mats as table cloths for the Friday family meal; bags of food wait close at hand. Throughout the country mosques and shrines are popular holiday destinations: the older and more venerable the shrine, the more intense the traffic.

Whispering prayers or verses from the Qur'an, or simply silent, knots of supplicants cling to the grill-work around the marble-clad bier which marks the exact spot where, less than three years before, Khomeini had been laid to earth. Some are weeping; others hold up infants. Most poke a few coins, or a tattered bill or two through the square-cut openings, adding to the heaps of money lying on the mirror-like dark marble. Here, in this huge semi-industrial shed kept cool in the torrid heat of summer and warm in the chill of winter, all the accoutrements of a traditional Iranian Shi'ite shrine are being assembled. Khomeini's injunctions for a simple resting place have been ignored. It is as though the old man's legacy of simplicity, austerity and self-sacrifice is being systematically cast in the concrete of his son's visionary neo-Islamic giantism, the message of intransigeance transformed into pietist rhetoric.

The thirty-year, multi-billion rial project will be the end point of the first functioning section of the long-promised Tehran Metro. Inside the vast, echoing space, we catch a whiff of the smell of poverty mingled with the scent of rosewater. Groups of day-pilgrims are arriving by minibus from the South Tehran suburbs: The men's faces are weather-worn, wrinkled, bearded, their hands are the hands of labourers and villagers; the women are tightly wrapped in their *chadors*, faces turned toward the ground, closed-off, remote. The faces and the mixture of sweet and acrid odours, touch off memories of the burial day. Kings and governments come and go; ideologies thrive then wither. Poverty and its handmaiden piety endure. Dust and roses.

Every night, a section of the huge enclosure is set aside for long-distance truckers, who sleep here in perfect safety before continuing on their journey. Throughout Iran — and the Islamic world — the mosque is the hostel of last resort, the community centre, the source of God's hospitality and nourishment to the rootless, the roofless and the wayfarer. Like the message of the Imam, the Khomeini mausoleum has now become part of the fabric of quotidian religious life.

MANY IRANIANS have been educated in American universities and speak excellent, if mildly accented English; but when I met Mohammad Ja'far, a tall, dark-skinned man with close-cropped curly hair, I was astonished by his perfect, idiomatic command of the language. In fact, if he had any accent at all, it was that of Black America. It all began to make sense a few days later when Mohammad confessed with a laugh that he was born in South Carolina and grew up in the Black ghetto of Washington, DC. But unlike many American Blacks who were drawn to the home-grown Black separatist variant then preached by the followers of Elijah Mohammad, Mohammad fell under the influence of Malcolm X in his last days, after his conversion to mainstream Islam, and thence to the fiercely anti-American positions of Iran's Islamic revolutionaries.

I never learned the precise circumstances which led Mohammad from the mean streets of Washington, DC to the sidewalks of Tehran, and he never volunteered the information. Besides, in Iran, he once cautioned me with his booming, explosive laugh, "There are some things you just don't want to know, man." Whatever the details of his background, he is well-informed, well-connected with several high-ranking Iranian officials, and highly respected by them for his quick wit and independence of mind, if not for his critical view of post-Khomeini politics.

I brought a tape recorder along to one of our many long and convoluted discussions over *kebabs* in a quiet restaurant. Although he's lived long enough in Iran to pass for a Pakistani immigrant, Mohammad didn't leave his shoot-from-the-hip American style at the door. Where Iranians may circle around touchy subjects, hedging, backing, filling and surrounding them with exquisitely polite ifs, ands and buts, Mohammad would speak his mind. After the table was clear and the machine running, the talk swung around, as it inevitably does when Iranian politics came up, to Ayatollah Khomeini.

"The Imam was a tremendously popular man and he shaped events in this country in a way that nobody else had shaped them before, not at least in living memory and not in the last I don't know how many hundreds of years," he explained.

"Many Iranians are not in love with the Imam, but they respect him, because whatever he said he believed in and he lived a certain way. And everything he said, he more or less did. The only thing that I'm aware of that he said and he didn't do was, he didn't win the war. But everything else throughout his history he accomplished. But my own feeling is that..." Pause. "Of course, they said that the Imam had a cancer — but my feeling is that the Imam died from a broken heart and that broken heart had to do with the war and it had to do also, I think, with his disappointment with the people around him."

The disappointment was probably inevitable. "The Imam asked us to climb all the way to the top of Damavand," a friend in Tehran told me with a rueful smile. "But we were only prepared for a short hike into the foothills."

THE FAITHFUL at Behesht-e Zahra come less to pay homage to the founder of the Islamic Republic than to spend a few quiet hours, perhaps an entire day, in the company of a man of proverbial ascetic purity and total devotion to the cause of God: a saint. They are less concerned that with Khomeini the cause found political expression, more that the laws of Islam ruled their lives, in form if not in spirit. They had always known, as we did not, that like the great martyrs of the Shi'ite tradition, Khomeini endured exile and public humiliation at the hands of the irreligious and the corrupt. They know this, which we contrive to ignore: unlike the Shah, who prided himself on being photographed in the company of every US president from Harry Truman to Jimmy Carter, Khomeini never travelled abroad to pay obeisance. Never bowed his head to any man. He is the first Iranian leader in living memory to be buried with honour in his own country, not driven from power or deposed by the machinations of foreign embassies and intelligence agencies. If sainthood can be defined as a combination of exemplary religious zeal and single-minded absolutism, Imam Khomeini — distant descendant of the Prophet — must qualify as a saint.[20]

His heirs will quarrel over his legacy, dispute the authenticity of his political testimony; each may well claim monopoly over the Khomeini heritage and declare the infallibility of his interpretation of the Khomeini corpus. It may be rejected. But the devout Iranians who come to the shrine are unlikely to be moved by such claims. They, after all, no less than the few clergymen who supported an obscure *Ayatollah*, were the first to respond, unquestioning, to his call to action on 15 Khordad 1342 (June 6, 1963) and, fifteen years later, to take to the streets against the Shah's police in the violent months before the overthrow. They marched off to war and martyrdom at his command, and when — finally overruled or abandoned by his pragmatic followers — he ordered the war to end, they stopped fighting. Now he has departed the realm of the political, the domain of violence and treachery, to become the interceder for those who seek the heavenly kingdom.

His legacy is Behesht-e Zahra, real and symbolic meeting place of the living and the dead.

Maessume Shrine in Qom, Iran. Photo © Michael Coyne / The Image Bank.

4

Moonlight in the Quince Groves of Isfahan

WINTER SUNSET COMES EARLY to the Iranian plateau. Evening stars are flashing on in the deepening turquoise firmament over the Isfahan oasis as Ingeborg and I stride briskly into the great square, the Meydan-e Imam; the call to evening prayer rings out, haunting and melodious in the distance. A few Isfahanis hurry by at a quick pace, collars turned up against the chill, bone-dry December wind. The shops which ring the perimeter of this immense public space are closed, the bustle of the bazaar stilled for the day. Here, where once Shah Abbas I (the man called "the Great" prior to the Islamic Revolution) reviewed his guards as they manoeuvred in tight formation on horseback, or cheered on his favourite polo players as they galloped wildly up and down the 700-metre-long square, a wind-blown mist from the water fountains draws a diaphanous veil across the arched spectator galleries, leaving the dome of the Sheikh Loftallah mosque to emerge, luminescent like a polished green stone against the pale indigo sky. A few more paces and we stand opposite the outer portal leading to the Masjid-e

Imam, the mosque of the Imam. The twin minarets tower over us as we walk slowly toward the arched entranceway, where the stalactite mouldings glint of burnished gold and turquoise in the floodlight. The massive wooden doors that open onto the inner court and the sanctuary are barred for the night. High in the upper reaches of the half-dome, night-birds flit in oblique trajectories, their shadows fleeting across the tile work which evokes a prayer rug hung in invitation to worship.

Next morning we wash down a breakfast of fresh Persian bread, honey and butter with cups of steaming lemon-fragrant tea, then strike out, breath frosting the air, excitement wrestling with anticipation, across the Bridge of the Thirty-Three Arches in the slanting sunlight, retracing our steps toward the great square. With dawn the city has come alive. In contrast with hilly, sprawling Tehran, Isfahan — a city of a mere one million inhabitants — is a relatively compact, even placid place. The rapid pace of pedestrians seems more a reaction to the frosty morning than any inclination to hurry. Workers glide by on bicycles, groups of young men and women clamber into city buses, businessmen hail taxis. On the steps to the bridge a lone beggar with the greasy, haggard, beatific look of a world-denying Sufi — or perhaps the glazed stare of an opium eater — has begun to stir. Isfahan has always been home to large numbers of Sufis, scraggly or humble beatifics intoxicated by God who stand at the far antipodes of the Islamic austerity preached by the Ayatollah Khomeini or the free market nostrums of his heirs. The man crawls from beneath his bright-coloured blanket, rubs his eyes and gets ready for another day's work of sitting motionless, hand extended, waiting for alms. He is still squatting there when we return hours later.

Now the northern extremity of the square, on our left, is crawling with dented Paykans, minivans, motorbikes and donkey carts gravitating around the bazaar entrance like fruit flies around an overripe peach. To our right, the main portals of the mosque are open now, and the complexity, subtlety and richness of their mosaic work stands revealed — gloriously — in the dawn light. We pause in the doorway, run our hands over the ancient silver trim of the doors, our steps suspended for an instant, balanced, like those of Ha'fez's Dervish, between eternity and infinity.

Our feet finally touch the smooth-worn stones of the entrance way and we edge forward into the courtyard. We are alone; the first rays of the early morning sun rising above the east *aivan* reflect off patches of thin ice floating on the ablution pool, touching with suddenness and delicacy the mirrored image of the sanctuary arch, the minarets and the delicately bulbous turquoise dome. The exterior walls give way to receding arches clad in turquoise tile; sweeping Arabic script quoting the Qur'an guides the eye toward the mihrab, the niche in the southeast wall which focuses symbolically on Mecca, while simultaneously sweeping it upward in an irresistible thrust replicated in the minarets toward the perfect, infinite azure of the sky. "Overwhelming" and "incomparable" are the words used by most foreign visitors, but in an age of bloated superlatives these words are insufficient. The power of the great mosque flows not from the interplay of volumes alone. Like music which echoes from the farthest point of the universe, so too does the architecture of the sacred speak directly to the emotions without the mediation of speech. The dome hangs seemingly suspended, weightless almost, above the bare floor of the sanctuary. I stand directly beneath its apex and clap my hands: The sound echoes seven times, sending the flock of resident doves fluttering in momentary fright from their perches in the finely-wrought arched lattice-work windows of the *aivans*. As the great lowering shell of the Aghia Sofia in Istanbul employs its mass to master and marshall the resonant vastness of interior space in a way never again equalled, so the Masjid-e Imam's gravity-defying structure focuses the eyes and diffuses the heart in the infinite sky, organizes the visual — and by extension the unseen, the unfathomable, the true and indifferent — universe.

Slowly we walk through the mosque, rejoicing in the sunlight pouring through the high east windows into colonnaded chambers which give onto the sanctuary. In the constantly shifting shafts of light the tiled interior surfaces of domes and walls glow with tones of blue and gold. Through an arched portal we enter a smaller, enclosed court, part of the theological school which once adjoined the mosque, where gnarled fruit trees and centuries-old grapevines overlook reflecting pools, where silence has replaced the whispered devotions of Qur'anic exegetes. Now the sunlight has reached the main courtyard floor; I sit down cross-legged on a low wall by the ablution pool and let my eyes wander at random across the panorama of abstract textual inscription intertwined with elaborate vegetable and floral motifs displaying the traditional Iranian invocation of fertility and abundance, its visual richness and complexity in counterpoint to the simplicity of the floor plan. Emotions flow in cascades of exuberance and humility, awe and the comforting sense of belonging. Individual worshippers cross the courtyard; a keeper rinses out an empty vessel in the pool, one or two tourists come, cameras clicking, and leave. A little girl chases the doves across the court in a sudden flutter of wings while her grandmother rests in the sunlight. This building, I realize in retrospect, is an immense and beatific mechanism for sensory dilation, a subtle and powerful manipulation of the stuff of the soul.

The British traveller Robert Byron, with the purism of the true eccentric, wrote disparagingly of the mosque's "huge acreage of coarse floral tilework," but did not see the tree for the blossoms, nor the field for the flowers. The Masjid-e Imam is flawed — only God may create perfection — by the haste with which Shah Abbas' architects and builders were exhorted to work by an exacting master. The mosque's imperfections may even be interpreted as a built-in defense against the vainglory of the mighty. Still, a surging creative power rooted in faith inhabits these precincts, as it does the rough-hewn, searing sincerity of Beethoven's monumental symphonies in their struggle to surmount the obstacles of worldly imperfection. The quality of the Royal Mosque is that which Islamic art places above all others: the Ultimate Degree, a symbolic evocation of the Qur'anic image of paradise, a garden enclosed against the encroaching desert and open to the sky. Belief in the God of Islam is not a requisite for grasping either the quality or the immanence: time, silence, contemplation are enough. Three hours later, when the sun disappears behind the sanctuary minaret I get to my feet, heart refreshed as by a drink of cool water on a hot day.

THE ZAYAND-E RUD oasis, named for the river that carries precious water to the gardens and quince orchards of Isfahan, has been a centre of trade and agriculture for centuries, perhaps millennia. Shah Abbas I, the ruler who assumed power in 1589, moved here from Qazvin in 1598, intent on transforming his new capital into the centre of the Islamic universe. It was to be the set-piece of an urban construction program never equalled in Islam, and rarely anywhere else: a harmonious, brilliantly conceived complex of bridges, public gardens, shaded thoroughfares, public markets, baths and monumental religious buildings — most of them still standing today — a great Qur'anic allegory proclaiming the glory of God and in its reflected splendour, the greatness of the Shi'ite Safavid monarchs. The Chahar Baq (Four Gardens), the great tree-lined main boulevard of Isfahan, bodies forth the Qur'anic theme of the four gardens of paradise.

Work on the Meydan — the climactic element in Shah Abbas' grand design — began in 1612. By then, after defeating the raiding Uzbeks in the east, he had driven the Ottoman Turks westward and out of Iranian territory, establishing himself as the first uncontested ruler of the historic territory of Iran since the pre-Islamic Sassanians of 1,000 years before.

By 1666, nearly forty years after Abbas' death, the French traveller Jean Chardin wrote that the city boasted 162 mosques, 48 madrasses, 182 caravansarais and 173 public baths. Isfahan was one of the world's great cities, giving rise to the popular rhyme *Isfahan nesf-e jahan* — "half the world is Isfahan." Isfahan is a monument to Shah Abbas. A ruthless absolutist, he handed out firm, impartial justice, yet was capricious and unpredictable toward his own family, causing his own son to be killed on suspicion of rebellion, and his two other sons blinded. Before his death, torn by remorse, the Shah wandered the narrow lanes of the city by night dressed as a beggar.[21]

Paradoxically the Safavids, creators of Isfahan and recreators of the Iranian national state, were not Persians at all but Turks, who, in the manner of previous — and subsequent — tribal conquerors, adopted Iran's superior culture and contrived to rule through the ancient Persian bureaucracy. (Iran, along with China, perfected the art of statecraft by a literate administrative caste.) But what set Safavid rule apart was its identification with Shi'ism, which the founder of the new dynasty, Shah Ismail, decreed as the state religion when he declared Tabriz his capital in 1501.

Ever since their crystallization into a permanent opposition after the martyrdom of Imam Hossein at the battle of Karbala in 680, Shi'ites had formed an urbanized minority in parts of predominantly Sunni Iran, notably in cities like Qom and, to a lesser extent, Isfahan. Radical movements such as the Assassins, or short-lived dynasties such as the native Persian Buyids, who collapsed in the mid-eleventh century, never succeeded in sending down strong roots among the population at large. Unlike the conversion of Iran to Islam, which was deliberate and relatively peaceful, the imposition of Shi'ism by the Safavids was sudden and violent: their troops marched across Persia, imposing the new doctrine at sword point. Sunnis who declined the Shah's invitation to convert were summarily executed.[22]

To bolster his claims to legitimacy, Ismail fabricated a fictitious lineage stretching back to the holy family of Imam Ali. But the new ruler soon encountered a serious obstacle: the dearth of an ideological apparatus to ensure the necessary uniformity of thought. As few Shi'ite scholars lived in the newly converted dominions and virtually no books had been written in Persian expounding Shi'ite doctrine, Ismail turned to the only remedy at hand: his Arab neighbours. Experts in law and doctrine were imported from the traditional centres of Twelver learning in Syria, Arabia and Bahrein. Did the Safavids impose Shi'ism to create a counterweight to the expanding Sunni power of their Turkish cousins, the Ottomans? The hypothesis is impossible either to confirm or disprove. Still, the fact remains that despite the bloodiness of the forced conversion, despite its imposition by a coalition of Turkic soldiers and Arab scholars, the doctrine found an abiding resonance among Iranians.

By the seventeenth century, Isfahan had become not only a seat of empire, but the metropolitan centre of Shi'ite learning. Over the course of a century Iranians had come to form the majority of Shi'ite religious scholars. Unlike the Ottoman Empire, where the religious establishment was incorporated into a state apparatus taken over virtually intact from the Byzantines, in Safavid Iran the Shi'ite hierocracy gradually distanced itself from the government while gaining unrivalled authority among the uneducated masses. This it accomplished by incorporating popular beliefs and practices, many inherited from pre-Islamic times, into religious dogma.[23]

So influential had the state doctrine become that Shah Abbas, a strong, determined and politically sophisticated man who expelled the Portuguese from the port city of Hormoz in 1622 with the help of an English fleet, maintained a richly endowed stable of well-groomed horses which were reserved for the use of the Lord of the Age were He to make Himself manifest.[24] But the Shah's outwardly pious behaviour belied the cruelty, absolutism and dissolution which prevailed at his court. The Safavids, culminating with the reign of Abbas I, believed that the monarch, who claimed to rule on behalf of the Hidden Imam, could do no wrong. However, egged on by malcontent clergymen, people whispered that the Shah secretly cultivated Christians while persecuting Sunnis, even tolerated a Carmelite mission in Isfahan. Certainly the Shah had caused an entire Armenian community to be relocated from Azerbaijan, on the Ottoman border, to the capital where it was to provide the skilled craftspeople and tradesmen needed to construct his great monuments. So sympathetic was the Shah toward Christians in general, and toward Europeans in particular, that several visitors argued that the monarch was in reality a crypto-Christian, complete with hidden crosses hanging about his neck.

As Shah Abbas' regal manner became progressively more capricious, the religious establishment — the *ulama* — began to turn their attention to the question of how to accommodate their inherently oppositionist doctrine to the temporal power which had brought them to new prominence. The earliest Shi'ites recognized no explicit separation of worldly and religious authority; the Imams descended from the house of Ali were considered the community's supreme guides, political and religious leaders combined. With the advent of the doctrine of Occultation of the Twelfth Imam, a divorce between Imamate — the rule of divinely invested authority in all matters religious — and political rule was concluded. Imamate became, over time, an abstract principle of Shi'ite theology. But no claims were made for it, either as a basis for public law or a political theory.[25] A second transformation would occur later, with the Shi'ite revival of the late nineteenth century which ultimately made straight the way for the coming of Ayatollah Khomeini. Even so, during the reign of Abbas I, the *ulama* had begun to formulate the theory of the illegitimacy of the monarchy, no matter its claims to piety or its claimed lineage. A certain *mollah* Ahmad Ardabili once encountered the Shah, so the story goes, and reminded him that his power was held not by divine right but as a trust on behalf of the Imam. If the trust were violated, he warned the Shah, the clergy would withdraw its support.[26]

Chardin, in his account of his long sojourn at the Safavid court, recorded the lament of an indignant *mollah* which epitomized the Shi'ite dilemma: "Our kings are impious and unjust, their rule is a tyranny to which God has subjected us as a punishment for having withdrawn from the world the lawful successor of the Prophet. The supreme throne of the world belongs only to the *mujtahid*, a man possessed of the sanctity and knowledge above the common rule of men. It is true that since the *mujtahid* is holy and by consequence peaceful, there must be a king to wield the sword, to exercise justice, but this he must do only as the minister and subordinate of the former."[27]

By the end of the seventeenth century, fissures had appeared, fault lines along which two tectonic plates — the spiritual power of the Shi'ite hierocracy and the temporal power of the political establishment — were to shift and grate, sometimes in collusion, more often in collision, touching off tremors, then earthquakes. The rapid decline and collapse of the Safavids after the death of Shah Abbas I ushered in a period of anarchy in Iran. In the absence of secular authority the Shi'ite *ulama* became more than spiritual guides and occasional critics of the king; they assumed the role of *de facto* local governors, arbitrators of disputes and executors at law — by default of the rulers they became, in fact, the authorities to which an abandoned populace increasingly turned. Isfahan, once seat of Persia's greatest empire since the Sassanians, entered into a decline from which it has never fully recovered. Yet it, along with cities on the desert road to the north like Qom and Kashan, played a leading role in the overthrow of the Pahlavis. The worldly glory of Shah Abbas, by a process which is still ill understood, fertilized the seedbed of Islamic revolution. Less than 400 years later the clerical institution, having withdrawn its trust from the monarch, replaced him.

OUR FRIENDS IN TEHRAN were insistent: When in Isfahan you must see the one-candle bath. One lone taper burning in a glass enclosure generates enough energy to heat not only the water but the bathhouse itself, they said. As guidebooks to the city are mute on this prodigy, we decide one brisk morning to try our luck at the local Islamic Guidance Bureau, which doubles as the Isfahan tourist office. As we stroll in the employees are huddled around a kerosene heater, rubbing their hands together, breath misting in the dank, frigid room. Dark blotches of humidity stain the peeling concrete walls; a small samovar hisses in a corner. Before I can finish explaining to the desk clerk what we wish to do, a balding man with a properly Islamic five-day growth of beard interjects: "I've heard about this place but I've never seen it. I will take you there myself. Come, we will go in my car."

The man is Majid Jamallamelian, the director himself. Without further discussion, swept up in a small tornado of enthusiasm utterly out of keeping with the studied diffidence, not to say indolence, of the Islamic Guidance bureaucracy, we soon find ourselves wedged into Mr. Jamallamelian's car, a venerable Iran-built rattletrap Citroën Dyane ridiculously nicknamed "furious" in Farsi, its air-cooled engine whirring like a great sewing machine in full stitch toward the Masjid-e Jomé, Isfahan's Friday Mosque. Reputed to be one of the greatest structures in the Islamic world, the mosque is also, so Mr. Jamallamelian believes, the site of the mysterious bathhouse. Islam is a religion of townsfolk and merchants, a belief system which stresses the responsibility of the individual for his own salvation and lays down rules of conduct for all aspects of life, including business practice and the handling of money. Commerce and trade were vectors for the spread of the faith, and today the great working mosques of Iran (and indeed, of the entire Islamic world) are located in the heart of the bazaar, surrounded by stalls, workshops, teahouses and public facilities, contiguous with them, partaking of their quotidian bustle and animation. Such is the perimeter of the

Isfahan Friday Mosque that its outer walls are indistinguishable from the market structures which have agglutinated around it, concealing, then effacing its original contours.

The Masjid-e Imam, the great mosque of Abbas I on the Meydan, is a monument to a man of vision, ambition and power. Modelled after the holy shrine of Imam Reza at Mashhad it is, in a sense, a political monument, an attempt to curry favour with an increasingly critical religious establishment, a building constructed with one eye to heaven, the other on the nascent religious opposition. Unlike it, the Friday Mosque is a triumph of accretion in which elements of the Seljuq, Mongol and Safavid eras combine in a breathtaking, overarching synthesis whose grandeur is exceeded only by the that of the Masjid-e Imam but whose complexity and subtlety are unsurpassed. Its vast colonnaded *aivans*, where slanting rays of sun play amongst the patterned columns in a geometric alternation of incisive light and blotted darkness, reveal a variety of vaulted ceilings, many dating back to the latter third of the eleventh century, when the domed sanctuary was built by order of Grand Vizier Nizam al-Molk, the quintessential Persian bureaucrat who later met death by an Assassin's dagger.

Beneath the great colonnaded halls lies an immense indoor prayer room, possibly anterior even to the great dome whose single fired brick structure has survived more than 900 years in a zone of high seismic activity. Illuminated by daylight filtered through paper-thin marble skylights, it remains naturally warm on all but the coldest winter days, and blissfully cool in the heat of summer. In a small exhibition hall near the entrance we inspect photographs of the most recent reconstruction of the masjid. At the height of the Iran-Iraq war Saddam Hussein targeted this, a world architectural masterpiece, for destruction. Soviet-made rockets scored several direct hits, killing worshippers and demolishing one of the great arcaded *aivans*. If ever a military decision was catastrophically counter-productive, this one was. The population of Isfahan erupted, stung by the outrage. A popular subscription quickly raised money and rebuilding was under way while the bombs were still falling on other parts of the city. Choice of target was, of course, consistent with the murderously rational character of the Iraqi dictator: the cultural equivalent of his chemical warfare attacks on Iranian troops and later, on unarmed Iraqi civilians at Halabja.

As we wander through the mosque courtyard, Mr. Jamallamelian comes running toward us, waving his arms in excitement. We hurry back through the entrance where we're joined by the doorkeeper, who is carrying a ring of massive keys. "Give him 1,000 rials," he whispers, "and he'll show us the *hamam*." The price — less than a dollar — still strikes me, accustomed by now to the Iranian value of goods and services, as a bit steep. But these are exceptional circumstances. The one-candle bath beckons. I slip the man a crisp note. At a brisk pace we leave the mosque and weave through several corridors of the cloth bazaar before issuing into a maze of open-air alleyways. We pass crafts-men at work hammering out brass and copper utensils, stamping patterns on the city's inimitable block-print calico with cushioned pads strapped to their forearms. Around a corner we go, down another alley-way, pressing up against the ochre clay walls to let an oncoming Paykan pass, until finally the caretaker locates the entrance, an unmarked wooden door in a blank wall. After trying several keys, he finally releas-es a huge, rusting padlock, pushes open the creaking door and leads us down a short flight of stairs into the *hamam*.

Fine reddish-ochre dust coats everything, the stone benches, the carved wood lockers, even the clothing which lies just as it had been discarded God knows how many decades ago. Bent double, we make our way up a narrow, grime-caked passageway toward the rear of the bath. Here is the chamber, explains the caretaker, where the candle burned. All we see is a sooty rectangular sink-like depression at the foot of the wall. "The truth," he says, "is that the one candle was really a wick. It kept the sewer gases piped in from the mosque's public latrines burning, plenty hot enough to heat water and keep the place warm in winter."

About twenty-five years ago, he continues as Mr. Jamallamelian translates, some foreigners — maybe they were archaeologists, Americans or Englishmen — tried to find out exactly how the system worked. They broke the glass enclosure which held the candle. The ancient system never worked again. I take the story of the one-candle *hamam* less as fact — for in Iran the line between fact and fiction is blurred and constantly shifting — than as the creation of collective imagination. A metaphor, too, for the way Iranians see their relations with foreigners (and in a larger sense, those of Muslims with the West) who must now bear blame and responsibility for the destruction of what once worked so well.

"You would like to see the shaking minarets?" Mr. Jamallamelian asks as we warm ourselves with a cup of tea in the caretaker's booth, re-compense for the generous emolument and our enthusiasm. After demurring the requisite three times to test the sincerity of the proposal, we agree and once again we find ourselves crouched in the tattered

Citroën rattling westward through the old quarter of the city, where high brick walls overlook stagnant irrigation canals, then past walled apple and quince gardens with windbreaks of poplars punctuated by the intense green of cypress trees. The minarets flank a small mosque built during the Safavid period, and are said to oscillate as much as thirty degrees from the vertical when leaned against. But when we arrive, we see them immobilized in wooden scaffolding. "The minarets only shake once a year now, at Now Ruz, the Iranian New Year," Mr. Jamallamelian tells us. Why? we ask. It seems that once again foreigners are the culprit. Engineers, British or American, attempted several years ago to ascertain why the minarets shook and did not collapse, and why their delicate turquoise tile cladding remained intact. The experts removed a brick here, a beam there, and suddenly the tiles began to pop off, the structure began to deteriorate. Now the authorities have had to stop the shaking.

A few hundred metres from the immobilized minarets stands a barren hill whose peak is crowned by the remains of a Zoroastrian fire temple. Presumably thousands of years old, the temple marked the point where heaven met earth, and served as sanctuary for the sacred flame. The structure, a dome supported by four columns over a square foundation, was later adapted to mosque construction when Islam overwhelmed the Sassanian state religion. We scramble up the steep, gravel-strewn slope, pass by the disfiguring hulk of a modern water reservoir and, panting from exertion, step onto the level clearing at the temple peak. A stiff westerly breeze is blowing and the air is brilliantly clear. The entire Isfahan oasis lies at our feet, the Zayand-e Rud glistens silver through leafless branches as it meanders among the fruit groves. In the distance the turquoise dome of the Masjid-e Imam looms over ochre rooftops.

On our way back to the town centre Mr. Jamallamelian suddenly remembers he must pick up some papers from his home. We drive north into a newly built suburb, where the streets are wide and dusty, swarming with children on their way home from school. We agree to wait in the car while he picks up his documents, but in three minutes he returns, beckoning us. The stopover for business is, it turns out, a pretext for an invitation to tea, an invitation as genuine as his enthusiasm is infectious. We cross the small courtyard with its few scraggly fruit trees, and enter the house. Here the living arrangements are typically Iranian: Mrs. Jamallamelian is at home but because of my presence she remains concealed in the kitchen, sending out plates of fruit, sweets and cups of fragrant tea with the couple's eldest daughter. An uncle wanders in to join us.

I notice a large portrait of a bearded young man hanging on the wall at one end of the room. Our host follows my eyes: "That is my brother," he says, his mood suddenly shifting. "He was martyred in the war against Saddam." The talk swings around to the war, to Iranian politics, to religion. But it is time for us to return to our hotel, and for Mr. Jamallamelian to put in an appearance at the office. President Rafsanjani will be making an official visit to the city shortly, he explains. There are meetings to attend, itineraries to draw up, decisions to be made. As we get up to leave another daughter appears through the kitchen door, carrying a box. We break into smiles: The box contains *gaz*, the perfumed chewy nougat candy for which Isfahan is famous.

A QUINCE GROVE by the riverside at dusk. Through the bare late-autumn branches the crescent moon and its companion, the evening star, are etched on the dimming sky like fine calligraphy on the porphyry-glazed tiles of a mosque dome. In the fading light we see the remains of an ancient dam across the Zayand-e Rud. Downstream from the stone-buttressed structure, part of the ancient water management works that dot the Isfahan oasis, a stork stands on one leg scanning the fast flowing water for fish. Over the murmur of the river we hear the distant tinkle of sheep bells and the yelping of dogs — squat, stocky mutts with powerful jaws who take their guardian's role very seriously and who, in contrast to their mangy, Islamicly unclean urban cousins, are prized by Iranian country folk for their fierce devotion. A twig fire is crackling now; we thrust tiny potatoes into the glowing embers. Shortly they will be charred black, their flesh cooked to a perfect fine-grained whiteness, to be pulled open, steaming, and devoured with mouthfuls of cheese and bread seasoned with the taste of burnt potato skin on our fingertips.

We've come to this place with our Isfahani friend Rostam Mehranzadeh, a young psychology professor who bears the name of the legendary Iranian hero immortalized by Ferdowsi in the *Shahnameh*. Rostam is a self-styled Sufi, fancier of modern Iranian poetry and frustrated idealist. Several days before, on arriving in Isfahan, we'd taken a taxi to Rostam's home in one of the city's winding alleys, armed with a letter of introduction from a friend in Tehran. The door had opened, we presented the letter, and within two minutes we'd been swept into the complex and enveloping whirlpool of Persian hospitality. Soon Rostam's wife Muzhgan joined us, without *chador* or headscarf. A teacher of "exceptional" children in a nearby school, she chafes under the proximity of her mother-in-law, and dismisses Isfahan as a hopelessly provincial place. Our host is in his late twenties, a wiry, dark-skinned man of sharply chiselled, hawk-like features and hardly less acerbic opinions. "What can I do," he says with a smile and a shrug as if flinging his desire for knowledge against the walls of Iran's isolation: "My country is a prison, but I am a free man."

So will you be attending the welcoming ceremonies when President Rafsanjani visits the city? I ask jokingly. Rostam shakes his head in mock sorrow, throwing me a quick sidelong glance: "I do not have time for Mr. Rafsanjani," he says. "For you I have time."

The architectural prodigies of Isfahan mean little to Rostam. They are, after all, the daily background to the mundane, gritty struggle for existence. I understand perfectly. During the three years I lived in Athens, I may have visited the Acropolis twice. It was overbearing, its mute presence dominated the city and intimidated an entire country, the simple fact of its existence a cruel reminder of the venality of the present and the glory of an unattainable, demimythical past, a place best avoided. "I do not want to show you old buildings," he tells us, tossing his head. "I want you and your wife to see nature, the nature of Isfahan."

Nature it will be. Rostam and his friend Abbas, a soft-spoken man who shows up with a Persian-English dictionary under his arm, escort us to his car, a Paykan of indeterminate age, and we head southeast from the city and into the countryside. Abbas speaks almost no English, but we soon understand his function. Whenever Rostam cannot find the word he wants, he fires the Farsi at Abbas who opens the dictionary, locates then enunciates the English translation one perfectly formed syllable after another. In excitement, our guides point out the broad cylindrical structures which, like stately plump Martello towers, dot the rural landscape across the great oasis. What are they? we wonder aloud as Rostam strains for the word and Abbas leafs furiously through the dictionary, its pages fluttering. Co-lum-bar-i-um, he bursts out. After a mystified instant, we understand. These massive yet harmonious structures are pigeon towers, monumental dove cotes once used as sources of the fertilizer which helped Isfahan's fields and orchards to flourish. Beyond them, in the distance we spy a lonely minaret thrusting sunlit against the dusk-darkening sky.

In the village of Charyan we pause to inspect the ruins of an ancient mosque. Judging from the graceful curve of its mud-brick dome it is probably a relic of the Seljuq period. Around the building, on a this-tle-grown expanse of flat ground, grimy, shoeless boys with gobs of opaque snot hanging from their noses are playing soccer. Dust devils whipped up by the cold wind go spinning off down side alleys. Across the road idle men have congregated in front of the teahouse, and are observing us with more than idle interest. "We should leave from here," remarks Rostam. "They are too curious. Maybe they think you are spies."

Back into the Paykan it is. The minaret on the horizon is drawing closer now, as we double back and forth along dusty, rutted rural lanes, through walled gardens and orchards, sometimes surrounded by flocks of sheep. Through a dense thicket we catch a glimpse of the river, and across a field of corn stubble a pigeon tower looms, its side cracked open as though by a blow from a giant's axe. A few moments later we pull to a stop in the quince grove.

WE ARE GUESTS that evening at Rostam's house for a family banquet served Persian style and eaten seated cross-legged on the floor. Just as dinner is about to be served, a friend arrives from Tehran, and Muzhgan's mother-in-law comes down from her first-floor apartment to the couple's basement flat. The feast quickly materializes: green rice, spinach and meat stew with dry tamarind, garlic-laced sour pickles, yogurt and a platter of *tadiq*, delicacy of delicacies — the buttery crisp-golden crust from the bottom of the rice pot. Before and after the meal we gorge ourselves with fruit washed down with tea, and as the evening wears on semi-illegal cassettes appear. Persian music fills the room; rhythmic, sensual music. With languorous movements, their fingers snapping in the two-handed Persian manner, the women dance for us, torsos swaying forward and back, hips rotating, hands coiling, beckoning, like a one of the brightly coloured murals of the Chehel Sotoun palace come suddenly to life.

During the early years of the revolution three of the palace's exuberant wall paintings were masked by the Islamic authorities, distressed perhaps by the scenes of drink and elegantly tempered full-costume debauchery which, along with vivid battles, they depicted. Not so today. All are now visible but one, and it is shrouded by a sheet which conceals not the content, but the restorers hard at work. Chehel Sotoun — Forty Columns — was Shah Abbas' pleasure palace, a place for worldly celebration, for enjoying the presence of women, the glitter of military finery and the delights of food and wine. A broad porch — entertaining at Chehel Sotoun took place almost entirely out-of-doors — gives onto a long pool lined with cypresses which, in reflection, doubles the palace's twenty carved wooden columns. Today, the morning after our modest carousal at Rostam's flat, the wind has sprung up, the reflected image blurred in the wind-riffled surface of the water.

Before the road network of modern Isfahan — a surrender to the ethos of cheap oil and the automobile — was laid out, a broad footpath led directly from Chehel Sotoun to the Meydan-e Imam, to the Ali-Qapu Palace, the administrative centre of the Safavid state. Like the Chehel Sotoun the palace has a colonnaded porch, but here the porch — as befits a permanent reviewing stand — overlooks the great square from on high, the entrance to the bazaar on its left, the perfect, compact dome of Sheikh Loftallah mosque directly across, and to the right, the great portal and dome of the Masjid-e Imam. Though small in size, almost intimate, Ali Qapu, and not the royal mosque, holds commanding position on the square. Though the Safavids boasted of the purity of their Shi'ite convictions their rule was that of God's vice-regent in its most worldly sense. But unlike the Ottomans, who gradually shifted the thrust of their royal construction away from the mosque and to the palace, a process which culminated in the eclectic neo-baroque tragi-comedy of Dolmabaçe on the Bosphorus, the Safavid dynasty, under the vigilant eye of the *ulama*, never abandoned the primacy of the house of worship.

For some Iranians, Isfahan's religious heritage is tainted by the heritage of empire. The Safavids had drawn on scattered popular resentment of the dominant Sunnis in their merciless campaign to make Shi'ism the official doctrine of their nascent empire; under their reign it became a quietist cult of mourning in the expectation of the Twelfth Imam. In one of his most inflammatory essays Ali Shariati, the impassioned conscience of the Islamic Revolution, counterposes the last insurrectionary upheaval based on "Alavite Shi'ism against foreign domination, internal deceit, the power of the feudal lords and large capitalists...under the banner of justice and the culture of martyrdom" against the entrenched pseudo-religion of the Safavids. The movement which Shariati describes as Red Shi'ism — "leaning toward the people and fighting relentlessly against the mosque" — arose in the impoverished countryside of Khorassan under Mongol rule 100 years before Isfahan was declared capital under the Safavids. The peasants, writes Shariati, have been inspired by the teachings of a certain Sheikh Khalifeh, and are prepared to resist the torment and inequity of their overlords. So when the retinue of a nephew of the ruler enters the village of Baashteen, near Sabzevar, they ask the villagers for food and are duly served. Then, they ask for wine:

For the villagers who are Muslims and Shi'ites, who have been deeply influenced by the words of Sheikh Khalifeh, the bringing of wine — and that too, under compulsion, for such rascals — is too much. However, they serve it. The guests become oppression, ignorance and poverty. [...] They ask for women. This was the beginning — very simple and speedy. The host goes to the people and calling the Shi'ite masses, exclaims that the Mongol ruler is asking for their women. What is their reply? They say, "We are prepared to die rather than be so defiled. Our women for the enemy shall be our swords."

The result is obvious. The masses have made up their minds; they kill the whole group in one lot. As they know that there is no turning back, as they know that they have already chosen death, they stop wavering. [...] The villagers overrun the town, fighting against the Mongol army and the decrees of the pseudo-clergy of the religion of the state. They are victorious.

A century later come the Safavids, and Shi'ism departs from the great mosque of the masses to become a next door neighbor to the palace of Ali Qapu in the Royal Mosque. Red Shi'ism changes to Black Shi'ism. The religion of Martyrdom changes to the religion of Mourning.[28]

BEFORE LEAVING FOR ISFAHAN we had heard rumours of the notorious character of the city's residents, and caught wind of its reputation as a breeding ground for sour-faced hardliners, parsimonious functionaries, grasping merchants and devious citizens. Of this we encountered little. As we were crossing the Bridge of the Thirty-Three Arches one evening, a bearded young man growled as he passed us, "Fucking Americans get out of Isfahan." This attitude we could understand. Before the fall of the Shah, Isfahan had a sizeable population of American military men, advisors and experts, not to mention their dependents. The city boasted an abundance of nightclubs, liquor stores, bars and diverse other amenities of civilization as we understand it.

Isfahan reached its summit under Shah Abbas; its deterioration and loss of status followed that of the Safavid dynasty. The capital was transfered, briefly to Shiraz, then to Tehran, leaving Isfahan as a living museum and, in the decades prior to the Islamic Revolution, an industrial city notable for a high concentration of foreigners. Isfahanis of a certain age still recall the common spectacle of drunken Americans abusing Iranian citizens in the street. Pitched battle between Iranians and Americans inevitably followed, with the Yanks eventually retreating to a fortified encampment outside the town, which further fuelled local hostility toward their overbearing and uninvited guests. Later, before the overthrow of the Shah, some of the fiercest fighting and most violent demonstrations took place here, all part of the collective memory which has undoubtedly shaped the city's modern-day reputation for *hezbollahi* rectitude.

Tourists may have been scarce, but handicraft merchants at the bazaar were as persistent and as engagingly single-minded, as their Istanbul counterparts. A clerk at the government handicraft store all but wept as he begged us to purchase some items from him at a "private price," it being understood that proceeds from the sale would go, not to the state, but into his more deserving pocket. But as we strolled along the tree-lined boulevards or meandered down the sidewalks in the market quarter, stopping off to sample quince jam being produced in huge bubbling vats, or watch *biriani*, an Isfahani delicacy made of mutton fat, being fried; or tasted rice-flour pudding spooned, still warm, from shallow trays, we encountered nothing worse than friendly curiosity. Still, Isfahan's ill-repute has endured for several centuries.

"An Isfahani buys a cucumber, paints it yellow, and sells it as a banana," Iranians say of the town's tight-fisted residents. In 1598, a certain Abel Pinçon, a Frenchman travelling in the company of the English adventurer Anthony Sherley, described the Persians he encountered in Isfahan as "very dangerous, extremely greedy for money, liars, wantons, blackguards, drunkards, cheats, and in a word, base, worthless and entirely lacking in courage."[29]

The brothers Sherley occupy a special place in the annals of Isfahan's magnetic attraction for Europeans. Anthony and Robert Sherley were spiritual kinsmen of Francis Drake: high-born pirates, exquisite brigands, international confidence men and swashbucklers who hoped to find at the court of Shah Abbas free reign for their acquisitive drive and lust for glory. But they, and the other Western visitors who made their way to the Safavid capital, also had what might today be described as a hidden agenda. Throughout the sixteenth century the power of the Ottoman Empire hung over Europe like a shroud. Well-trained, highly motivated Ottoman troops staged armed incursions into the heart of the continent and extended their control of the Balkans. European statesmen prayed for heavenly deliverance while they schemed and manoeuvred to exacerbate existing hostility between the Ottomans and Persia in the hope of dissuading the Grand Turk from further aggressive action.

As the sixteenth century came to a close the brothers set out for Persia with the approval of the crown. The aim of the mission was to develop commercial relations; more important, to persuade Shah Abbas to make common cause with Christendom against the Turks. If the plan worked, so the reasoning went in London, a wedge would be driven deep into the heart of the Islamic world. The empire's commerce could flourish untrammelled.

The brothers arrived in Iran late in 1598, reportedly accompanied by a British gun-founder in whose skills the Persian court showed rapt interest. Insinuating themselves into the Shah's confidence, aided by their fortuitous arrival only months after Shah Abbas' victory over the Uzbecks to the east, the Sherley brothers convinced the monarch that they were the official ambassadors of European royalty charged with conclusion of an alliance against the Sublime Porte. In the spring of 1599, after arranging to leave his brother behind as hostage to guarantee his return, Anthony Sherley departed overland for Moscow, duly empowered as Persian ambassador to Europe. The mission eventually collapsed in Rome two years later, and Anthony ended his life as an admiral in the Spanish fleet.

His brother Robert, who had stayed on at the court of Shah Abbas, finally succeeded in having himself appointed Persian ambassador to the British court more than twenty years later. In 1624 he arrived in London, bearing a letter from the Shah to King James I which stated that "the Turke ought to be assaulted by dyvers waves" and that Christian Europe and Persia must combine to "ruyne him and blot out his name." The message was apparently well received, and Sherley gained rapid accreditation at court. The Levant and East India Companies, however, who then held the monopoly on trade with the near and far East feared incipient commercial rivalry. They began to whisper that the Persian envoy was an impostor. In March of the following year Robert's fortunes took an even more sombre turn. His protector James I died suddenly; overnight he lost his lodgings and a generous weekly stipend — but worse was to come. Early in 1626 an East India Company ship carrying an illustrious visitor landed at Portsmouth. The visitor's name was Naqd Ali Beg, and he claimed to be the real Persian ambassador. Sherley, so the story goes, made a courtesy call upon his rival. He unrolled his precious credentials, and in the Persian manner touched his eyes with them and kissed them. As he handed them over for examination, Naqd Ali leaped up from his seat, tore them from Robert's hands, ripped them to shreds and punched the Iranicized Englishman in the face.

The dispute was never settled, the alliance between Europe and Persia against the Ottomans never concluded. Robert Sherley fled London, to die in Qazvin in 1628, far from the capital, one year before the death of his royal patron Shah Abbas.

IN WINTER THE CITY of wine, nightingales and roses has none of these things. When we arrive in Shiraz after a short flight from Isfahan a light rain is falling; the air is cool and damp. The rain is still falling, gently now and intermittently, as we set out next morning for Persepolis in a pre-revolutionary vintage Chevrolet accompanied by a guide called Hamid, a short, obsequious man given to impulsive tittering and cere-monial handwringing. Hamid teaches high school English to augment his meagre earnings: though tourists are slowly returning to Iran, they are too few to pay a guide's wages. What, I ask, about the strikes of two years ago when thousands of poorly paid teachers paraded in silent protest through the streets of several provincial towns — including Shiraz — pockets turned inside out, bearing handmade banners quoting Imam Khomeini? Giggling nervously Hamid says "Yes, yes, the strike.... We must not talk about it if we do not want to lose our heads," and makes a short eloquent gesture of the forefinger being drawn across the throat while throwing a quick sidelong glance at the driver. Later we learned that the driver has done time for narcotics offenses: would that make him more or less inclined to offer the information ministry reports on the conversations of tourists and their guides? Out of deference to Hamid, I change the subject, laughing in turn. No gesture though.

Shiraz is set among mountains whose snow-capped peaks are obscured by clouds. The road to Persepolis winds its way uphill out of the city, and through a series of narrow valleys where most of Fars province's petrochemical industry has been located. Long tendrils of stinking yellow chemical smoke curl through the rocky landscape and drift across the highway, burning our nostrils. We pass slow-moving Iran-made Mercedes Benz buses spouting murky diesel fumes which blend with the low-lying clouds and smoke into a choking, abrasive air-born soup.

Suddenly we swing off the main road. Now we're speeding between long rows of pine trees. Dead ahead are the ruins of Persepolis stark against the mountainside. We alight from the Chevrolet and Hamid leads us between the monumental columns and immense carved figures whose faces, he says with a grimace of theatrical disgust, were disfigured by the invading Arabs. Our guide, not in the least troubled by the inherent dissonance of his position, dismisses the conquerors as barbarians, forgetting that the Arabs, in spite of their alleged anti-figurative zeal, were the bearers of Islam, which was to become an inseparable component of Iranian identity. The "victory of victories" was won before stern strictures against representation became the rule. Furthermore, he cannot explain why the victors contrived not to touch the exquisitely carved stone friezes showing representatives of twenty-eight nations gathering to pay tribute to the Achaemenian rulers whose empire spanned the Middle East, from India to Greece. Reliefs, startling in their animation, depict Nubians, Arabs, Armenians, Jews, Assyrians and Greeks, each in national costume bearing gifts from their lands to the great king. As we stroll through the ruins, we notice a sudden flurry of activity at the main entrance. A tour group of Japanese has disembarked from its bus and now comes marching up the ceremonial staircase, Iranian guides scurrying along behind attempting to keep pace. As if from nowhere, impromptu outdoor stands selling Fuji film and postcards have materialized.

Persepolis, the Greek name for Takht-e Jamshid, was never a political capital. The mighty columned halls and their monumental surrounding precincts were designed as a religious site glorifying not only the divinely sanctioned dynasty, but concentrating the empire's appeal to the celestial powers for fertility and abundance which would culminate in the main festival of the ancient Persian calendar, Now Ruz, to this day celebrated virtually unchanged in Iran.[30]

The Arab invaders, with all due respect to Hamid, were the lesser destroyers of Persepolis. Perhaps history's greatest master of the vendetta, Alexander the Macedonian, having subdued the Persians by blood and iron, arrived at the sacred city and burnt it to the ground, presumably in retribution for the depredations of the empire in the course of its repeated campaigns against the Greek city states. To Alexander's credit, he did cause the library to be translated before destroying it, too, then moving on to enshrine himself as a Persian god before whom all prostrated themselves. When I mention this to a group of Greek tourists we encounter at the hotel, back in Shiraz, they bristle with indignation. My information is clearly flawed, they say. That great emissary of Hellenism would never have done such a thing.

Persepolis, with its monumental sculpture, huge columns, ceremonial ramps and staircases, is an exercise in the architecture of magnitude, power and wealth. As befits a sacred structure, the workmanship and finish are meticulous, knife-edged in their precision. Polished marble walls which once shone with mirror brilliance are still glass-smooth to the touch 2,500 years later. Stone carvings breathe with the highest degree of artistry in their finely chiselled detail. But I find myself unmoved by the monumentality, by the carvings of Ahura Mazda, the Zoroastrian divinity atop soaring columns, the cuneiform inscriptions reading "I Darius have caused all this to be built for the glory of God." The God of Darius seems remote, overwhelmed by the invocation of might and obscured by history: time has completed the work of deconstruction begun by Alexander and continued by the Arabs. The secret of Islamic architecture, for all its monumental, ceremonial thrust and its evocation of a heavenly model, lies in its openness to human concerns and human commerce. Great or small, the mosque stands at the heart of civilization; not as a remote and overpowering monument but a living social organ, a part of the city.

Built on a series of terraces each housing its own ceremonial structure, Persepolis commands a wide, fertile plain ringed with mountains. In the pine grove at the foot of the hill, a few hundred metres from Xerxes' cyclopean Gate of All Nations, stands a cluster of blue and yellow tents: the remains of the tent city thrown up in 1971 by the defunct, self-proclaimed heir to the power and glory of the Achaemenians, Mohammad Reza Pahlavi, when he celebrated the erzatz 2,500th anniversary of the monarchy in Iran. The festivities, staged for an adoring audience of world royalty and dictatorship were catered by Maxim's of Paris, who laid on tons of caviar to be washed down with champagne, and concluded with a prayer to be recited by all Iranians:

> O, God Almighty, Creator of Universe and Man, The bestower of intelligence and thought on Man, The Creator of countless blessings in our Noble Land, Thou has appointed the Just Aryamehr as the Custodian of the Land of Iran![31]

The public prayer was one of those calamitous errors that can only be traced to hubris. In February of that year the Shah had played a leading role in setting up OPEC and raising world oil prices. Now in October, drunk on soaring oil revenues, with one stroke he eradicated nearly 1,400 years of living history, ignored the Islamic identity of Iranians, and symbolically linked himself with what, for the mass of the subjects he believed docile and submissive, was a remote, semi-mythical past. The ambiguity of the message — and adoption of a calendar based on the founding of the Achaemenian Empire — even touched off speculation that the Shah would soon announce a return to Zoroastrianism as the state religion.

Totally excluded from the event were the people of Iran, who looked on in sullen rage as thousands of dignitaries, and of course the most craven foam-flecked crust (might one say the scum) of the international media establishment wined, dined and fawned over the short-wicked "Light of the Aryans." Military units patrolled the tightly sealed-off area, while in the cities the Shah's police rounded up potential protestors by the thousands. Student demonstrations did break out and were met with savage repression. From his exile in the Shi'ite shrine at Najaf, Iraq, Ayatollah Khomeini spoke in support of the demonstrators: "They said: 'We do not want these celebrations, do something about the famine, we do not want you to celebrate over our people's corpses'."

The Shah had a particular affection for Shiraz. It had a reputation as an easy-going place, the wine was good, and it shared little of the sour-faced religious intensity of cities like Qom or Isfahan. He, then-Empress Farah, and a steady supply of one-night mistresses flown in from European capitals as befitted a man whose sexual appetite was exceeded only by his ego, would spend two weeks a year at a small Qajar-era pleasure palace in the Baq-e Eram, the city's most celebrated rose garden from which thousands of rare varieties had been uprooted in order to construct concrete helicopter landing pads. Now the building houses the Shiraz University law faculty, set among centuries-old cypresses and fruit-laden orange trees. Under the rule of the hapless Qajar ruler Fath Ali Shah, in the early years of the nineteenth century, the façade of the pavilion was decorated with murals showing one of the king's favourite wives in the near-altogether, bathing in a bucolic setting. The *Shahbanou* is protected from the curious eyes of the monarch's court by a red velvet curtain discreetly held by two eunuchs with downcast eyes, but she is exposed to ours. In Iran, where pictures of scantily clad ladies are enough to draw the wrath of censorious *mollahs*, the fresco of Fath Ali Shah's bathing wife remains free for all to behold.

For a brief and almost blissful interlude in a land where history and violence are most often synonymous, Shiraz was the capital of Iran under an ephemeral dynasty founded by Karim Khan-e Zand in 1750. Karim Khan refused the title of Shah, calling himself instead *vakil* (regent), whether on behalf of the people or of the Hidden Imam is difficult to determine. His rule was an enlightened one, and is still visible in the urban fabric of Shiraz, from the massive central fortress to the great bazaar where teahouses in hidden courtyards planted with orange trees shading gracious reflecting pools tempt the idle stroller.

Shiraz had reached its peak several centuries before, under the Mongol and Timurid regimes. It was then that Ha'fez and Sa'di, the city's two great poets, flourished and along with them legions of calligraphers, craftsmen, architects and builders. In a driving afternoon rain we stride quickly toward the portal of the shrine of Seyyed Mir Ahmad, the holiest place in the city. The mausoleum marks the spot where, according to legend, the brother of Imam Reza (he who is buried at Mashhad) died — or was killed — in 835. Six hundred years later, the present structure was built. Ingeborg borrows a *chador* — made of the synthetic print fabric affected by women of lesser means — at the ladies' entrance and disappears into the shrine, carried along by the steady flow of pilgrims. Hamid and I check our shoes and enter through the men's door. The interior is small yet overwhelming: the inside surfaces — walls, ceiling, columns — are coated with cut mirror fragments which reflect and multiply the gleam of the sanctuary lamp into a dazzling, kaleidoscopic fragmentation of light. From opposite directions, men and women pilgrims slowly converge on the gold and silver encrusted tomb, thrusting coins or small bills through the grating, whispering a short supplication for intercession of the saint called Shah-e Cheraq — the King of the Lamp. The air inside the shrine is thick with the smells of sweat and damp cloth mingled with rosewater. In a dark antechamber several penniless men are curled up on the carpeted floor, fast asleep. Squatting close to the catafalque a white-bearded *mollah* intones verses from the Qur'an in a strong, sweet voice.

Early winter darkness is creeping over the city but the steady rain has stopped as we reach the shrine of Khajé Shamseddin Mohammad, the thirteenth century mystic poet better known as Ha'fez. Every year thousands of Iranians visit the poet's grave, set in a formal garden north of the city centre, and many more practise *fal-e Ha'fez* — divination through his poetry. One of the two books almost sure to be found in an Iranian home is a *Divan* of Ha'fez; the other is, of course, a Qur'an. Not every literate or illiterate speaker of Persian may be conscious of the literary merits of Ha'fez's poetry, even though his works are still widely read and admired. The *Divan*, however, has an extraliterary function, to help an individual or family to make important decisions. The book is opened at random and a poem found on that page is read. Based on the mood of the poem and on one's interpretation of it, the crucial decision can be taken.[32]

What other country, we wonder, so sustains a cult of its best-loved poets, to whom it turns for spiritual guidance? Abruptly the spell of the place is broken. A gaggle of Japanese tourists — the same aggressive, camera-wielding swarm we'd encountered at the ruins of Persepolis — wheels into view. But they turn quickly away from the engraved marble plaque marking the tomb of "him who recites the Qur'an from memory" and gather instead around a table filled with postcard images of it. In the gathering dusk the mirror image of the fruit-laden orange trees that overhang the twin reflecting pools bursts into a quiet infinity of particles as the rain starts to fall again.

WHEN WE WALKED through the gates of the Baq-e Fin, the jewel-like Persian garden of Kashan, we thought for a moment we had stepped into an earthly replica of paradise. Quince, pomegranate and walnut trees line its geometric paths. In the near-indigo shade of ancient cypresses, clear, cold water tumbles down channels lined with turquoise tile, catching the glint of late-December sunlight, while birds flit overhead, wheeling and darting against a pale blue sky. So exquisite is the setting that we almost expect to come upon the languorous almond-eyed beauties in diaphanous veils and the turbaned, mustachioed warrior-huntsmen of a painted miniature.

Designed for Shah Abbas I four centuries ago, the Baq-e Fin shelters behind high burnt brick walls from the hot winds sweeping off the Dasht-e Kavir, the salt desert. The master builder of imperial Isfahan, who often transited via Kashan on his way to the important military post at Qazvin, so loved the city that he chose it for his burial place. Today, in the mild winter sunlight, old men lounge on benches overlooking the arcaded pavilion where water gushes from a subterranean spring, while a couple strolls hand in hand along the cypress-shaded paths. Further off, an amateur photographer scatters handfuls of yellow walnut leaves to the wind, leaving them to flutter to the walkway

No matter how idyllic, few Persian monuments are far removed from treachery or tragedy. Next to the garden is a small, prettily tiled *hamam* with a complex network of concentric passages surrounding the central pool. It was here that Mirza Taqi Khan, known as Amir Kabir and esteemed by many Iranians as the enlightened counterweight to dissolute Qajar tyrant Nasreddin Shah, was murdered in 1852 at the height of his power as grand vizier. Amir Kabir was a low-born servant who acquired his political education by listening at the keyhole of the Shah's antichambers. By a combination of native intelligence and shrewd political instinct he gradually won the capricious ruler's confidence. Appointed vizier, he undertook an ambitious reform program, creating institutions on the European model. Soon a clique of landed nobles, threatened by the upstart's ambitious plans to modernize Iran, began scheming against him. They succeeded in swaying the monarch who, one night in a drunken rage, dispatched a military detachment with the order that Amir Kabir, then in Kashan on state business, be killed. They found him in the evening, at the *hamam* in the Baq-e Fin and served him with the death sentence. The vizier refused execution by pistol and insisted that his wrist veins be opened. The Shah, when he emerged from his stupor the next morning, sent a rider from Tehran to Kashan to countermand the order. The scene was an archetypal Iranian tragedy. As the messenger galloped up to the main gate, Amir Kabir's lifeless body was being carried out of the garden.

The road to Kashan passes through Qom, the city with Iran's greatest per-capita concentration of *mollahs*, a place so sacred that aircraft are forbidden to overfly it. The idea of a holy city had always conjured up in my imagination an ethereal silhouette of domes and white spires shimmering in the desert like a mirage. On my first visit, in 1985, the approach to the city had all the elements of high drama. An hour out of Tehran, as the sun rose over Damavand, the contours of the desert began to take shape against a forbidding backdrop of jagged peaks. Gullies, wind-eroded ravines, gravel moraines and barren hillsides sloped toward the distant salt flats. Midway across the horizon a cloud of dust rose into the sky, thrown up by a migrating flock of sheep. But as we approached Qom the mirage dissipated: Such cities may be the stuff an Orientalist's fantasy; they are not of this world.

The war was at its height; anti-aircraft guns scanned the skies, and Revolutionary Guard check-points scrutinized all vehicles. It was July then, and by 7:00 a.m. the temperature had passed the 40° mark. I rested in the shade of a teahouse, a lump of ice pressed to my forehead in an attempt to stanch the flow of blood from my nose. The sunlight glinting off the gilt of the squat sanctuary dome bored into my retinas like a rusty ice pick. After several hours devoted to moving from one patch of shade to another, surrounded by crowds of pilgrims impervious to the heat, I retreated to Tehran.

Today we are passing through, on our way to Kashan. On entering the outskirts of Qom the first thing we see is an enormous amusement park Ferris wheel stark against a curtain of smoke billowing from the city's brick kilns. The early morning air is thick with the stench of diesel fumes. Groups of bare-legged boys are playing in the muddy rivulet flowing down the middle of the dry riverbed which separates the suburbs from the historical shrine and theological seminary. Our driver Reza manoeuvres his Paykan into a parking spot in a narrow alley, and we make our way rapidly through a crowd of pilgrims toward the shrine of Fatima, sister of Imam Reza. The religious gatekeeper, dressed in a fraying blue serge uniform and holding as badge of authority an enormous silver-tipped staff engraved with Qur'anic verses, satisfies himself that Ingeborg is in proper Islamic attire — a *chador* borrowed from thoughtful friends in Tehran — then waves us through with a smile. On this brisk morning the faithful perform their ritual ablutions quickly before hurrying through the mirror-encrusted archways to the sanctuary. We go no farther: only Muslims may enter the Holy of Holies.

Feeling ever so slightly like interlopers, we retire to a teahouse which advertises Tehran water on its sign. Clever marketing strategy. Boiled or not, Qom's brackish water is barely fit to drink. I think back to my first visit, and its gut-wrenching consequences. Between sips we warm our chilled hands on the steaming tumblers as we watch pedestrian traffic hurry by. The street is lined almost entirely with food shops and minuscule stalls specializing in religious items and artefacts: images of Ayatollah Khomeini who taught here for several decades, prayer rugs, prayer stones made from sacred local clay, black Ashura flags commemorating the martyrdom of Imam Hossein, *tasbis* (chaplets), small scourges used in ritual self-flaggellation and more. Only a few hundred metres away, along the river road, is the Faizieh Madrassa, the seminary where Khomeini's fiery 1963 sermon against the Shah launched the revolution. Today the seminary, one of the Islamic world's most sophisticated institutions — currently in the process of computerizing — houses theological students from all over Iran, as well as most Muslim countries.

Improbably (although this being Iran, we were prepared to admit that the rules of probability are, like everything else Iranian, models of elasticity), Qom is a city with a sweet tooth. Revile or envy the city for other reasons, but never impugn the quality of its local speciality, the confection called *sohun*. This pistachio-laced brittle, as irresistible as Qom is ugly, is sold not only by the lump from hundreds of street stands, but in elaborately decorated tins bearing the picture of religious dignitaries. Pilgrims quite commonly walk away with five, ten or even more such tins, explains Reza as we pull up at a huge, echoing *sohun* emporium to lay in our own, more modest provisions.

Though the dour, dare I say fundamentalist, atmosphere of Qom might seem certain to put off the fun-loving, this is not an entirely accurate reading. How, for instance, are we to interpret the amusement park on the outskirts? Emotional ardour, some say, is a natural outgrowth of religious intensity. Young men in turbans may be at their most attractive while they are at their most ecstatically devout. Qom, alongside Mashhad, enjoys a certain, though discreet, reputation as a place where, from a woman's viewpoint, temporary marriages can be advantageously concluded with handsome *seyyeds* — direct descendants of the quite Arab Prophet Mohammad, another of the paradoxes of Aryan Iran.

After another hour skirting the western rim of the Dasht-e Kavir we begin to encounter pomegranate orchards. Before long we enter Kashan, an ancient oasis town founded in the Sassanian era, but with archaeological remains dating back to the fifth millennium BC. Unlike Qom, whose dismal appearance only the arrival of the Lord of the Age could redeem, Kashan has a certain faded grace. Built around precious supplies of running water from natural springs and hand-dug underground *qanats*, the town learned long ago to live in harmony with the desert and developed a unique architecture and building style to match its harsh, bone-dry environment.

After departing the Baq-e Fin, we wind our way through a maze of back streets and alleys and finally come to a stop beside a high ochre brick wall. Following Reza's lead, we pass through massive wooden doors, each side bearing its distinct knocker — one for men, the other for women — and enter into a cool, dark, winding corridor. No sooner have our eyes become accustomed to the darkness than we step into a bright courtyard, its high walls surrounding a reflecting pool teeming with plump, indolent goldfish. This is the Borujerdi mansion, one of the finest dwellings in a town renowned for its sensually curved roofs and enigmatic *badghirs*, the tall wind towers from which extend slender rods, perches for resident and itinerant birds. The wind towers channel the merest breeze to the rooms below, and provide natural, noiseless cooling far superior to the modern air-conditioning systems whose rusting hulks disfigure the roofs of Iranian buildings.

At the western end of the court, shaded from the summer sun, a domed chamber gives onto the pool. Each of the recessed alcoves along its perimeter is connected to an air shaft. Doves nesting in the cylindrical wind towers which mark each corner of the building take flight when I step onto the second-floor terrace. No high-rise buildings block my sight-line as I look out toward the desert across the city's billowy rooftops. Today the Borujerdi mansion is a museum; but though this is my first trip to Kashan, I have an overwhelming sense of having been here before. Would this place have been used as a film set? I ask the doorkeeper. Ah yes, he beams, many times they have come to film here. Now I remember the film: *Nar o Ney*, a haunting, impressionistic evocation of the city at the turn of the century seen through the eyes of a poet.

A few minutes' away, through side streets thick with fine amber dust, stands another of Kashan's architectural wonders, the Aqa Bozorg Madrassa. With its graceful dust-tinted dome and twin minarets barely rising above the surrounding rooftops, this once-flourishing theological seminary set around a deeply recessed reflecting pool echoes with our footsteps. Like the Borujerdi mansion, the Aqa Bozorg Madrassa reflects the inward-turning nature of Kashan's oasis architecture: the colonnaded underground prayer hall, ventilated by air shafts, opens out onto the light and greenery of the recessed court, a place of calm, refuge and meditation.

Ravenous by now, we circle back toward the town centre. Reza has located what he claims is a clean restaurant. The lunch hour is long over: Iranians are quick, voracious eaters and restaurant meals are usually wolfed down with minimal formality and maximum speed. Now the staff is toting up the take on an abacus. A power failure is in progress, the owner informs us apologetically, and the water has been cut off too; but the food hasn't run out. We wipe what dust we can from our hands with the flimsy tissue which passes for table napkins and order a platter of *kebab* with soup, yogurt and ersatz Iranian coke. Within fifteen minutes, hardly a crumb is left. Fortified, we bundle into the car and head for the bazaar.

Kashan is famous far beyond Iran as one of the world's great rug-weaving centres. The weaving itself is done in homes or village workshops scattered throughout the region. As we approach the bazaar, we spy patches of dark blue and red on the domed rooftops; from closer range we see that they are huge skeins of freshly dyed wool spread out to dry. In the corridors of the ancient market wool merchants offer weavers the tools and the essential raw materials of a craft which has been practised here without significant technological change for more than three thousand years. Kashan's carpets are still crafted with the vivid colours and extraordinary patterns no chemical dye, artificial fiber or machine could ever duplicate, each one indelibly marked with the tiny imperfections that bring a carpet to life.

In another stall two ancient men, looking as venerable as Kashan itself, are slowly, painstakingly assembling furniture. One holds a length of wood in gnarled but trembling hands while his co-worker wields a wood-cased plane. The sweet smell of fresh shavings mingles with the pungency of rosewater. The local product is the most intensely fragrant in Iran: Each bloom concentrates the quintessence of hot sun and precious water into a dizzying elixir.

We stroll idly down the winding corridors, now up a few steps, now down a gentle incline. Through open doors we glimpse empty courtyards lined with workshops. There are no handicraft shops here, no hard-sell polyglot pushers of carpets, kilims and tourist trinkets. This is a working bazaar, the heart of the ancient Islamic city. Reza — whose driver's work keeps him away from home a lot — stops off to buy an expiatory offering of sugary Kashan shortbreads for his wife and infant son.

Tourists are still an uncommon sight anywhere in Iran. Here they are a true oddity. Two small boys stand and gawk at us in disbelief, while a group of idle Afghani refugees pretends to price the individual cigarettes on sale at a tiny table behind us as they sneak fascinated glances. "Salaam" I say to them. "Salaam," they reply, hands applied to the heart. It's mid-afternoon and the bazaar is just stirring after the midday siesta. Shutters roll up, ancient wooden doors creak open. From a distant cassette player comes the haunting throb of the *santur* over the rattle of cups. Tea is served. In and around the stalls conversation quickens. The Kashan bazaar, as it has been doing for fifteen centuries, begins to hum with life.

Friday prayers at Tehran University. Photo © Michael Coyne / The Image Bank.

5

Mollahs and Philosophers

ON A BLUSTERY FRIDAY MORNING in December, 1992, groups of demonstrators converge on Tehran University. They've come to protest the demolition by Hindu fanatics of the Babri mosque in India. Waving placards printed in English and Farsi issued by the Islamic Propagation Organization and chanting halfheartedly, they amble down Enqelab Avenue in disparate knots of three or four hundred, drawing indifferent glances from the crowds on the sidewalks. The demonstration is a flop: critical mass has not been attained and, more to the point, there's not a television camera in sight. Quickly the marchers lower their placards and mingle with the crowd moving quietly toward the University for the weekly public prayer, their ever-fainter shouts drowned out by the amplified voice booming out over the public address system. I follow them in, leaving my business card in lieu of a press pass. Security is not what it used to be. An impression confirmed by a perfunctory, even friendly, body search before I climb the short flight of steps to the obser-vation platform overlooking the amphitheatre where the man they call the "Minister of Slogans" is working the crowd.

I can never think of the Minister without a surge of nostalgia. His booming voice and sense of the inherent drama, of the richness and rhythm of spoken Farsi have made him a spellbinder for years of public events. From Army Day rallies during the heroic war years to weekly Friday prayer meetings, the melodic cadences of his voice evoked, in sound, the lurid reds and purples of revolutionary Islamic iconography: paintings of bleeding tulips, or the dolorous images of the suffering and death of Imam Hossein at Karbala in all the uplifting, graphic detail of blood catharsis. As the words tumbled out the minister would hold them up to the light like luminous spheres, turning them to reflect now the glint of steel, now the smooth resilience of silk. Then, caressing them with his tongue, he would send them rushing off into a towering crescendo that culminated in the explosive, near-orgasmic release of 10,000 or 100,000 voices shouting *God is great, Khomeini is our Leader!* or *Death to America!*, the perennial favourites.

At the foot of the rostrum large groups of men in uniform — revolutionary guards and army officers — deliver tangible proof of their unwavering devotion to the Islamic regime: They shout loudest and longest, or break into the ritual invocations of peace upon the Prophet Mohammad and his companions which take the place of applause at the call of *takbir* from somewhere in the crowd. During the war Iraqi prisoners, too, were a prominent part of Friday prayer meetings, erupting into long, aching roars of fury in Arabic at the mention of the arch-demon Saddam. Strategically placed throughout the crowd are the cheerleaders, strong-voiced authoritative men whose job is to make sure everyone is shouting in tune, or to silence the throng with a wave of the hand. The prayer meeting also has its individualists: men who suddenly leap to their feet to recite grievances or bellow last year's slogans. Heads turn, ushers scurry over. After a flurry of gesticulation, the voice falls silent. But no one is asked to leave. Beyond the compound wall, behind a barrier of bushes, the women worshippers are concealed, their soprano voices faintly audible over the dominant male bass line.

IN THE NEXT day's newspapers the gathering is described as "huge." Was this a step up or down from the more usual qualifiers "numerous" or "multitudinous"? That day in December, however, worshippers numbered only in the tens of thousands — a far cry from the immense throngs that used to pack not only the University but the surrounding streets. And now that the Imam is dead, and the Islamic Revolution transformed into a holding action, the Minister of Slogans — like the demonstrators — seemed to be going through the motions.

In Islam the devotions of the faithful are private except on Fridays when the crowds gather on the grounds of the University of Tehran and in the courtyards of mosques in every Iranian city for public prayer ceremonies. Directly inside the main university gates, across the street from the academic bookstores which give this three-block stretch of working-class Enqelab Avenue an intellectual veneer, an entire section of the inner campus has been transformed into an outdoor amphitheatre sloping downhill and southwestward toward Mecca, its focus an elevated, enclosed podium overlooking a shallow pit into which the prayer leader descends to direct the congregation.

When they instituted Friday prayers at Tehran University shortly after the triumph of the Islamic Revolution in 1979, Iran's clerical leaders were not only affirming their commitment to restore to Islam its long-lost public, political role. They were intent on demonstrating the ideological primacy of religion in what had been the bastion of Western intellectual influence throughout the last decades of the Pahlavi dynasty. The symbolism was as patent as the defeat of the Shah had been decisive. In the early days of revolutionary upheaval, while fervent Khomeini supporters from the slums of south Tehran battled groups of leftist students for control of the campus and later of the streets, Friday prayers were at once a show of force and a public forum. The new leaders of the regime, bearded men in clerical robes wearing turbans, used the pulpit to analyze the week's political events and to inspire their zealous followers. Urbane uptown Tehranis reacted with shock and bemusement. Who were these *mollahs*? Where had they come from? But unlike the Westernized intellectuals who had formed the provisional government, the *mollahs* knew how to hold and move a crowd. Trained in the arts of oratory and rhetoric, fluent in the language of the common people, the clergy quickly proved its mastery of the Friday prayer pulpit as its armed supporters were soon to prove their mastery of the streets.

To a population accustomed first, under the repressive reign of the Pahlavis, to pronouncements and edicts from a disincarnate court and palace, and then to near-anarchy in the heady months that followed the collapse of the monarchy, Friday prayers were a unique occasion to listen in on the affairs of state. Who could have imagined? The president himself explaining government policy and offering religious guidance? The weekly gatherings also provided the regime and its strongest supporters — the same devout and intensely partisan *hezbollahi* who fought the running street battles and attacked rival demonstrations under the benign eye of the revolutionary guards — an opportunity to measure their power. They came in their thousands, tens, hundreds of thousands, spilling out into the side streets around the university, lining up their prayer rugs and tiny prayer stones along diagonal lines painted on the asphalt, rain or shine, heat or cold, to hear the message of a new kind of Islam. It was an Islam which had already made them masters of the great city, released them from their poverty-stricken back alleys, set loose their overflowing energy against the Shah's police and army, then against those whom they believed would deliver Iran over to the capitalist West or the communist East, the twin poles of Godlessness and Corruption, and finally, by proxy in the war against Iraq, against World Godlessness and Corruption. They were the kind of people Marxists were wont to call the lumpenproletariat and dismiss as a mob for hire. The Imam, as they called the Ayatollah Khomeini with single-minded reverence, had given them their marching orders; theirs but to obey unquestioningly. Once, at the height of the "war of the cities" between Iran and Iraq, Saddam Hussein threatened to bomb Tehran University during Friday prayers. On that day, following an appeal from the Imam, the turnout was enormous. Saddam, true to form, was bluffing. The prospective martyrs were not.

AS I PORE through my files, I come upon an old photograph showing former Prime Minister Mehdi Bazargan, former President Abol-Hassan Bani-Sadr and former Foreign Minister Sadeq Qotbzadeh kneeling on prayer rugs beneath the midday sun, surrounded by worshippers. Today only Bazargan still lives in Tehran, his muted voice critical but still respected. Bani-Sadr resides in Paris, where he fulminates against the conspiracy of the Ayatollahs which scuppered his political career, and caresses the overweening ego which blinded him to the incontrovertible fact that Khomeini, not he, was the drummer to whose beat most Iranians marched. The unfortunate Qotbzadeh is dead, executed in 1982 for his role in an alleged coup attempt, or possibly, some say, as part of the general elimination by design or by "accident" of the revolution's militant Third Worldist leadership.

Hunting for leaders of the regime among the front ranks of worshippers has long been a favoured pastimes of guests and journalists attending Friday prayers. Over the years, I managed to spot officers of the Revolutionary Guard Corps, important *mollahs*, government ministers and members of the Islamic parliament. But the weekly event is not an Iranian version of the Red Square reviewing stand in Moscow, much less of the meticulously airbrushed group photos of the Chinese Communist Party leadership. Even the most diligent Tehranologists, cosseted in their CIA-funded think tanks, must find it a daunting task to chart the ins and outs, the ups and downs of the fractious religious establishment. "The order of the clerical community is in its disorder," the Iranian saying goes.

The Friday prayer ceremony at Tehran University stands at the apex of a country-wide organizational pyramid distinct from, yet intertwined with the state apparatus. Each city and town has its Friday prayer leader, and the main sermon is replicated and preached across the country, with the appropriate local and rhetorical variations. Friday prayer, apologists argue, is a form of direct democracy. But the gathering of the faithful is no deliberative assembly, no more than the opinion of the believers has been solicited. Now combined, spiritual and temporal authority here come before the congregation to explain, instruct, reveal, edify and motivate. The sermon may deal with foreign policy, may discuss sexual morality (always a popular subject in Iran, especially when President Hashemi Rafsanjani, with his great comic gifts, is preaching) or the regime's plans to liberalize the economy. But individual worshippers are free only to choose between acceptance or silent disagreement, beneath which may lurk skepticism and indifference toward both messenger and message.

GINGERLY I PICK MY WAY across the campus of Tehran University through ankle-deep snow toward the philosophy faculty. A few workers are attempting to make sense of a mass of twisted scaffolding covering the public prayer grounds — all that remains of the flimsy shelters which had collapsed a few days earlier under the weight of snow only hours before the weekly prayer ceremony was scheduled to begin. Once inside the building my footsteps echo on the stairs; it's midterm exam time and the usually crowded corridors and lecture halls are deserted. Pale yellow winter light is streaming in through the windows. As I enter the faculty lounge a lithe man with a salt-and-pepper beard, strong hands like those of, say, a carpenter, and small, intense eyes, clad in the turban and robes of a *mollah* rises to greet me. Dr. Ahmad Ahmadi, dean of the faculty, is the man appointed by Imam Khomeini himself to wield a new broom during the 1982 Cultural Revolution which turned Iran's educational system upside down.

A product of Iran's fiercely independent and frequently rambunctious theological school system, Dr. Ahmadi studied for twenty-one years under Ayatollahs Borujerdi and Tabataba'i, who was his master in Islamic philosophy and Qur'anic interpretation. He continued his studies under Ayatollah Khomeini for two years, completing his doctorate in Western philosophy at Tehran University while commuting from Qom, all the while translating works of Descartes, Etienne Gilson and Kant into Farsi.

When I hear "cultural revolution," images of fire-eyed Chinese Red Guards brandishing the sayings of the Great Helmsman spring to mind. But, Dr. Ahmadi hastens to assure me, Iran's own cultural revolution was not at all like China's. If the schools were closed, they were quickly reopened; an entire generation was not deprived of higher-level education. Iranian universities before the revolution were models of diversity, an eclectic mishmash from every country and every culture in which Islamic thought was one discipline among many. The program was consistent with the Shah's regime, but not with an Islamic one. "It was the beginning for us; we had to take a decision to clear our path," he says. "Also, the country itself was in a revolutionary state, with every possible group contending for power in the university, right down to the faculty level, as they were in society at large. The struggle was a political one."

It was guided from the summit by Ayatollah Khomeini. The few students who followed the discredited Shah posed little threat to the integrity of the new regime. Not so the supporters of the richly diverse Marxist and Islamic leftist groups which had flourished on campus during the revolution and fought the *hezbollahi* students and their outside allies for control of the lecture halls and common rooms.

In March, 1980, five days after elections to Iran's first post-revolutionary parliament, the Islamic Majlis, had given the Islamic Republic Party an overwhelming majority of seats, Khomeini called for Iran's universities to undergo a proper revolution of their own, and for a purge of all professors connected with the West or East. "Our dear students should not follow the misleading footsteps of faithless university intellectuals," he said. Adding, one month later: "When we speak of reform of universities, what we mean is that our universities are at present in a state of dependence, they are imperialist universities and those whom they educate and train are infatuated with the West."[33]

A Cultural Revolution Headquarters was set up in June of that year, and given the task of determining appropriate cultural and education policies for the country. The group was to draw up an Islamic education system which would be compatible with other aspects of the Islamic State. Degree of dedication to Islam became a criterion for university admission, and has been one ever since.

Dr. Ahmadi's version of events predictably emphasizes the initiative of university students. He does not mention Khomeini's denunciation of the faithless intellectuals, nor his ringing call to arms. In the aftermath of the revolutionary upheaval, according to this sanitized version of events, neither a coherent teaching program nor a university curriculum was possible. Revolutionary young people gathered together, closed the universities and insisted that a revolutionary Islamic program be established. "This did not mean we should extinguish anything, nor make all subjects conform to Islam. No. It meant that every revolution must have a program consistent with its overall strategy. This was the core of our cultural revolution."

Twenty months later, in October, 1982, the task of drawing up new programs was complete; the universities were reopened. The ideological and religious selection process had achieved its aims: Curricula remained virtually intact. The main impact of the cultural revolution was born by students and faculty. Iranian government statistics for 1979-80 showed 175,000 students were enrolled and 35,000 graduated from the country's universities; in 1982-83, 117,000 students were enrolled, 6,000 graduated. Teaching staff was cut almost in half, from 16,000 to 9,000. The process was neither smooth nor pacific, mirroring the state of virtual civil war that prevailed in Iran's cities as the revolutionary guards fought well-armed opponents in pitched battles on the streets. Ayatollah Hossein Ali Montazeri, whose following grew each time he publicly criticized the regime's excesses and abusive behaviour, equated the methods of the cultural revolutionists with those of the urban guerilla opposition: "Maybe these people have good intentions, but the adverse effect of excesses such as accusing and harassing professors in universities is no less than the blows we receive from counter-revolutionaries...."[34]

Today, concludes Dr. Ahmadi, who radiates the composure of authority, many, perhaps most Tehran University faculty members continue to teach. Some realized that they would be unable to do so in an Islamic environment. Marxist professors understandably did not feel at home, while supporters of the Shah's regime preferred to join their families abroad. Perhaps one thousand left altogether. But many who offered no resistance to the revolution are still teaching today. "You will even find Marxists in such disciplines as the physical sciences. Of course, Marxist economists had no place to go, and they themselves understood this."

THE TEHRAN UNIVERSITY philosophy department is quite distinct from the faculty of theology and Islamic science, Dr. Reza Davari explains as we sip hot tea and nibble on sweet cakes in that self-same faculty lounge. "Here we teach philosophy and literature. The theology faculty teaches religious science and jurisprudence, and the history of religion. But these students will not become clergymen; that is the role of the theological seminaries at Qom and Mashhad, where the curriculum is strictly based on Islamic science. Our courses cover the history and problems of Islamic and Western philosophy," he says in halting English beneath which I detect an undercurrent of existential malaise. "How we teach? That depends on the individual professor, on his views. I take a phenomenological approach," he adds, not implausibly for a man with a reputation as an admirer of Martin Heidegger. "I search for the intuitive perception of the thing."

Probably the most politically (and emotionally) charged philosophical controversy in Iran today focuses on modernity: can a society guided by divine revelation, as Islamic Iran claims to be, integrate Western technique and methodology, seen as the quintessence of this modernity? Iran, Dr. Davari insists, is not separate from the world, meaning the world created by the West, even though the Islamic establishment imagines that there exists another world view: its own. "There is only one dominant world view, and the essence of it comes from the West. No one can say precisely whether the Western social, cultural and economic model is inevitable. We don't see any clear answer. We are in a period of crisis."

Despite the official premise that the religious and the political are inseparable in Islam, a *de facto* separation between religious discourse and the practical work of governance seems to have taken place, I venture. There is no contradiction here, counters Dr. Davari with something less than unshakeable conviction. "If one does arise, it will come to us from the West." (This was the only hint of what may have been a note of crypto-Heideggerian anti-Westernism I was to glean from a frustratingly polite conversation.) "Our need for modern technology is so great that we have no choice but to emphasize scientific research. Our officials will have to take this into account."

The contradiction, some Iranian intellectuals say, has already arrived. Nasrollah Pourjavadi, scholar, philosopher-poet and free spirit, gazes out the window of his north Tehran office across the huge, roaring city, then turns back toward me, with an inimitably Iranian expression of spiritual anguish mixed with quizzical humour: "Modern Western civilization is the dominating civilization, and it will continue to dominate. It is the future of the world. All other civilizations must adjust themselves to this dominating force, even though they may themselves help to shape it. I don't want to sound as if I like this situation. I once resisted it. But it is irresistible; it has language and it has power."

Mr. Pourjavadi, a bearded man in his late forties, directs the Iran University Press, which publishes scientific and technical textbooks, most of them translations from American editions. The mission of the Press is to develop Farsi — which is primarily a language of poetry — into a suitable instrument for expressing modern scientific ideas and concepts, and stimulating Iranians to develop new terminology. "We asked specialists to translate foreign textbooks and to coin new words. This is not only a question of language, but a deeper cultural and intellectual activity which reflects our philosophy of life."

Iran is a traditional society, an ancient one with a strong cultural identity in language, in the arts and in philosophy, he continues. "Our ties to this past are very deep and very strong. Suddenly, in the twentieth century, we were confronted with a new civilization, that of the West, in science, philosophy and general outlook. You realize its power, its will to dominate, and you become dominated by it. Beyond the power you eventually discover the culture. But you see its strength before you see its beauty."

For the Orient, which first encountered the West through its power, the ultimate question is not knowledge, it is that only knowledge can be used to acquire power. The Orient's dilemma is that to acquire this knowledge it must turn its back on itself: Iran's two revolutions, particularly the Islamic Revolution, are the result of this struggle deep within Iranian society, deep within the Iranian mind. "We were living in a medieval world, to use the Western term. As a child, I lived in a world which was that of my ancestors. And this was in the middle of the twentieth century, right here in Tehran."

While Europe had three or four centuries to emerge from its medieval mentality and customs, Iran, like the rest of the Islamic world, has had no time to digest the changes, to accommodate them, to integrate them. Paradoxically, Mr. Pourjavadi suggests, the Islamic Revolution, which drew its immense power from the rejection of forced Westernization, may even have accelerated the trend. Throughout the world, Islamic civilization is facing a struggle to readjust to the modern Western model, to change over from an agricultural society to a modern industrial one. "This is not an easy task," he says, pausing to look at me over the top of his glasses. "You have to exchange your identity, everything. You find yourself in the middle of nowhere. You are no longer an Iranian or a Muslim, nor are you a Westerner."

"It's a difficult thing to go through a revolution; it's like being cooked in a pressure cooker. Your chemistry has changed; first you were raw, but now you are cooked. The process has been a painful one; you've been turned inside out. You've had to abandon some of your deepest beliefs and ideals, and you see that you have abandoned them, painfully. Your horizons have shifted. You're a different being, yet you remain the same. I have felt it. Deeply. And each individual feels it differently. It's like standing at the seashore: Some only get their feet wet, others take a boat, some dive down deep and sink to the depths."

ON THE SIDEWALK outside a nondescript apartment building in a middle-class suburb, a grizzled middle-aged man with several days growth of stubble clutching a tattered brown envelope under his arm comes up to me, smiles, and says in heavily accented English: "You come to see Dr. Rajai'e, yes?"

Indeed I had. We shake hands, introduce ourselves, and when the buzzer releases the street door, we climb the stairs together, like old acquaintances. Such is the nature of Iranian sociability that, by the time we've climbed the stairs, I have the overwhelming feeling that I know this man. But when Said Rajai'e Khorassani greets us at the third floor landing, he laughingly disabuses me of my illusions. The gentleman is a judge from his home town, Kerman, a place I have never visited. "You have never seen this man in your life, Mr. Reed," he says with wide-eyed grin. "Though you may have met someone like him."

By this time we're all laughing. It's hard to avoid laughter when you're in the company of Rajai'e Khorassani, a rarity among practitioners of the political (I avoid the word "politician," understandably pejorative to our ears in this era of disillusionment with representative institutions and their ways) in his unassuming good humour. Dr. Rajai'e has little of the self-serious gravity of *mollahs* come late to power and overburdened with the certainties of God's word. His skills are those of a debater, polished to a fine lustre through years in New York as revolutionary Iran's first long-term ambassador to the United Nations, and the constant ordeal of facing hostile television cameras and generically aggressive anchormen.

Rajai'e Khorassani is a stocky man with a penetrating, almost hypnotic gaze and a mellifluous, incantatory, elegantly modulated high voice. After tea and exotic sweets "just arrived from Kermanshah precisely for you," wherein the host snares the guest in a web of obliging hospitality, we retire to his office to leave free the modest dining room table for his son's homework. The small cubicle's furnishings consist of four large bookcases stuffed to overflowing, a carpet and several large cushions. So this is where the former ambassador and head of the powerful Foreign Affairs committee of the Majlis handles the business of state. The hyperactive Tehran rumour mill would have Dr. Rajai'e revelling in an ill-gotten fortune and extravagant lifestyle. All that must be somewhere else: this is not the house of someone who has transformed political connections into wealth and privilege.

We sit down cross-legged on the floor. "Try these, you've never eaten anything so delicious!" he exclaims as his wife appears with a bowl of Kerman tangerines and sweet lemons. Dr. Rajai'e then launches into a comparative analysis of church-state relations in Islam and in the West. All the while, the judge squats beside me, listening intently, occasionally nodding his head or sighing in approval at a point well made.

My first encounter with Rajai'e Khorassani had come several years before at his New York office, in the course of interviewing for a CBC radio program on the Islam-West nexus. Several years later we met again in Tehran, at the Majlis, and once, unexpectedly, at the home of Mohammad Taqi Ja'fari, one of the few leading Iranian *mollahs* to remain untainted by blandishments of power and the charm of elaborate titles. The discussion with Mr. Ja'fari was going badly that night. Our host, a plump man whose turban slipped off his head when he laughed, was in an expansive mood, overwhelming Reza, the friend who had brought me, with the nuances of religious doctrine. Sharing our frustration, Mr. Ja'fari telephoned a friend of his who, he assured us, would soon come and act as our interpreter. Within a half-hour, to my surprise, Rajai'e Khorassani walked in the door. (Naïvely, I was astonished at the apparent inversion of roles. A young Iranian I encountered in Canada later told me that he would leave without hesitation on the next plane for Tehran if he got a telephone call from Mr. Ja'fari.) The next two hours were given over to a faithfully detailed translation of Mr. Ja'fari's responses to my questions. Does the path to faith pass through the mind or the heart, I had asked the theologian. At the end of a lengthy exposition, in which he quoted Bertrand Russell and Auguste Comte, he touched his index finger to his chest, smiled and fell silent. Driving back to the hotel that night, Dr. Rajai'e's car passed three young men puttering along on a tiny motorbike. They recognized him and, as they waved and shouted in recognition, their motorbike nearly veered off the road into the ditch.

Today, I've come to ask Dr. Rajai'e about how Islamic Iran can shelter its culture from Western influence while seeking rapid technological development. How, I want to know, can Iran have one without the other? Does not modernity, particularly in its avatar of technoscience, represent an absolute contradiction of Islamic belief? Will it not entail the necessary and ineluctable end of faith as the founding component of society, as I understand Iran's Islamic doctrine.

"Aha, you have it backwards: You see," he responds, "your Western culture is the prescientific one. *It* is responsible for the secularization of science. But God cannot be eliminated from science; in fact, a totally secular world view represents a presupposition about science."

When the Romans converted to Christianity, he argues, the Church was established as an institution. For centuries, it was the only institution; but it was an institution with no political doctrine. Jesus Christ established neither a government nor a political tradition; he formulated no doctrine. Here was the germ of church-state separation. The role of the Church had no basis in Christian theory. Lacking a political doctrine, the Church assumed political leadership on the basis of its spiritual monopoly. Their reasoning was this: "As we are responsible for telling people how to live, we are also responsible for administering the affairs of state." But in the absence of an underlying political doctrine, this institution could not produce workable solutions. To maintain control it monopolized education and information. Had the Church been able to produce solutions the approach might have been successful; but it was not. Ultimately, spiritual matters were left to the Church, political administration to the lay authorities. In the West, Church and state separated because political doctrine which could have been developed, amended and strengthened was not a component of the religious heritage.

In contrast, the followers of Islam must act on the basis of a moral doctrine. If they do not, they are committing sacrilege. For Christians, separation of Church and state is a necessity, based on the Bible. But for such a separation to be possible in Islam, Muslims must ignore the doctrines of their faith. In fact, the Qur'an cannot be properly followed unless there is an administration which is able to implement its laws. "Do Europeans want to impose on Muslims ignorance of an important part of the Islamic heritage? If they do not expect us to ignore a part of our faith, they should realize that our political doctrines must also be respected."

As Dr. Rajai'e ends his sentence with the smile of a man who has just crafted a particularly telling response, the phone rings in the next room. His wife pops her scarf-covered head through the door: "It's for you, from Kerman." As our host offers long-distance advice on a home-town political problem the judge and I sip tea and share a tangerine; it is delicious, all the heat of the desert concentrated in the sweet juicy essence beneath the thin layer of aromatic peel.

"Now where were we? Ah yes. Islamic doctrine," he says, following our lead and peeling a tangerine which he promptly pops into his mouth — now the whole room is redolent of citrus oil — "covers individual spiritual discipline, communal acts, and obligations related to social functions. In our era, these things fall under the heading of government duties — land ownership, mining, forestry, water resource use, ecology, the treatment of animals. Should our Western friends have expected us to ignore all this? If they did not, we had no choice but to depose the Shah and set up a government."

"No, separation cannot be envisaged in Islam. Even acts of worship are collective acts, like the Friday prayer, which must be led by the state authorities whose obligation is to report on the functioning of the state. The 'Day of sacrifice' in the month of Moharram includes a special ritual which can only be carried out by someone with state authority."

The problem, insists Dr. Rajai'e, lies not in the contradiction inherent in Islam, but in the West's inability to recognize faith and belief as motors of social change, both in Iran and throughout the Islamic world. The role of faith in shaping man's inner life has a powerful and incontrovertible impact on his outer, social and political life. This concept may not be so easily expressed in Western scientific language, but Muslims have no problem in grasping it. Religious consciousness operates at several levels, all the way from Imam Khomeini to the most common of common men and women. But there is a unifying element: disaffection with the gap between religious ideals and dominant, primarily Western social norms. "Isn't it strange that Western secularism, which insists on freedom of conscience, cannot accommodate our standards?"

The Islamic revolution has touched off a revival of interest in religious and spiritual values throughout the world. "You may either like it or dislike it, but you can hardly deny it. The Islamic Republic, by its very existence, has brought about a change in the world order, whose shape is now slightly different than that imagined by Washington. Now there are two systems: the still powerful, dominant Western one, and the emerging Islamic order. The West may believe itself the model for the entire world, but Iran has shaken that belief. A new political space has taken shape under our very eyes. It's up to Westerners to understand this political space. Certainly, it is remote from the West. But differences need not always be sources of discord and enmity. We can enjoy them, and even view them as a source of wealth."

Everyone, he says with a good-humoured lilt in his voice, must ultimately surrender to truth (*Islam* means "surrender to God"). Both East and West can agree that happiness and prosperity should be our general goals. "Islamic values can be as helpful in attaining this goal as Western ones. Of course, there is no need for Westerners to become Muslims — they hardly lack for a spiritual tradition of their own. Besides, acceptance of truth is not a defeat, but a victory for the human spirit."

IN A NARROW back street just around the corner from Neuphle-le-Château Avenue, named for the Paris suburb where Imam Khomeini directed the crucial final phase of the Islamic revolution, stands a stately turn-of-the-century Tehran mansion surrounded by a formal garden complete with reflecting pools overhung with fruit trees and cypresses. A plump peacock — what would a Persian garden be without one? — is perched on the baroque plaster balustrade, preening its feathers in the late-afternoon sun.

Despite a hectic cross-town taxi trip with a driver who cannot find the street, I'm on time for my meeting with Abdolkarim Soroush, the director of the Iranian Academy of Philosophy, formerly known as the Royal Institute of Philosophy. The meeting has taken several weeks to organize, with the help of recommendations from discreetly dissident friends. While business relations under the Islamic regime are open and cordial, especially if there are lucrative contracts to be signed, intellectual contact outside government-approved channels can be tentative, difficult and sometimes risky. Iranians, particularly those holding official positions, remain cautious in their dealings with foreigners. Mr. Soroush, I had every reason to suspect, was doubly so.

Abdolkarim Soroush was born in Tehran in 1945, and studied pharmacy and chemistry, history and philosophy of science, in England. "I did two things," he says with a chuckle, "analytic philosophy and analytic chemistry. The science degree was as necessary as the degree in the philosophy of science." And all the while he read assiduously in Persian and Arabic literature, and Islamic philosophy. As he speaks my eyes peruse the bookcases that line the walls of his office. Among the hundreds of Persian titles I spot I. F. Stone's *The Trial of Socrates* and Christopher Lasch's *True and Only Heaven*. Tea arrives. From the garden comes the croaking of the peacock.

When he returned to Iran six months after the outbreak of the Islamic revolution, he began teaching the philosophy of ethics, science and religion at Tehran University, gradually gravitating toward the human sciences. The author of seventeen books on topics ranging from philosophy to literature, with more in progress, he has also participated in learned seminars as far afield as Greece and Canada. Today, his prolific pen turns out essays for newspapers and periodicals, and, in a country where the unmediated spoken word has lost nothing of its subversive power, he is a popular public speaker and lecturer. And seen by the hierocracy as a threat.

A few hours before our meeting, he tells me, he has been served with a gag order from the authorities. The decision, which prohibits him from publishing or speaking in public for an indefinite period, was the result of a particularly outspoken speech at Isfahan University, in which he challenged the clergy over its easy access to power and its lack of openness to criticism. (Several months later, I asked Ayatollah Ahmad Janati, Head of the Islamic Republic's Cultural Revolution Committee, why Mr. Soroush had been banned from public speaking. The Ayatollah denied the existence of such a ban and pointed to Soroush as an example of the tolerance of the regime.) The full text of the speech, published in the Tehran Islamic radical daily *Salaam*, has set tongues furiously aflutter.

"The clergy," declared Dr. Soroush, "assumed the country's management after the revolution.... Religious sciences now have the potential to bring to power someone who has learned them.... The clergy have always been an organized party and now they form a party which has set other opposition parties aside."

Iran's theological seminaries, he went on to warn, face three dangers which arise when science joins hands with power: using the language of force and not logic, using power when one is short of science and logic, and justifying power instead of fostering guidance and criticism of the rulers. "If the right to discuss the Rule of the Jurisconsult is not observed at the seminaries and views for and against are not expressed freely, it indicates a plague which should be eliminated.... I am aware that what I am saying would not taste sweet for some, but I speak this bitter fact out of sympathy."

The same issue of *Salaam* carried — *objectivité oblige* — a rebuttal from Ayatollah Naser Makarem Shirazi, of the Qom theological seminary. When Dr. Soroush began expounding his views five years ago, disagreement from Ayatollah Shirazi, one of Iran's few senior Ayatollahs, was, as he describes it, "friendly." Not today. The Ayatollah's January, 1993, article contained one sentence —"What he [Soroush] has done is similar to what those like Kasravi did in the past" — which was an encoded warning whose intent could not have been lost on anyone familiar with the last fifty years of Iranian political, intellectual and religious history, Dr. Soroush least of all.

This is what "those like Kasravi did in the past": in the early '40s, the violently anticlerical Persian nationalist Ahmad Kasravi published a series of pamphlets calling for the rationalist purification of religion. One such pamphlet, written by a former cleric, challenged his former colleagues of Qom to respond to precise questions on the most sensitive points of Shi'ite theology. Ayatollah Khomeini, then teaching at the Qom seminary, took up the challenge in his book *The Unveiling of Secrets*. Though Ahmad Kasravi, who had inspired the pamphlet, was not mentioned in Khomeini's reply, there was no doubt that he was one of its targets. Five years later, in 1946, Kasravi was murdered as an apostate by the *Fedayin-e Islam*, an extremist religious organization which practised the physical elimination of its opponents.

Dr. Soroush's critics, particularly theological students with close ties to the religious establishment, argue that he is an agent of cultural infiltration. Western culture, they claim, is a humanist culture, that is, man-based and Godless, and thus a bitter enemy of religion. Soroush has been attacked as a handmaiden of Freemasonry, which, along with international Zionism, heads the catalogue of ideological forces inimical to religion. "Religious intellectuals cannot exist, they say. Therefore I cannot exist. They accuse me of following Calvin and Luther, of being an agent of the Western cultural onslaught."

"Of course this is bitter news," he says in a soft voice, with a shrug of his shoulders. "But you have to cope. No, I'm not that worried. Freeing ourselves from the heritage of dictatorship is a long process."

Abdolkarim Soroush's problems began with a series of philosophical essays entitled "Expansion and contraction of religious knowledge" which he later compiled and published in book form. They insisted on the necessity of seeing — in the classic Kantian formulation — the thing for ourselves, the *phenomenon*, not the thing for itself, or the *noumenon*. In religion, he argues, both aspects are in a state of constant dialogue. Although religion can only be apprehended as it appears to us, all our doctrinal claims and our faith necessarily belong to the sphere of phenomena. But religion "in itself" is silent. "We have to make it speak. To do this, we must use the full content of our reason."

Religion, he wrote, is not one and undifferentiated. We have the religion of the layman, that of the learned; mystical religion, scientific religion. But these many manifestations are merely phenomena. The individual believer's perspective — mystical, philosophical — determines his definition of religion in itself, as *noumenon*. One's religion is proportionate to one's understanding of it. Human beings cannot attain more than an understanding of the world, and this realization should lead to a plurality of understandings, opinions and sects. The two main Islamic doctrines, the Shi'ite and the Sunni, are an example. "My main point was this: We must see the difference as natural. If you assume absolute right or wrong for one or the other, then Muslim unity is a myth. But if you assume a dialogue, then opposition is both legitimate and natural."

In the same spirit, he flatly rejects the "inevitability" of the Western cultural model invoked by Tehran's technocrats as they attempt to justify the new free market orthodoxy, and by the traditionalists as they attempt to seal off Iranian culture from the influence of the West. "Historical prophecy is utterly unimaginable. To claim otherwise simply demonstrates the poverty of the imagination. How can we assume that there is no potentiality to be actualized? This is a throwback to Hegel — who is still alive and well in our country," he says with a sardonic smile.

No one can deny the greatness of Western achievement. After all, every civilization sees itself as the final, culminating point, when in fact it may well be the beginning of something else, he says, adopting Kuhn's theory of the history of science as a series of consecutive closed-system paradigms. Does not divine revelation, the very core of the Islamic belief system, then become merely a "monotheistic paradigm?" Yes, he answers himself in the next breath, and so does every religious system, even though its adherents and followers believe it to be the only one possible. "To such people, relativism based on paradigms is distasteful. But, there must be a last paradigm. You may well view your own as the last, the ultimate. But you must still argue your case."

"What gives me the greatest pleasure," he continues, walking over to one of the bookcases and pulling out several of the volumes generated in response to his work, "is not disseminating a new theory, but starting a dialogue, as I attempted to do in my speech in Isfahan. But some serious, and sometimes harsh, people will do their utmost to stop the game."

As he pushes against the outer limits of what may be said, not merely within the confines of school or seminary, but in public, Dr. Soroush is expanding the boundaries of public discourse. In his Isfahan lecture, which drew an enthusiastic response from the thousands of students and faculty members present, Dr. Soroush declared that since religious leaders were human their decisions should be treated as the work of human beings: open to criticism and analysis. "In our country, religious issues have become so politicized that scientific and philosophical discussion is impossible in public. We'll be driven into politics in spite of ourselves."

Avoiding politics in Islamic Iran, where under official doctrine, religion and politics are one, is not a foregone conclusion, however. The doctrine of *Velayat-e Faqih*, central to the Islamic Republic's religious legitimacy, is a particularly sensitive issue. Dr. Soroush dismisses with a wave of his hand the clergy's accusations that he seeks its abolition. "The theory of the Rule of the Jurisconsult is no longer discussed, as though it were divine revelation. But it is nothing more than a theory, a doctrine — however respectable. It can be argued, especially at places like the theological seminary in Qom. Several of the doctrines and theories which are linked to power should be debated, and held up for examination. What I did was to warn the clergy of the danger of proximity to power. Be on your guard, I warned them. This will be fatal to you. Power and thought are two distinct things. You must convince with reason, not with power. If the religious establishment continues to use this language, it will lose its base of support."

AT THE HEART of Khomeini's appeal and peculiar power (he, like the Pope of Stalin's ill-advised aphorism and unlike the Shah, commanded no battalions) lay the uniquely Shi'ite invention of an Islamic ideology of state power which made possible the establishment of a theocratic government. This was to be achieved under a radical new institution devised by Khomeini, called the Rule of the Jurisconsult. Traditional Shi'ite doctrine had for centuries held that legitimate authority belonged neither to the secular rulers, the caliphs and the sultans, nor to the *ulama*, the clerical establishment — but only to the infallible Imams, direct descendents of the Prophet through his daughter Fatima and her husband Ali. This lineage — the Holy Family of Shi'ism — continued until the twelfth Imam, al-Mahdi, the Lord of the Age, who went into Occultation in 874. The doctrine of Occultation both shaped and reflected the Shi'ite propensity for quietism and withdrawal in long-suffering expectation of the Day of Resurrection; in the absence of the Twelfth Imam the *ulama* shunned worldly affairs. Simultaneously, it masked an undercurrent of insurrectionary indignation directed against all temporal rulers, who were, by definition, corrupt and irreligious.

A resolution came some 200 years ago, after a debate among Islamic scholars over what, today, might strike an observer as an abstruse matter of Islamic jurisprudence, the equivalent of the medieval theological debate about the sex of angels. The outcome, however, was radically different. A movement of Iranian *mollahs* known as the *usulis* provided Shi'ism with the conceptual tools it needed to break with the conservatism of centuries and permit "innovation" (*ijtihad*, whose doors, according to Sunni orthodoxy, were irrevocably closed). The *usulis* argued that even in the absence of the last Imam it was permissible to apply independent reasoning to problems of scriptural interpretation in the real world. When they emerged triumphant in the debate against their conservative adversaries (called *akhbaris*) at the end of the eighteenth century, the *usulis* had established the authority of the *ulama* — the clergy — to act, albeit in limited ways, until the reappearance of the Hidden Imam. Crucially, the *ulama* were empowered to exercise this limited authority to guide the religious functioning of the community. Since Islamic law and tradition impinge on all aspects of individual and political life, direct involvement in the affairs of the world was but a short step behind.

The *mollahs*, who over the last several centuries had become virtually a hidden, parallel government, began to speak out on political issues — and played a critical role in Iran's first constitutional crisis. In 1892, the most eminent religious leader of the day, Mirza Hassan Shirazi, led a powerful and effective protest movement against the granting of a monopoly on tobacco production and marketing by declaring that it was forbidden to the faithful to consume tobacco as long as it was so cultivated and marketed. So effective was the religious edict that even the women in the royal household refused to use tobacco.[35]

When the Constitutional Revolution broke out in 1905, with the demand for election of representatives, the Shi'ite *ulama* took the position that power held by an elected assembly was preferable to the absolute and arbitrary power of a tyrant. A half-century later, another religious leader, Ayatollah Kashani, called for nationalization of Iran's oil industry and the limitation of royal power.

However, a doctrine which would allow the clerical establishment actually to govern was lacking until Ayatollah Khomeini, in the early 1970s, asserted that the Jurisconsult's mandate included a general right to rule. His injunction abolished at one stroke the dichotomy between religious/legal and temporal authority. Originally conceived as belonging to all Shi'ite jurists, or at least to the senior, highest ranking members of the hierocracy known as "sources of emulation" (*marja-e taqlid*), this prerogative Khomeini distilled into a single, unitary leadership to be achieved by Islamic revolution. "If one such [just Jurisconsult] succeeds in forming a government it is incumbent on the others to follow him. If the task is not possible except by their uniting, they must unite to undertake it."

Succeed he did. The Constitution of the Islamic Republic confers leadership upon "the just and virtuous jurist." The progression from passive withdrawal to oppositionism, to interventionism and finally to state power made possible the total integration of religion and politics, and placed the Shi'ite clerical establishment in the position of absolute political and religious domination. The doctrine of *Velayat-e faqih* is now taught in Iran's schools, and Friday prayer leaders enjoin the faithful to obey the *ulama* as a matter of religious obligation. Shortly before his death in 1989, Khomeini, in a decision which was intended to sacralize secular rule, decreed that all governmental ordinances were henceforth to belong to the category of primary rules incumbent on all believers. Clerical rule was officially termed the Absolute Mandate of the Jurisconsult.[36]

Paradoxically — and, lest we forget, Islamic Iran is the realm of the paradoxical — the doctrine which permitted Khomeini to assume uncontested political and religious leadership may have proved less to sacralize life in the Islamic Republic than to secularize religion. The dismissal of Khomeini's appointed successor, Ayatollah Hossein Ali Montazeri, in early 1989, following his increasingly outspoken criticism of the failings of the revolution, created an acute constitutional impasse. The constitution was clear: the spiritual and political leader of the Islamic Republic could only be a "source of emulation" — a qualification which Montazeri fulfilled. Ostensibly at Khomeini's behest, the constitution was revised to separate the function of leader from the highest religious authority. The result was to undercut the role of the religious establishment in the governance of the Islamic state. Anti-regime authors Ali Rahnema and Farhad Nomani claim that with the nomination as leader of Ali Khamene'i, a relatively junior religious figure who is not such a source of emulation, a *de facto* separation of religion from politics took place.[37] Others claim that the weakening of religious authority has obliged the regime to rely increasingly on the high clergy of Qom — the profoundly conservative gerontocracy which Imam Khomeini had ridiculed as "petrified" (*mottahadjerin*) — for its legitimacy, reversing in one fell swoop Khomeini's policy of alliance between the disinherited and the militant clergy — the policy that gave birth to the Islamic revolution.[38]

"OF COURSE WE ARE FUNDAMENTALISTS! And proud of it. Every house must have a strong foundation to stand on. Do not Christians and Jews believe in the fundamentals of their religion? Why should we not also?" I am listening to a man who wields the language of power with self-assured bluntness: Seyyed Hadi Khamene'i, publisher of a daily newspaper called *Jahan-e Islam* (World of Islam) and member of the Majlis, is big-boned, dark-skinned and taciturn; a man who wears authority as naturally as he wears his cleric's robes, listens attentively and occasionally bursts into booming full-throated laughter. Like all those whose bear the honourific title of Seyyed, the younger brother of Iran's current leader Ali Khamene'i wears a black turban indicating his descent from the family of the Prophet Mohammad.

I've been introduced to Mr. Khamene'i by a mutual friend, a devout and wealthy businessman who maintains close ties with several members of the "radical" wing of the clerical establishment. The snowstorm which swept through the city only two days before has left the steep-pitched streets in the northern district slippery with frozen slush and ice. After several minutes of wheel-spinning frustration, I dismiss my taxi and hike the last half-kilometre north through the crystalline cold night. Now, as I sip a steaming cup of tea, the warmth slowly flows back into my chilled hands and feet.

One of the most striking results of the concentration of political and theological power in the hands of Iran's religious establishment has been an ebbing of Shi'ism's claim to supra-Iranian, or pan-Islamic universality. Though both minority Shi'ites and majority Sunnis share the same core dogma of the oneness of God, the same sacred Book, the same Prophet, the same belief in resurrection and final judgement, and the same basic obligations — prayer, fasting, pilgrimage, alms and *jihad* — Shi'ites also believe in God's justice and in Imamate, the institution of the Imams, the twelve pure and infallible Guides of the community who belong to the lineage of the Prophet. But the Iran-Iraq war and the Gulf

War dealt a crushing blow to the historic centres of Shi'ism at the shrines of Karbala and Najaf, in Iraqi territory. When Saddam Hussein's loyal troops recaptured the holy cities after the brief but violent Shi'ite uprising which followed Iraq's Pyhrric defeat at the hands of the Western coalition in Kuwait, his bloody repression was praised with faint damns by Iran.

The death of Ayatollah Kho'i shortly afterward (August, 1992) signalled the disappearance of the last of the Grand Ayatollahs to reside outside Iran, while Khomeini's development of the doctrine of *Velayat-e faqih* had strengthened the clerical establishment's control of the state machinery at the expense of the Shi'ite clergy's traditional independence from politics. Whether these developments were symptoms or causes, Iran's adversaries in the Islamic world, led by the Saudis, achieved some success in emphasizing the differences between Sunnis and Shi'ites, depicting the latter as more Iranian than Muslim. Still, Iran's Shi'ite hierocracy has always paid fulsome lip service to unity through the Qur'anic origin of all Islamic thought and practice.

Mr. Khamene'i doesn't want to discuss the rift. But, he adds, only in Iran can true Islam be found today. True Islam is not to be defined as Shi'ite as opposed to Sunni, but in terms of the relation of its practitioners to World Arrogance — that is, the United States. Islam as practised in countries like Algeria, Tunisia, Egypt and above all Saudi Arabia he contemptuously dismisses as "American" Islam. "Here we have Muslim Islam," he booms. "Before the revolution we had 'American' Islam too, but now we are creating a true Islam of our own. American Islam claims only a handful can exercise economic control, while the rest can go begging. We believe that if we show the face of Islam in the Islamic Republic to the people of the world, the idea will progress on its own. We are not exporting our ideas by force."

But this does not mean that what happened in Iran cannot happen anywhere in the world, he adds bluntly. "We are telling it like it is and we really don't care what the Americans think. They won't even give us the time to present our views in any case."

We move to the dining room. In traditional fashion, our host serves the guests from heaping platters of roast chicken, fried Caspian white fish and steamed rice while his wife remains carefully concealed, stage-managing from the kitchen in deference to the high-ranking clergyman.

Radicals like Mr. Khamene'i and moderates both swear by the fundamentals. Religion and politics cannot be separated, they protest.

Religion is the glue that holds society together, the force that illuminates all of its component parts. But beneath the façade of unity — both main political factions, the Society of Militant Clergy (the radicals) and the Society of Militant Clergymen (the moderates) insist on their devotion to the heritage of the Islamic Revolution — there is bitter disagreement.

Before the revolution, economic pressure was stiff, says Mr. Khamene'i. Now the pressure is even greater, but the people are tolerating it because of their attachment to Islam and their confidence in the leadership. Once past the commonplaces and on to the controversial issue of foreign investment — the touchstone of the Rafsanjani government's reconstruction policy — he becomes suddenly animated and incisive. Pushing aside his plate, he leans back in his seat, deliberating on his choice of words: "We welcome investment as long as it does not destabilize our Islamic integrity. Some people believe it will undermine us, but the leadership does not think so. Even so, some oppose this policy, and if they held ministerial positions, if they had power, they would reverse it," he says, pausing in such a way as to leave no doubt where he stands. "We are concerned that continuing this policy will exacerbate our problems. Investors come under the guise of assisting us, but their remedies are worse than the illness they seek to cure."

IRAN MAY BE GOVERNED by the Rule of the Jurisconsult, but the Jurisconsult by and for whom the doctrine was conceived is now dead, safely buried and out of harm's way beneath the gilded dome and minarets of his immense mausoleum. The *mollahs*, as a distinct class, have quickly grown accustomed to the ways of power and have been seduced by its blandishments. Whatever remained of the clerical establishment's unitary singlemindedness, a myth which was once able to conceal internal rifts in the face of outside danger, has been neutralized by its promiscuous relationship with power. The *mollah* who preaches the Friday prayer sermon is not merely the representative of state power: he actually holds and wields that power.[39]

But the hierocracy itself may be at risk as Iran struggles to integrate the Western technoscience it is convinced it must have to survive in the world. The *mollahs* may rule Iran, but the country owes its survival to a group of Western-educated technocrats, technicians and engineers: the men, and few women, who actually make things work. These new Islamic experts, far more than the clergy or the traditional intellectuals, have given credibility to the alliance between the positive knowledge which changes the world and supernatural revelation. They are the draughtsmen of the government's economic and cultural policies; its junior ministers, technical experts, representatives on international bodies.

These Muslim technocrats have taken over the Islamic revolution, a dissident political scientist told me as we walked through a downtown park, far from potential eavesdroppers. "They are superficial Muslims, affiliated with the clergy or raised in traditional families. This is the Islamic middle class, with its ingrown respect for the *mollah*, and its subservience to authority. Each is connected to the *mollahs* in power, and they are very innocent in the deepest sense of the world. They don't have the faintest idea what the West is, what the modern age is. They have never examined their own beliefs and values. The net effect will be to accelerate the progress of Western technology and technique. Unfortunately," he says in a low voice, "the political situation is such that we are not free to discuss openly. I want to be able to say these things, but I do not dare."

AS REVOLUTIONARY ARDOUR cools, the inevitable compromise between religious purity and the exigencies of translating moral precepts into practical politics can only sharpen dissatisfaction both within the hierocracy, and with religion itself. Proximity to power may have already compromised the *mollahs* as a class: in assuming state power they may have surrendered their independence as an institution. Clerical income was formerly based on revenues from the voluntary tax which is one of the five pillars of Islam, and from the *vafq*, or religious endowment properties. Its independence made the clergy responsive, if not always responsible, to the concerns of the people to whom it ministered and on whose alms it depended. Its responsiveness was the principal factor in its ability to weather the attacks of the Pahlavi regime. Today, as disillusionment with the Islamic regime grows, these revenues have entered into sharp decline, forcing the state to introduce income taxes to offset the shortfall. At the same time the Leader, Ayatollah Khamene'i, who many in Tehran view as the president's religious alter ego, is attempting to bring under the direct control of his office the great theological schools of Qom and Mashhad, the heart of the conservative Shi'ite religious establishment.[40] If the strategy is successful, Iran's rambunctious clergy will soon be metamorphosed into docile handmaidens of an increasingly secularized power structure. It would be an audacious rewriting of the Shi'ite tradition of visceral mistrust in government, as well as a serious challenge to the fiercely guarded autonomy of the religious establishment. The result, warns Ayatollah Montazeri, is likely to be a lapdog "official" clergy prepared to issue *fatwas* to match the dictates of political authority.

BUT THE GREATEST ERROR Western visitors to Iran and the Iranian dissidents they meet may make would be to dismiss too hastily the Shi'ite clerical establishment as intellectually retarded throwbacks to a dark age. The *mollahs*, unlike their Westernized critics, still enjoy widespread contact with all sections of Iranian society. They have mastered the art of persuasion and acquired sophisticated tactical skills over the course of their decades-long struggle first to overthrow the Shah and his regime, then to institute an Islamic order. They are protected by a devoted, disciplined para-military apparatus which owes its welfare and social status to the hierocracy. They can rely on a cadre of intensely, if superficially, religious technicians, researchers and scientists to keep the machinery of state functioning at minimal efficiency levels as long as oil keeps pumping. The factional infighting for which the clerical establishment is famous is, after all, an expression of clerical independence, and, some say, the quintessence of the unique Shi'ite institutional structure and source of its extraordinary resilience.

Iran's clerics range in attitude from modest and self-effacing to vulgar and pretentious. But they share an unshakable devotion to the survival of their institution, and the conviction that they alone can speak to — and for — Iranians. And, unlike the Shah and his courtiers, the *mollahs* and their rank-and-file followers have nowhere else to go, no fall-back position, no powerful foreign friends. They are on their own, and they know it.

School assembly in Kharzan, Iran. Photo © Michael Coyne / The Image Bank.

6

Daughters of Fatima

WHY THE SUDDEN UPROAR when I climb into the bus? Why are voices shrilling in protest, hands reaching out to jab at my shoulder, fingers pointing at *chador*-clad heads? Why are the expressions on the passengers' faces wavering between indignation and amusement? Strange. The faces are all women's. Slowly, what has happened penetrates my consciousness: obsessed with escaping the omnipresent press of humanity, I have boarded the less crowded women's section. Forbidden zone. Males keep out. Sorry, O so sorry. With mumbled apologies I back out the door and rush chastened to the fore-compartment. No seats here. Nothing but a mass of male bodies crushed up against one another like bruised tangerines in a crate. The women are seated at the back, gazing imperturbably, primly now, out the windows. I catch a man's eye. His expression is one of resignation mixed with sympathy, as if to say: "This is Iran."

MY HOTEL IS JUST AROUND the corner from the textile shops on Felestin (Palestine) Street with their show windows full of bright patterns and weaves, metallic cloth, diaphanous fabrics. The shoppers here are all women; some clad in *chadors*, the traditional Iranian black garments that cover the head and body, others dressed in headscarves worn with square-cut, loose dark blue or brown unbelted calf-length coats. One long block east, on Vali-ye Asr Avenue, shoe store windows display local knock-offs of the latest in Italian elegance — footwear which, if worn in public, would bring their wearer a stiff reprimand from the Islamic dress patrols that still scour the city. Some stores have been padlocked and their entrances hung with banners proclaiming "Closed for un-Islamic behaviour." I could only speculate on what the offense might have been: perhaps a timid display of ladies' undergarments — never shown in shop windows though reputed, on the best authority, to exist — or failure to respect the rules of *hijab*, ill-defined in Islamic writ and tradition but generally understood as properly modest attire for women. Signs prominently posted near the door in restaurants inform diners: "Ladies without *hijab* are strictly forbidden." Restaurant proprietors, who know that they risk having their premises closed if they serve improperly clad women, post such signs as much to assuage police suspicions as to demonstrate their own commitment to Islamic propriety.

At Friday prayers at Tehran University, half of the faithful are out of sight — but not out of mind — of the dignitaries who preach the sermon. Behind a white curtain, on the side streets to the west, sit the women worshippers, unseen and virtually unheard, but whose presence the Islamic regime cannot ignore. More than passive support for the Islamic regime, the presence of Iranian women occupying the streets at the Friday prayer ceremony expresses, in its way, a shift in social behaviour every bit as radical as the imposition of *hijab* after the Islamic revolution of 1979. On Friday, while their husbands turn homeward after the week's work, these women — in their tens of thousands — abandon household tasks to converge, alone or in groups, on the downtown area to join the ranks of the daughters of Fatima. Unknown before the revolution, this presence reflects the refusal of the country's most militantly religious women to be excluded or isolated from society, their determination that their own existence be respected in and of itself. It also offers a silent but eloquent contradiction to the Western view of Iranian women as voiceless, faceless and repressed.[41]

WARNING AND DISCLAIMER. Writing about women may be, in our era of gender studies, a perilous enterprise for a man. Writing about women in an unfamiliar and profoundly different culture, where even the dangers of voice appropriation pale before those of ignorance, is even more perilous. Then, too, the objectivity syndrome must be factored in. By immobilizing the subject, wrapping it in a straightjacket, the writer risks turning it against himself. He who would immobilize is immobilized, made prisoner of what he presumes to master: the commonplace and the conventional. Between objectivity and objectification there lies but a short, and possibly fatal step, into a conceptual quagmire. The objectifier enters a hall of mirrors, an exhibition of the tragic and the unconventional, a world cultural supermarket, where he picks and chooses, discards and obscures, integrating unconnected and unrelated fragments, the better to reduce and ultimately digest them. To chew them up and spit them out. All of this by way of acknowledgement that I am about to enter uncharted and perhaps dangerous territory. Proceed, however, I must.

The Woman Question, along with its sub-categories Dress, Propriety and Behaviour (and including the silent but implied category of Sex) is sensitive for another reason: It is one of the dominant world culture's most precisely focused points of attack against Islamic Iran, and against Islam in general. (Salman Rushdie realized what the other one was — but that's another story.) The reasons for this both conflict and converge. Women in Iran, so goes the modernist Western stereotype, are forced to take the *chador* as a distinctive garment of oppression which stifles self-expression; they are excluded from society, relegated to their narrow, biologically-determined duties as mothers and their socially-determined role as housekeepers, at the mercy of abusive husbands and tyrannical families, all reflecting the generalized and pervasive inferiority of woman enshrined in the 1,400-year-old Qur'anic message and the life of the Prophet Mohammad himself. Islam, thus defined, negates a woman's identity; her profession of faith can mean only her subjection.[42] At the same time, the Orientalist vision created by and inherited from the past has, in Western eyes, cast Muslim women as mindless, sensual creatures lounging in harems, at the beck and call of shadowy male despots who wield over them the absolute power of life or death. The two images converge in their common belief in an all-encompassing female passivity and concomitant lack of intelligence, even of essential humanity. Seductively, unctuously, both assumptions flatter our assurance that as wielders and possessors of a value-free world culture we need not question the origins of our own founding myths, which, as Thierry Hentsch has demonstrated,[43] we must now recognize as no less determinant for being grounded in myth.

My reading of Islamic history and my experience in Islamic Iran combine to convince me that these images are contrived, flawed and grotesquely false. And yet, as even the most scurrilous libel may contain a grain of truth, so there may be some grounds for the West's charge against Islam. In Iran, I set myself the task of seeking this grain — or certifying its absence — through observation and discussion with official spokeswomen and oppositionists, with professional women and students and mothers of martyrs. The difficulties, while not insuperable, are substantial. In traditional Iranian households male guests may never see the lady of the house, who remains behind closed doors while her husband serves; or, if present, is closely wrapped in her *chador*. Unrelated men — especially Westerners — do not approach women in public places, although on several occasions I faintly dared convention by inviting female acquaintances to lunch. In Westernized households, of course, women move about without *hijab*, even in the presence of male guests, but such women are likely to share Western views and be unsympathetic to their religious, *hijab*-observing sisters whom they dismiss as either tradition-bound or Islamist diehards.

AFTER THE FIRST SHOCK of encounter with a society which consciously withholds the beauty of women from public view, which removes all overt expression of sexuality from the public domain, which dictates behaviour not only through consensual social norms but, where norms fail, through harshly enforced religious regulation, I gradually grew accustomed to the prospect of black-clad, formless bodies. I began to appreciate the subtleties of recognizing a fellow human's character through her eyes or her speech. Scantily clad or nude women in seductive poses are not used to sell or promote anything in Iran: in fact, such practices are illegal. This, I happily admit, I found refreshing. So much so that whenever I leave Iran I am briefly astonished at how provocatively Western women are dressed, how closely they resemble the commodities their bodies are displayed to promote, how blurred the dividing line has become.

In its modernizing zeal the West has contrived to forget, even to suppress, Islam's accomplishment in bringing women, 1,400 years ago, a social status which Western societies only achieved in the late nineteenth or early twentieth centuries. The combination of forgetfulness and suppression was even greater in an Iran fascinated with overtaking the West and building a Great Civilization. Shah Mohammad Reza may have been a despot but he was a "progressive" despot, positively enlightened when he ruled that Iranian women must discard their *chadors*. In so doing, he was only carrying on the work begun by his father Shah Reza, whose wife first appeared with head uncovered in the late '30s, or by Nasreddin Shah, the late nineteenth-century Qajar tyrant who returned from Paris so enchanted with classical ballet that he dressed the women in his harem in short-skirted ballet costumes, then made them descend a long slide to his private quarters, the better to admire their frilled underwear.

With the Shah's final marriage to Farah Diba, the daughter of the Otis Elevator empire's Iranian concessionaire, duly consummated, women began to emerge smartly from polished lifts dressed in miniskirts with high-heeled shoes, and to stride rapidly into all walks of life: professional status for the wives of a chosen few, the office or the shop floor for the many, by the grace of his Imperial Majesty. Women's liberation was rushing ahead full speed, gaining momentum, unstoppable. The ruler had so decreed. In 1966, the Iran Women's Organization was founded. Ten years later, it had more than 70,000 members in local sections throughout the country. Membership was made up primarily of the wives of high-ranking civil servants and the Westernized bourgeoisie. And, as in every Iranian institution, SAVAK was at work, promoting pro-government women to key positions.

Mrs. S was one of those on whom fate — and royal indulgence — smiled. She educated in England, her husband in France, the couple moved effortlessly between Europe and Iran, their passage lubricated by high-level connections at the royal court. I meet them in their downtown Tehran office, a place whose dark wood panelling and dusty leather furniture exude the musty, claustrophobic scent of hopelessness. Mrs. S is an ebullient, vivacious woman whose headscarf covers only the absolute minimum of her raven-dark hair. Emancipation? "The Shah handed it to us on a silver platter," she says. "There seemed to be nothing we couldn't do, nothing we couldn't aspire to, no position we could not hold." She shows me photos from an old album. "Look! Here I am, twenty years ago." The photograph shows her addressing a management meeting of the semi-public organization she directed. Her head is uncovered, hair trimmed short; she is wearing a chic European business suit, Chanel maybe. On the wall behind her is an organizational chart; the name of the firm (whose name she asks me not to reveal) is written in English. Many of those in the audience are women. Could have been London or Los Angeles. That, I reflect, was the idea; more Los Angeles than London, reflecting the shift in protecting powers.

Come the revolution, she continued working until she was forced out by "Islamic zealots." *Hijab*, already a badge of revolutionary honour, had been enthusiastically adopted by administrators who wished to demonstrate their allegiance to the new regime; it became obligatory in the public service in 1980. Women who did not wish to comply either left their jobs or were sacked. She left, hoping to ride out the storm until things improved. They never did. Now, despite what she terms the "fifteen terrible, wasted years," Mrs. S radiates the kind of fierce intensity that I imagine would have kept recalcitrant subalterns in line and the organization humming at peak efficiency.

What was then the limelight is, today, the penumbra. "Our life is private, insular. We come here every day to the office. We try to do a little business and live off of our savings, which hopefully will last us a few years longer" — here she breaks into laughter — "and spend our time with a close circle of friends we can trust. Of course, we have to be careful about what we say, and what we do. Some of our friends have spent time in prison; some have had their property confiscated. But no matter what happens, I'm not giving up. I'll keep on trying until my last breath. This is my country, and I'm too proud to leave."

The imperial regime's efforts to win over women were, for people like Mrs. S, a success. She and thousands of women like her were the incarnation of a certain modernity, of a life-style which was promoted as uniquely appropriate to public life. At the same time, traditional family values continued to dominate the private sphere. Public life, however, was narrowly defined, highly selective, and closed to all but a tiny, privileged minority. The rhetoric of technological and economic integration into the world market — the avowed aim of the Pahlavi state — was matched by the cultural exclusion of most women from society. The imperial system conflated modernity — Western, desirable, inevitable — with a supremely oppressive political system in which social change was imposed by edict from above.[44] Women who had no inclination to discard tradition, and who had no access to the emerging public sphere defined as "modern," recoiled. Most of the country's women had never abandoned Islamic dress; they prefered to remain indoors rather than face dishonour on the street. Families kept their daughters out of school rather than send them unveiled into the world.

The contradiction rapidly turned volatile. At a drama festival held in the city of Shiraz several years before the revolution, a visiting European experimental theatre troupe performed in the nude not on stage, but in a public place. For years Islamic preachers, reviled by the regime as black reactionaries, had equated lack of *hijab* with nudity.

Now, suddenly, what had been metaphorical became virtual. Shock waves ripped through Iranian society. The incident touched off an outcry which was quickly caught up in the spiral of discontent.

While the beneficiaries of imperial reform prospered, other well-educated women from middle-class families had already begun to return to the *chador* as a badge of protest first against absolutism and the rampant Westernization which accompanied it, then in solidarity with the oppressed, and finally, the ultimate step in the progression, as an affirmation of a new-found Islamic identity. The *chador* had a practical side too; it provided even non-believers with anonymity and ample space for carrying leaflets, emergency food supplies, and, in the heat of combat, weapons. This the Shah's advisors belatedly realized, and the police began to rip off women's Islamic garb. In the desperate despot's final months in power his police stripped girl high school students to the waist at a school in Kerman. In another town, female students were raped by SAVAK agents. Nothing now, not humiliation nor public shame could stem the onrush of anger, much of which was now focused on the hypocrisy of the palace which had liberated women only to have them harassed, molested and raped.

Of this modernity women would have none. They turned out massively in the great street marches that led to the Shah's downfall, in the process establishing themselves as a force to be reckoned with after the corrupt ruler had been cast down. How forceful this movement became was revealed in a speech by Ayatollah Khomeini, later omitted from his collected writings on women, in which he revealed with some surprise that "the women come out into the streets even without it having been decided on beforehand."[45] The Imam, who like many clergymen had objected to the enfranchisement of women by the Shah as "un-Islamic" in the early '60s, quickly revised his position. "What they say," he thundered, "that for instance in Islam women have to go inside the house and lock themselves in, are false accusations. Islam is not opposed to women in universities. It opposes corruption in universities.... Islam empowers women. It puts them next to men. They are equals."[46]

For the women who joined or supported the movement, the Islamic revolution was not the revenge of tradition against the Shah's bungled attempts at modernization. The institutions of the state which replaced the Pahlavis were anything but traditional: women were to see to that. Women in full *chadors* carrying guns on their shoulders, sitting in parliament, piloting airplanes or directing films contrast sharply with simplistic, medievalist definitions of womanhood.

JULY, 1985. Since her husband's death Atekah Raja'i has lived alone in a small, one-storey house in east-central Tehran, a traditional Iranian dwelling with a small reflecting pool surrounded by fruit trees in the middle of a high-walled garden. While we wait cross-legged in the midsummer heat on the carpets of the living room floor, a housekeeper serves a tray of watermelon and glasses of ice water. On the wall is a lone portrait of her husband, Mohammad Ali Raja'i, Iran's second president, whose brief term and short life were ended by a bomb explosion on August 30, 1981.

With a soft rustle of fabric one of the first four women members of the Islamic parliament enters the room; joints creaking, we rise to our feet. We exchange no handshake, no eye contact; the three of us — filmmaker Ron Hallis, an interpreter and I — bow slightly and offer our greetings and appreciation for the cooling fruit. Atekah Raja'i is a small, slender woman with an angular face, intense eyes and a direct, self-assured manner; her barely modulated voice becomes more animated as the interview progresses. When she and her husband, whom she calls simply "Raja'i" were schoolteachers in the early '60s, he decided to join the Islamic movement. "After Imam Khomeini's speech on 15 Khordad (June, 1963), he asked me to help him. We worked together until 1973, when they arrested him and then I continued on my own, until he was released with the revolution," she says, *chador* held tight over her chin, eyes carefully averted.

Mohammad Ali Raja'i typified everything that was distasteful about the Islamic regime in the eyes of its opponents. Born into the poverty of a rural migrant family, he scratched out a living as a street vendor and errand boy, struggled through high school and finally graduated from teachers college in the capital: a survivor. He was a small man with wiry hair; quiet, persistent, and single-minded in his devotion to Islam. Iran's sophisticated secular politicians, many of them the sons of the country's self-assumed natural rulers, the great families, could hardly believe their eyes. Raja'i's political ideas bore the unmistakable stamp of the *Fedayin-e Islam*, a militant organization founded in the mid-'40s, whose aim was to purge Iran of corrupting Western influences.

But Raja'i was no one-dimensional man. He later joined Mehdi Bazargan's Liberation Movement, spent five years in that great revolutionary preparatory school, the Shah's prisons, and in the early days of the revolution revealed his political talents as he outmanoeuvred then-President Bani-Sadr for the support of parliament and of the Ayatollah Khomeini. Bani-Sadr had been shown, by compromising documents discovered during the occupation of the United States Embassy, to have entered into secret communication with the Great Satan. (This happened while the *mollahs* were in close contact with Ronald Reagan's Republican Party, arranging to hold the embassy hostages until after the US elections of November, 1980, the better to guarantee Jimmy Carter's defeat.) He was declared unfit to continue as president, and fled into exile. The bomb which destroyed Raja'i's office ended the new president's term less than a month later.

"Up until Raja'i was martyred," she says, "I was only a simple schoolteacher. But I always believed I had a duty to defend the rights of the oppressed and fight against tyranny. After the revolution, I saw no reason to change my ideas. So, after his death, friends and colleagues came visiting to offer me their condolences. But they also encouraged me to run for parliament. At first I declined, but they convinced me. I stood for election, the people voted for me, and now I represent them in parliament."

Colonialism, Mrs. Raja'i insists, has learned that the best way of penetrating a country is through its women. It creates superficial concerns, far removed from the society they live in, from political life, from women's own role in society. "As soon as women in Iran discovered the conspiracy, they became involved in political and social action. The fight was particularly ferocious under the Shah's regime. Women encouraged their husbands to go out into the street, then they went out into the streets themselves, taking their children with them. We found out what it meant, to sacrifice our husbands and our children."

When I ask her what the *chador* means for Iranian women, I detect a note of impatience — an attitude most women officials I interviewed seemed to share, as if to say that Western journalists are obsessed with the superficial at the expense of the essential. "Our dress laws are from the Holy Qur'an," she says. "The woman's body should be covered from the head to the feet, in such a way that her natural contours do not show. We do this to protect society, to protect social and moral values. After all, women are the opposite of the animals, which have nothing to constrain their physical impulses. If women are exposed to men, human values are transformed into animal impulses, into sexual desire. I'm not saying this to draw undue attention to sexual desire, but to show that for us, Islamic dress was our own choice."

WHERE THE SHAH'S REGIME tried, and failed, to remove women's *chadors*, the Islamic revolution has been entirely successful in restoring *hijab*. A woman's bare head — or arms, for that matter — cannot be seen in public in Tehran, or in any Iranian city or town, with the tolerated exception of brides making their way to the wedding ceremony. For Imam Khomeini's devoted and pious followers, anything else would have been unthinkable — a violent rupture of tradition and a betrayal of Islam. For the newly devout women of the middle classes who joined the revolutionary movement, turning away from *hijab* would have been a denial of themselves. But for the the women who identified with the Westernized, cosmopolitan outlook of the Shah's regime, the advent of obligatory Islamic dress was a negation of all they had achieved — and a crushing symbolic defeat. A few months after the revolution, thousands of women marched through the streets of Tehran, joined by American feminist Kate Millet, as if to certify their estrangement from the religious and social movement surrounding them — to protest the new government's determination to enforce Islamic dress. Predictably, the protest and its colonial feminist thrust only strengthened official determination to press on.

As the Islamic revolutionaries consolidated their grip on Iranian society, posters began to appear on walls, their message ranging from the calm voice of reason: "Sister, *hijab* is not only the *chador*," to the shrill voice of coercion: "the headscarf or the club." Women of the Islamic *Komitehs*, the neighbourhood-based civil surveillance and morality squads known as the "Vengeance of God," would stop offenders on the street. Too much hair showing, high-heeled shoes, visible make-up, or revealed body contours could mean an on-the-spot lecture on Islamic propriety, or worse, being bundled into a waiting unmarked car for interrogation at *Komiteh* headquarters, and possibly a lashing.

More serious offenses against public and private morality were quickly brought under the Law of Retribution (*Qesas*), one of the first major legislative acts adopted by the Islamic parliament. The law set out draconian penalties, including stoning for adulterers of either sex, and established blood money (the "blood price" paid for women is half that paid for men, opening the door to the possibility of wealthy wife-murderers avoiding punishment) for victims or their families. It also made such matters difficult to prove: conviction before a religious judge could only be obtained by the testimony of four righteous men, or three righteous men and two righteous women.

AT THE MENTION OF hijab, Sorraya Makhnoun bristles. It's 1988, and I'm interviewing Ms. Makhnoun, director of the Centre for Women's Studies, for Ideas, the CBC radio program. We are doing the interview in her conference room, a threadbare place with nothing on the walls and a fraying, machine-made rug (O sacrilege!) on the floor. Maybe it's because I'm a half-hour late. My excuse is the Tehran standard: the taxi driver could not find the address. But it may not be good enough. Though they will probably be kept waiting, visitors in Iran are expected to be prompt. Or perhaps Ms. Makhnoun is simply having a bad day: "Why is it that foreigners always ask the same old questions?" she snaps. "We speak about *hijab* from two different points of view. Some people see this as only a head covering; we believe it's more than that — a way of showing what is going on inside our head. The West is not interested in the philosophy behind *hijab*. And one of the advantages is that it keeps women from being used in media or propaganda as a tool for spending money on Western products that come into the country."

In Iran, the sight of a tape recorder, or even a reporter's notebook, is usually enough to set off a well-composed, often lyrical exposition which might or might not answer the question but is invariably fascinating, sometimes even dazzling, in its eloquence. This is, after all, a culture which has always revered the spoken word and whose poetic tradition is one of the world's greatest. But Ms. Makhnoun is carrying out a full-scale preemptive strike, seizing all the high ground before I can get the proverbial word in edgewise, rattling a withering fire of concepts, principles and statistics off of my ears, and sending my Sony's sound level indicator leaping off the dial.

What are the limits to equality for women in Islamic Iran, I ask. "There are none," she answers. "Women can do anything they wish." Well, I ask, can women become judges? The question is a delicate one. In Islamic Iran, four professions, including that of judge, are closed to women for reasons relating to what Islamic tradition cites as their more emotional nature, or, in the case of high religious offices, to the physiological differences which differentiate males and females. Because of the menstrual cycle, women may not lead Friday prayers or become models for emulation (*marja-e taqlid*).[47] "If women cannot make the last part of the decision, it is because Islam believes that there is so much responsibility involved that it should be removed from women's shoulders. In the West, you may see the inability to become judges as a disadvantage. We see this as an opportunity for women to do other things that they can do better."

Westerners are making a mistake if they expect Iranian women to become like them and consider that to be progress, she adds after a pause, her tone more reflective now. "We have seen what's happened to women in the West, and we don't want it. If people outside Iran want to see whether Iranian women are behind or advanced they should learn the meaning of concepts like happiness, freedom and equality according to Islam, not compare them with the meaning that other countries have made for us. The same people have always said that after the revolution Iran is behind, Iranians are fanatic, Iranian women are old-fashioned or whatever." Then, with a mixture of scarcely concealed bitterness and complaint: "Why don't they let us be the way we are? Maybe the world has made some mistake in their judgement toward Iran after ten years now. Behind this *chador*," she says, fingers plucking at the black fabric that envelops her head, "maybe something else is happening."

§

O mankind! Lo! We have created you male and female and made you nations and tribes that ye may know one - another...

— The Qur'an XLIX, 13

THE DIFFERENCES BETWEEN MEN AND WOMEN are a matter of symmetry, not of imperfection or perfection; superiority or inferiority, argues a leading Iranian Islamic theorist. Each sex possess its distinguishing biological and behavioural characteristics, each one the natural complement of the other. Man, in this interpretation, is the slave of his own passions while woman remains steadfast in the love of man.... A man's sexual drive is aggressive, a woman's is passive and inciting. In Islamic doctrine, man and woman were created in need of each other with a view to fitting man and woman more firmly together, and making the home, which is the basis of the real happiness of man, stronger and more secure.[48] The equality of rights and responsibilities promised by Islam does not mean identical rights and responsibilities, however. Just as the complementarity of the sexes leads to a stronger home and family, where the woman's role is to ensure the reproduction of life within the family, and that of the man to ensure the production of wealth in order to meet the needs of the family within society, complementarity must provide the foundation for a society based on equality and justice.

How could it be otherwise, reflects Zahra Shojae'i, head of the women's section of Iran's Cultural Council, a para-governmental body which answers to the country's Supreme Council on Culture and Social Affairs. As the equality of men and women before God is decreed in the Qur'an, it must be respected by every Muslim; nothing in Islamic scripture and tradition shows women as "inferior" to men. "Women, like men," she assures me, "can aspire to the highest human accomplishments."

Accompanied by Fatima, an interpreter from the Islamic Guidance Bureau, which has emerged from its political torpor long enough to arrange the meeting, I meet Mrs. Shojae'i in the offices of the Cultural Council on a pleasant, tree-lined section of Felestin Street in December, 1993. Large official portraits of the late Imam Khomeini with the obligatory diagonal black mourning band and of his successor Seyyed Ali Khamene'i, are the room's only decorations, except for a vase of fresh-cut flowers and a plate of sweets on the table. A grizzled old concierge wanders in and out carrying trays of tea, begging pardon in the flowery language of subordinal obligation for his repeated interruptions while the ladies grow increasingly exasperated. At most official interviews in Iran the conversation is recorded not only by the interviewer but also by the interviewee's assistant. Today I am using primitive information gathering technology — a pen and reporter's notebook — but the interview is still being recorded by two tape machines. At every creak of the opening door, at the muttered obsequiousness of the manservant with his trayful of rattling tea cups, at the snap and pop of stop-start buttons my concentration falters.

Mrs. Shojae'i is constantly adjusting and readjusting her head covering, a black cowl worn over a dark brown coat, as she explains how *hijab* is related to the nature of women, and is a constant in monotheistic religion. The natural corollary is that men, of course, should also dress in such a way as to show respect for the opposite sex. (I have heard reports of *Komiteh* action against men wearing short sleeves, but never witnessed such action.) There is no law against variety and colour in Islam, she adds. Black *chadors* are traditionally Iranian — simply the local variant of a cultural tradition. A comparison with Western divorce rates, she suggests, may indicate that modest dress can have a stabilizing effect on the most fundamental institution in society, the family. "Here in Iran, men can see only their own wives; they learn to keep away from temptation."

The dress code has actually encouraged women to enter the labour force, she explains. The number of women in technical jobs has increased by more than 40%; in public administration the increase is 12%; in higher education, 45%. Today, more than one third of the work force is made up of women, rising to more than 50% in sectors like health and education. No gender gap in wages exists. In fact, while base salaries and wages are the same, and discrimination is prohibited by the Labour Code, male workers are paid a differential because they must support their families. Women remain economically independent in marriage under Islam, and can claim payment for housework, which is not one of their marriage obligations. If Iranian women usually don't request such payment, it's because social custom and respect for women among men make the practice unnecessary.

"We still have a long way to go to reach our main goals. But we, as women, have made a strong contribution to the fight against illiteracy and for strengthening motherhood as an institution — which is women's main responsibility. These are the areas where we've made the greatest progress."

Yes, she acknowledges, there are still inequalities in Iranian society. It comes as no surprise to hear her describe these as remnants of the old system. But, I ask, are there not voices in Iran today, voices from the clerical establishment, who oppose a wider role for women, who would like nothing better than to define as narrowly as possible women's God-given role as devoted wives, nurturing mothers and dutiful daughters. "Some people, religious conservatives in particular, would like to limit women, but they don't have much influence. They may oppose our work and write articles against us, but they can't stop us," she warns. "Our leaders, the government itself, are strongly pro-woman. They've made it clear that only three things can serve as criteria for judging people; only three things can set the sexes apart: knowledge, piety and respect for human values."

THIRTY-TWO YEARS OLD, divorced, and the sole supporter of her nine-year-old son, Narghes lives far from the rarified world of religious politics and its often abstract discussion of women's nature and rights. Our meeting place is my friend Majid's around-town car, a dusty cream Paykan, one late afternoon in autumn. She is seated alone in the back seat, the two of us in front to allay suspicions as we drive through the dusk of north Tehran.

This is Narghes' story. Her monthly wages — 60,000 rials ($50 CDN) teaching English at a high school in south Tehran — barely cover the rent on her tiny two-room apartment. When she discovered her husband's drug addiction (not uncommon among Iranian men, Majid whispers: "They just crack under the pressure of trying to support a family.") she sued for divorce and won. The man is now in prison for drug-related offenses. Despite a court judgement requiring him to do so, he cannot pay child support. To survive, Narghes supplements her income by taking in private pupils, and spends her nights producing sweaters on a knitting machine. "I just want to take my son and leave this place," she says haltingly, looking down as her slender fingers fidget on her lap.

We pull up at a fast-food outlet for a rubbery Iranian hamburger and a glass of lukewarm domestic cola. Under the bleak fluorescent lights she looks drawn, almost ashen, her dark brown eyes dart back and forth. Classes begins at 7:30 in the morning, after a one and one-half hour bus ride from home. With food, transport and incidental costs totalling at least another 60,000 rials, Narghes needs twice her present wage simply to survive. "Without a husband, life is hard for me, very hard," she says, as tears glisten in her eyes. "But I'll never give up. I must keep trying, for my little boy. I must bring him up the right way."

Later, Majid tells me that she survives by the grace of discreet assistance from a distant relative, who bought her the knitting machine and helps pay the rent. Her handwritten appeal to President Rafsanjani went unanswered. Unlike the mothers and wives of war martyrs, whose needs are met by government programs, women like Narghes have almost nowhere to turn. Her family is too poor, and too embarrassed, to support a daughter whose marriage has failed. Islamic women's organizations provide first-line consultation services and sometimes run small handicraft enterprises, but they are few and receive little state support. Narghes and her son, in a country whose constitution has enshrined the family as the cornerstone of society, are on their own.

For a few desperate women, the only alternative is the unthinkable. Statistics from 1986 — the latest available — showed a surplus of two million women in the prime child-bearing ages: women of the generations which lost their husbands in the war, or who will never find a marriageable man. In the intensely family-oriented society of Islamic Iran, single women like Narghes must bear, in addition to their loneliness, the social stigma of spinstership.

NARGHES THE SCHOOLTEACHER is a real person, though her name, like many in this book, has been changed — a necessary precaution when writing about Iranians encountered outside official channels. But on my visit to Tehran, in January of 1993, I encountered another Narghes: this one a fictitious character in a remarkable film of the same name by Rahkshan Bani-Etemad, perhaps Iran's best-known woman director. Economic conditions have created a series of acute social problems in Iran, she explains over coffee at her office in the Tehran documentary film centre as she outlines the documentary film she is currently finishing. "After divorce, low-income women — poor women — face huge financial problems. They cannot work, they usually have no support, and cannot return to their families because of the burden they would cause. They must support their children and fend for themselves at the same time."

"The problem is a twofold one. Our traditions make it hard for women to live alone. The financial pressure is so acute for poor women that their children must leave school to work. Such women are often forced into a second marriage; it's their only way out. But such marriages create new problems. The husband will be from the same class, and cannot support the first husband's children. This is my subject. What flows from the film is the necessity of providing housewives with an income, of considering work done in the home as labour. With financial security, women would not be intimidated by divorce. If something is not done, women will turn in desperation to prostitution."

The following day I see Mrs. Bani-Etemad's best-known feature on video cassette at her office. *Narghes* depicts a peculiar, lower-depths love triangle set in the seamy south Tehran slums. The film is, at the same time, a finely detailed examination of the social conditions which shape the lives of its characters. They are Iran's "forgotten people," those from the bottom of the social ladder destined to be left far behind in the rush toward market-driven prosperity and untouched by the pious platitudes of official religious doctrine. *Narghes* tells the story of a young criminal emotionally (and sexually, although this is never shown, only suggested) dependent on an ex-prostitute. Adel, the young man, falls in love with a hard-working poor girl called Narghes, who tries, and fails, to change his life. "When we show such conditions, questions will follow," she says. "We had a favourable response from the authorities; the film definitely touched a nerve."

Narghes has the gravelly texture of the dust-filled streets it so starkly depicts. Unsentimental, but with the power of a blow to the stomach, it portrays the effects of poverty, leaving the viewer to reflect on the causes. The film is as closely observed as it is compassionate, and full of small, telling touches. In one scene Narghes and Adel are strolling through the bazaar. Suddenly the "Lambada theme" is heard in the background, blaring from a storefront loudspeaker, a kind of tinny hymn to to the fleeting nature of happiness and a siren song of Western pop eroticism. One of dozens of ephemeral mini-trends in the West, the music was an underground hit in Iran for most of 1991, and can still be encountered in stores and restaurants. Though sung in Brazilian Portuguese, a few lines actually sound like Farsi, including one that seems to say "Why is he growing a beard?" To which most Tehranis would reply: "to apply for a government job."

THE SAME LAMBADA THEME is throbbing from the speakers of Mohsen's car as we swing off the Karaj road for Dizin, Iran's former world-class ski resort. The late January sky is a deep blue turning to purple at the meridian and the morning sun glints off the snow-covered peaks of the Alborz range. A journalist with one of Tehran's largest dailies, Mohsen is my contact point with the rough and tumble world of Iranian politics. He is also my friend, a man now entering his mid-thirties with a deliberate sense of mission: to create the conditions needed to embark on marriage. For most Iranians — men and women — life without marriage is inconceivable. Still, the institution, especially for men whose role is that of sole provider, is not entered into lightly. You need several things, Mohsen is telling me as his Saipa hums along the sinuous mountain road: a good job or perhaps two, a car, a house and good family connections. So far, he laughs, he's got three out of four. But women are demanding, not at all like they used to be in pre-Islamic days when the rial amounted to something and a civil service job was a sinecure.

The Dizin resort lies at the head of a perfect bowl-shaped valley ringed by the jagged summits that stand between the Iranian plateau and the Caspian depression. Today it provides Tehran's leisure-class with the ideal refuge from the dull cares of Islamic conformity. Dizin has no chador-clad ladies from the working class hurrying to make the south-bound bus, no demobilized militiamen in frayed uniforms hawking cigarettes, no poor families crowded — kids and all — onto 125cc Honda motorbikes, no milling throngs of transplanted villagers or Afghan refugees squatting, waiting for a day's work on the construction sites. None of the dusty monochrome of south Tehran. Dizin is a riot of colour, thronged not with religious fanatics but with leathery-skinned ski enthusiasts as single-minded as the most intense revolutionary guardsmen. English can be readily overheard, spoken with both British and American accents, by pudgy-faced pimpled adolescents and their plump and solicitous parents, and by sleek ladies sporting designer sunglasses and well-heeled consorts.

Today is a religious holiday — the Ascension of the Prophet Mohammad — and the parking lot has long since spilled over. We leave the car at least a kilometre down the road and hike in past expensive four-wheel drive vehicles, several immaculately preserved American cars, and ranks of flashy new BMWs and Mercedes Benzes: the kind of wheels you won't see in the rough and tumble traffic of Imam Khomeini Square. As the call to prayer rings out over the outdoor loudspeaker system the skiers clomp on in their massive plastic high-tech boots, oblivious to the word of God crackling through the mountain air. Around the hotel at the foot of the slopes men and women mill about, gaudy in their fluoroluminescent ski-wear and proscribed signature clothing. Not a *chador* in sight: most women have tossed a casual scarf over their heads, as if good intentions could replace the thing itself. Even Mohsen, a dispassionate but fascinated observer of sexual politics, is surprised.

At more than twelve million, Tehran's population today surpasses that of many United Nations member-states. On any given winter holiday thousands of them can be found on the ski slopes. We even encounter a *mollah* escorted by a deferential army officer. He may have come to Dizin to expose himself to the sinful ways of the rich, the better to hone his self-abnegation. More likely he's enjoying the fine day and the warm sun. But he and his escort disappear rapidly in the throng jockeying for position around the gondola entry.

Sexual segregation starts here, Mohsen whispers. Women, unless they are accompanied by a husband, brother or father, must travel in separate cars, which they must enter through separate lines. I follow his eyes to the other side of the shack, where the women are jostling and giggling. Once at the top, they ski down equal and parallel runs divided from the men by a flimsy fence. There are certain advantages. Separate toilet facilities are not necessary: at any given moment a line of men can be seen lined up at the nearest precipice, pissing into the void as they stare across the snow-filled valleys toward the sacred peak of Damavand. The women, we understand, take similar liberties. Once on the down-slope, male trespassers can be whipped if apprehended by the morality patrol on skis. "The *mollahs* are worried about mass copulation on the slopes," he hisses as our gondola passes high above skiers of varying degrees of proficiency, from the falling crawlers to the speeding kamikazes. Of ski-equipped *Komiteh* patrols we see not a sign.

Faced either with swimming and playing tennis in their *chadors*, or sheltered behind high fences from the lascivious stares of men, Iranian women have few opportunities to show their athletic ability in public. The ski slope is one such opportunity — and they don't waste a moment. Far below, we see the "zorros" as their male counterparts call them, schussing downhill at breakneck speed with shrieks of mock terror and delight, their short black capes flapping behind them in the wind.

SAYEH AND I MEET for lunch in a quiet downtown restaurant. I am nervous, fidgety, acutely aware of the delicacy of appearing in public with a younger, unmarried woman who is certainly not related to me. Life at street level in Islamic Iran means accommodating every waking moment to injunctions and interdictions. Since even the smallest details of everyday life have been invested with political significance, neglect of or resistance to these injunctions inevitably becomes a political act. But with the impetuosity of a zorro on the ski slope she brushes aside my cautionary remarks.

By the time we've finished the chicken *kebab* I've found out that Sayeh is more than a full-time English teacher and university student. A striking woman with — who am I to feign unawareness? — breathtaking brown, almond-shaped eyes, she has acted in several films. Now, with a laugh so crystalline that I look around me in apprehension — not to worry, the place is nearly empty and I am a regular customer — she admits to playing the guitar in her scant spare time. Her dream is to visit Spain, where the people, she feels certain, have the same fire the Iranians do. Young people of her own generation she heaps scorn on. "All they care about is getting into Med School, graduating as fast as they can and making money. But for me, life is much more — it's beauty, love, creative work, the search for God."

But wait. This is an interview, I remind myself before plunging my spoon into a bowl of *bastani*, saffron-flavoured ice cream. What about *hijab*? How do educated young Iranian women deal with the exigencies of the dress code? Sayeh's mood abruptly shifts; with a dismissive wave of the hand she says that for most women it is a shell, a superficial covering that means only inconvenience. "I've got nothing against women who want to dress Islamicly. But for me, my religion is between me and God. I don't need anyone's mumbo-jumbo to tell me what to believe. In Iran, people behave like they're wearing blinkers," she says, her voice vibrating with the sudden turbulence of youthful rebellion. "The only really safe thing to do is keep your head down, look straight ahead and be quiet." And if you're too critical? "You may lose your head," she says with a flash of innocent smile and a flicker of her dark eyelashes.

I SUPPOSE THIS IS WHAT IRANIANS call a party. It's really nothing more than an extended family gathering at a private home in one of Tehran's northern suburbs. Western pop music is playing on a tape deck, people are discreetly sipping alcoholic beverages with no apparent concern about a *Komiteh* raid. (Stories of morality squad officers knocking back home-brew vodka or smuggled whisky at drinking parties are one of the staples of the Islamic rumour mill. Iran, which used to produce enough agricultural products to feed its entire population, Iranians joke maliciously, is now self-sufficient only in illicit alcohol.) The women move casually about in clothes that would not be out of place in any urban social gathering in Europe or North America, chatting among themselves or with men who may or may not be their relatives. The atmosphere is quiet, cultivated, infinitely distant from the other Iran of black-clad women crowding the sidewalks. "Come on over," says my host. "I want to introduce you to my niece Parveh. She's studying medicine in Germany." Despite the language barrier — we communicate in a mixture of her rudimentary English and my beginner's Farsi with a few words of German thrown in — I quickly realize that I have happened upon (was this by my host's design or was it coincidence?) someone who roundly detests the regime and all its works. Islam, she says, her face twisted in theatrical disgust, equals oppression. People can only think of escaping "this insane asylum." Eyes flashing, she describes the *mollahs* as "animals." Their system is "the worst thing that's ever happened to women in Iran."

Taken aback, I ask her opinion of the Islamic theoretician Ali Shariati, whom she immediately dismisses with a scornful wave of the hand. Forget him then. Forget Islam too; hopelessly, irredeemably mired in the Middle Ages, Islam has nothing to offer women. "You're talking to me about Islam?" Parveh asks rhetorically. "What do you Westerners know? We have to live here; you — you can leave whenever you want."

She smiles a sweet, venomous smile. Somebody has slipped a video cassette into the VCR: *Silence of the Lambs*.

ONE OF THE MOST ESSENTIAL COMPONENTS of the Islamic revolution was the contribution of young, Western-educated Iranians who came back, won over to a radical new vision of Islam by the writings of Ali Shariati. Graduates in engineering and medicine and business administration from universities in Texas and California, Ontario and Québec, London and Birmingham, Bologna or Stuttgart, they flocked back to Iran in the waning days of the Pahlavi dynasty and poured their pent-up idealism not into reconstructing a nostalgic's utopia, but into building a new society. At first glance, the wellsprings of this movement seemed far removed from the all-consuming thirst of the dispossessed for justice and divine law promised by Shi'ite tradition. But the teaching of Shariati, who died in London in 1977, reputedly at the hands of the Shah's secret police, provided the bridge across which tens of thousands of young Iranians, at home and abroad, travelled to join the mainstream of the uprising. They also gave it its peculiar stamp, a melding of fiercely sectarian religious intensity and a technologically sophisticated commitment to modernity.

Shariati's impact on this, the first revolutionary generation of middle-class students, intellectuals and technicians, was as decisive as was Khomeini's denunciation of the Shah on the simmering masses of the disinherited, and on the pious *bazaaris*. The effect was galvanizing — all the more because, for the first time, women were being addressed as both sentient and religious beings. At the core of Shariati's militant credo was a woman, the daughter of the Prophet and wife of Imam Ali. Fatima represented

> a halo for the visages of all the oppressed who later become the multitude of Islam. All of the usurped, extorted, oppressed sufferers, all of those whose rights have been destroyed and sacrificed by pressure and force, and have been deceived, had the name of Fatima for their slogan.
>
> [...] She herself is an imam, a guide, an outstanding example of someone to follow, an ideal type of woman, and one who bears witness to any woman who wishes to "become herself" through her own choice.
>
> She answers the question of how to be a woman with her wonderful childhood, her constant struggling and resistance on two fronts — inside and outside — in the home of her father, in the home of her husband, in her society, in her thoughts and behavior and in her life.[49]

Sussan Parsa is one of the returnees. When her middle-class family sent her off to university in the United States in 1970, she, like most Western-influenced Iranians, had heard nothing of the Islamic revolution. It was not until several years later that she started reading books by Dr. Shariati, and developed a keen interest in the rights of women in Islam. Soon after, Iranian students abroad began receiving "night letters" from religious leaders. Her favourites were those written by Ayatollah Taleqani, whose openness had won him a strong following among the intensely patriotic, increasingly religious young technical professionals. She returned to Iran three months before the revolution, intent on putting her skills in public hygiene at the service of the down-trodden.

Today Dr. Parsa, who covers her head with a starched white cowl worn over a well-cut dark blue coat, lectures on family planning at Shahid Beheshti University in north Tehran, and practises in a down-town private clinic. In sharp contrast to the heady, early days of the revolution, she has now given up active involvement in politics. On each of the several occasions we met, she spoke with great frankness, often a risky enterprise in a country where tolerance of criticism does not extend to the public domain. The Islamic revolution did put an end to the subversion of Iran's traditions, particularly regarding women, she tells me; on the other hand, the religious establishment went too far, to the opposite extreme. "I was expecting that after the revolution, these people that say they know Islam should have known more about women in Islam, but unfortunately, they never paid any attention."

What particularly rankles is the widely-held and intensely promoted proposition that the *chador* makes the woman. "I'm not scared of saying it: Some people may have a *chador* on but they don't have any brain. They just say they believe in Islam or they pray or they observe the fasts. Some people trust them a lot and support them. But because you don't have a *chador* on but you believe in Islam, you respect Islam, you really love God and you respect all the aspects of Islam and you really work for Islam..." She pauses to catch her breath. "Well, they don't believe you anymore. They are scared to support you if you don't have a *chador* on."

AZAMEH TALEQANI CONTRIVES TO BE as casual and good-humoured as most Iranian official spokeswomen are punctilious, formal, austere, distant and dour. She agrees to meet on short notice, just a few days after my telephone inquiry. By the time my taxi finally finds her south-central Tehran address the hour is late and everyone but the elderly woman gatekeeper and her personal assistant have gone home. Ms. Taleqani spends the first twenty minutes of our meeting asking me questions about my life story, educational and professional background, taking assiduous notes all the while, punctuated by gently self-deprecating jokes at which she is quick to laugh herself, rapidly creating a climate of confidence. A short, plump woman in her fifties whose natural friendliness quickly reveals an alert, probing mind, she has spent most of her life fighting not only to improve women's place in Iranian society, but to reform society itself. Instead of the regulation *chador*, she is wearing a bright print headscarf over a dark brown cloak.

On the wall behind her hangs a portrait of her father, the late Ayatollah Taleqani, one of the most respected, and open-minded, of Iran's revolutionary clerical leaders, who died at age sixty-nine in September, 1979. Taleqani was, along with Ayatollah Montazeri, one of a handful of high Shi'ite Muslim clergymen within Iran to take an openly confrontationist approach to the imperial regime, which resulted in years in prison and torture at the hands of SAVAK. He understood Islam as a revolutionary ideology which could not only be used to overthrow the imperial regime. Correctly interpreted and applied, he believed, Islamic rules would inevitably bring about a society based on equality, social justice and fraternity. Taleqani may well have had the attitudes of several illustrious clergymen in mind when he wrote: "Nobody has been given the right to impose his will on the people or suppress them and exert control over society. Even prophets were not given this right. Similarly, no single individual or party has any right to impose his self-righteous control over others. In the Islamic system of government, it is possible for a person to be in a position of leadership, but he has no right to control and dominate people."

Her father's daughter by upbringing and by temperament, Ms. Taleqani was arrested, imprisoned and tortured by SAVAK. In 1978, when she was released, the old regime, veering wildly between brutal repression and clumsy liberalization, was entering its last phase, that of terminal decomposition. When it collapsed, she established the Islamic Women's Institute as a successor to the disbanded Iran Women's Organization and was one of the four women deputies elected to the first revolutionary Majlis. But the religious authorities grew increasingly ill at ease with her direct, no-nonsense style and independent spirit. The organization, which had chapters in most cities, was forced to scale back its activities after it was criticized as "oppositionist" during the bitter, bloody days of 1982 when the label could mean a death sentence in front of a revolutionary tribunal. Oppositionist she certainly was. Hers was one of the few voices raised in criticism of the abrogation, in 1979, of the family code inherited from the imperial regime, leaving Iran with no family protection act; her spirited criticism helped block the separation of the sexes at the university level: all of this deepened the conservative clergy's resentment against her.

Today the Institute — housed behind the high walls of a once-aristocratic villa, since surrounded by the working-class apartments and mercantile alleys of south-central Tehran — gets not a *toman* of assistance from the government. "We insist on being self-supporting," she says, looking me straight in the eye, as if to make sure I understand both the virtues of necessity and of freedom from government interference. "When I was in parliament, all kinds of organizations applied for and got funds. But not us. We want to be independent, not influenced by any outside interests. In fact, recently we've been certified by the government as a political organization in our own right."

When I raise the question of *hijab* with Ms. Taleqani, her vigourous response seems quite in character: incisive and compassionate. "Look" she says, "from the beginning of the revolutionary movement, many women accepted *hijab* not only voluntarily, but gladly. It's part and parcel of our beliefs, so it should be our practice too. But I don't agree at all with the way in which it was done. Women who did not want to cover themselves should have been persuaded, not forced. Of course, we women should wear *hijab* because it's God's law; to understand the philosophy is to understand *hijab*."

But since women were and are not persuaded, but forced to adopt *hijab*, isn't there a danger that it will become an empty shell? I ask. "Yes, the danger exists and it is real. The only answer is to persuade women, to bring them to believe in Islamic values, and in the philosophy of *hijab*. In itself, *hijab* is not the problem," she says, choosing her words carefully.

Ms. Taleqani listens intently as I relate having seen lone women waiting along the streets at night. Could some of them possibly be ladies driven into prostitution by personal misfortune in Iran's eroding economy. Such women do exist, she admits, but prostitution is not really a problem in Iranian society. "We have institutions which help destitute women — at least one million women are receiving help of some kind. Even before the Islamic Revolution, prostitution was not a serious problem because of our strong cultural beliefs. Our culture sees it as an ugly thing; we are doing whatever we can to counteract this ugliness."

Does she have anything to say to women in the West, I ask. She laughs and shakes her head: "I wouldn't presume to give anyone any lessons. But for me, the most vital thing is to see ourselves as human beings first — not as men or as women. In the Qur'an, God says that men and women have been created from one cell; thus men and women should help each other. This is their main responsibility. Gender-based thinking and analysis is strictly physical — but we should go beyond this, and concentrate on ourselves as humans. The greatest danger we face today is the search for immediate satisfaction of our physical urges and needs, when instead we should be concentrating on helping one another."

In her eyes, the main accomplishment of the Islamic Republic has been the preservation of the heritage of Imam Khomeini and the other leaders, including her father: "We must never accept oppression of any kind. Women should know themselves, and the power they can wield if they are determined to do so. Today, women in Iran know that they must never go back."

As I drive back to my hotel in a taxi, we pass the new Bank Saderat headquarters only a few blocks from Ms. Taleqani's institute. The marble-clad skyscraper surrounded by a tall steel fence and illuminated by powerful floodlights epitomizes the Islamic regime's social and economic priorities: the bank's massively assertive presence towering over the venerable, ill-kept, neglected but once-proud building far below which houses the Islamic Women's Institute.

THE DRESS ISSUE, say some observers of the Islamic Republic, is a kind of barometer showing the wax and wane of "radical" political influence in Iran. This may be an illusion, however. Political infighting centres on economic and political issues, less on the amount of hair a woman shows beneath her headscarf or *chador*. The *hijab* question may well be a diversionary tactic to focus attention on the narrower issue of Islamic public morality, with the aim of strengthening the regime's grip on the citizens, something both "radicals" and "moderates" agree should not be loosened.

As Iran's leaders wrestle with the theological and political implications of Islamic feminism, including massive participation of women in the labour force, growing disenchantment with the country's sputtering economy and polarized social climate is strengthening the hand of ultra-conservative Islamists who are now challenging the post-revolutionary consensus. The ruling establishment's efforts to strengthen women's role in society are coming under fire. On my last visit to Iran, Tehran municipality's decision to train women bus drivers was drawing sharp and indignant criticism from defenders of the separation of the sexes: How can women drive buses when the buses themselves are segregated? they asked in letters to the editor and on open-line radio programs.

Although the Majlis has approved legislation which would institutionalize obligatory *hijab* and draw up computerized files on repeat violators, in two months in Iran in the winter of 1992-93, I saw or heard of no incidents of women being taken aside for "unbecoming attire." Six months later, the dress patrols were back at work. The policy is becoming increasingly risky for the regime, however. Such incidents can quickly turn into confrontations between frustrated citizens of both sexes; the Islamic morality squads can find themselves outnumbered and unable to act.

In the early days of the revolution, men and women studiously avoided looking at one another. Now they seek out each other's eyes, flirt on the sidewalks, banter good-naturedly or vituperate the government as they cross Tehran wedged elbow to elbow in collective taxis in the intimacy created by economic and social distress. Mohsen my journalist friend told me one day as we strolled along a downtown street: "The regime has done everything it could to break women's resistance, but it has not succeeded."

No foreign observer can assess, even imagine, what goes on in the intimacy of the home, where the woman, as wife and mother, bears primary responsibility both by virtue of her biological function and her social status in Islam, for the rearing of the family. But today even a foreign observer can certify that, in the public domain, *chador*-clad women exercise both independence and assertiveness. For this, they have *hijab* to thank, an otherwise conservative gentleman told me, with a detectable note of ruefulness in his voice. "They can come and go as they please, and nobody can bother them." How far they are prepared to go was demonstrated at a recent official event staged by one of the regime's most conservative and least respected *mollahs*. Justice Minister Yazdi, who had come to speak on women's rights, was silenced, then forced to leave the podium by students in *chadors* praying loudly. The minister's male bodyguards looked on, helpless.

Iran, as the Islamic Republic's supporters correctly note, is neither Saudi Arabia or Kuwait. True, women are subjected to a seemingly endless catalogue of irritants, from dress regulations to restrictions on travel, which strike Westerners as anachronistic. Women also drive their own cars, hold jobs and build careers, own property, vote and are elected to public office. However sternly Iran's "hard-liners" may wish to crack down on women by imposition of rigourous Islamic dress, the objects of their attention are clearly not intimidated. On the sidewalks, younger women contrive to display hair so well-coiffed that it sometimes rises several centimetres above their scalp. More than shoes and ankles are visible — while students wear the now universal jeans and running shoe uniform, including the arch-American name brands.

To Western eyes the bargain seems one-sided. Women in Iran, whether voluntarily or not, have abandoned a part of themselves in return for the all-enveloping protection of a religious ideology which claims exclusive knowledge of their nature. For virtually all women in

Iran, putting on a *chador*, or some form of head covering, has become as routine an act as wearing a raincoat on a rainy day. Except that in Iran, for women, it rains every day. Still, to put the question in these terms is to accept too hastily the encrusted ideological assumptions of Western culture, and to ignore the power of custom and belief in shaping consciousness — theirs as well as ours.

For Islamic intellectuals, religious law has provided Iranian women with a framework for the struggle for their rights, and with a more equitable distribution of power between the two sexes. *Hijab*, as the Islamic expression of the distinction between the public and private spheres, has at the same time armed Iranian women with a way of dissimulating biological differences, and of creating a new and dynamic continuity between public and private worlds. But even some of its strongest supporters admit that the Islamic regime, by politicizing through narrow interpretation a religious concept and by forcing women to comply, has generated resentment not only against itself but against the religion in whose name it rules, and for which it claims universal legitimacy. Forced *hijab* may have created a legion of empty *chadors*. Sorraya Makhnoun's warning that many things are happening under the *chador* may one day be turned against itself.

"The Scholar Who Does Nothing" by Habibollah Sadeqi. Photo by Fred A. Reed.
The original painting is held by the Art Center of the Islamic Propagation Organization.

7

Searching for
the Ultimate Degree

ROCK 'N' ROLL MUSIC IS BLARING from the speaker of the car
driving me south toward the bazaar. No taxi, this. What Tehran taxi
driver would be foolish enough to take the risk? The year is 1985, and
the music of the Great Satan is forbidden. In fact, all music not created
or approved by the regime to stimulate the war effort or to lull late-
night test pattern viewers on state-controlled television is proscribed.
At the wheel is my journalist minder from the Islamic Guidance
Ministry, the cultural arm of the regime, and protector of the clerical
establishment's current, though continuously shifting, definition of
Islamic propriety. Let me be candid: I am no fancier of this particular
sub-genre of world pop-culture. I cannot even recognize the performers.
But this is my first trip to Iran and, like a deer caught in the beam of a
poacher's spotlight, I am frozen in fascination. Only a few days later, on
a stroll through Imam Khomeini Square amid the slow-moving crowds
of soldiers on leave, beggars, unemployed young men on motorbikes

crowded around open-air *kebab* stands grilling lamb hearts and livers and sidewalk merchants selling socks or cigarettes, I stumble upon a collapsible table laden with cassettes of Kurdish popular music. A sample is wailing and clanging out over a tiny loudspeaker propped on one corner. The proprietor's eyes dart back and forth in apprehension, scanning the horizon of bearded, close-cropped heads for any sign of the *Komiteh*, ready to fold and flee at a second's notice.

AS IT CONSOLIDATED ITS POWER the regime led by Ayatollah Khomeini moved quickly to obliterate all traces of Western cultural influence from public life. The nightclubs with their belly dancers, the discotheques with their sexually-charged dance rhythms and morality-sapping promiscuity, and even places like the Café Naderi, which offered its patrons live Iranian traditional music in its garden, were summarily closed down if they hadn't already been burned out in the street fighting that sealed the fate of Shah Mohammad Reza. All public performance, from traditional Iranian music through the European classics, was banned. Music of any kind, but especially lascivious rock 'n' roll, with its glaring sexuality, was henceforth illegal. More than illegal, it had been declared forbidden to Muslims by the Imam himself in a series of decrees as sweeping as they were detailed. Even a non-Muslim could see the point, I admit: After all, the beauty of music might divert the believer's attention from God toward the creation of man instead of the opposite, its stated goal. (There is a certain confirmation of this view even in the West. The renegade Austrian playwright and novelist Thomas Bernhart claims, correctly in my view, that Mozart and Haydn were the sons of God.) Measured against the same standard, Western popular music could reasonably be seen as the devil's work. Whatever the argument, music, be it celestial or infernal, quickly retreated deep underground, to the depths of private existence, where it subsisted in the well-muffled confines of the home or, daring fate, in a fast-moving car with the windows cranked up. Iranian drivers rapidly developed the reflex of switching off their tape decks whenever they approached an intersection or passed any car whose bearded male or austere *chador*-clad lady passengers might be *Komiteh* members on morals patrol.

Audio cassettes were impossible to control, of course, and the *mollahs*, who had used them to propagate the revolutionary message, knew it. Video cassettes, being easier to detect, were banned outright. The effect was predictable: they became dangerous, and highly profitable, contraband. Clandestine video clubs sprang up to service a brisk trade in everything from the latest American feature films, often available in Tehran only days after release, to the most sordid pornography. Behind a stall deep in the bowels of the bazaar, one such outlet charged prospective customers $50 (US) to "inspect" the merchandise; the amount could then be applied toward purchase. Anyone caught in possession of such material risked more than a reprimand, more likely a whipping. Video cassette raids carried out by the Revolutionary Guards received the same media coverage as narcotic busts. Page one photographs and evening news features showed huge piles of the offending objects under the stern surveillance of groups of guardsmen.

DR. MOHAMMAD MOHAMMADI's apartment on a quiet street off Vali-ye Asr Avenue in Shemiran is a discreet, small-scale temple of late-Pahlavi, neo-Western baroque interior decorating style in which rattan furniture, mirror-encrusted window frames, lacquered Chinese-style cabinetry and lush Persian carpets coexist peacefully, if not harmoniously. A man of exquisite manners, as befits a retired professor of theology, Dr. Mohammadi belongs to that segment of the Iranian cultural establishment which gravitated toward France as toward a mother lode of international intellectual inquiry. I had arrived with a letter of introduction from a mutual friend in Montréal, an essential precaution. Over a steaming cup of Nescafé and sweet biscuits he speaks in precise but halting French, which he ruefully admits he's had little chance to practise for the last fifteen years. Like many such conversations, this one begins cooly, with sparring in fulsome courtesies and a perfunctory display of diffidence...or is it caution? But as the discussion progresses, the tone shifts. Both of us warm to the subject; gradually the professor's stern demeanour relaxes into affability. More coffee? his wife asks, tiptoeing into the room.

Like most members of the pre-revolutionary Iranian intelligentsia I encountered, Dr. Mohammadi is acutely allergic to the present. "I don't understand it at all," he smiles in wan resignation. His subject is the past; his passion, the violent encounter between the cultures of Persia — the superior — and Arabia — the inferior — which culminated in what the Arab conquerors called the "victory of victories." It was a confrontation, he insists, which totally recast Persia and at the same time transformed Islam: a supreme moment in the history of the Islamic world, as Persian thought and science provided new foundations of an emerging world culture. It is also a question which weighs heavily on the regime's efforts to cast itself as the champion of all Muslims.

As Dr. Mohammadi pleads for a retracing of cultural and literary influences back to their points of origin, frustration with the fifteen years of undifferentiated Islamic public piety bubbles to the surface. How can we speak of one Islam in social, ideological or political terms? he asks with a rhetorical flourish. Each society produces its own, often highly contradictory version of Islamic culture. Cultures cannot be kept hermetically sealed off from one another, as if they ever could, he says, alluding perhaps to his area of mental allergy, present-day Iran. But Dr. Mohammadi's patience will be rewarded: Iran is slowly awakening to the apparent futility of cultural suppression, and to the inevitability of cultural exchange.

RESURGENCE OF AN IRANIAN national identity is both a reaction and a challenge to the monopoly of a narrowly defined, all-embracing state Islam. Questions avoided in the early years of the Islamic Republic over what is Iranian and what Islamic are hovering at the edge of public discourse. The conquest, which began almost 1,400 years ago when the armies of the mighty Sassanian Empire, and along with them the Zoroastrian religious order, collapsed before the inspired Arab cavalry wielding the subversive power of Islam, looms as large in the consciousness of a new generation of Iranians, stung by the faint Arab response to their Islamic Revolution, as it does for scholars of the old school like Dr. Mohammadi.

Over the millennia, the ebb and flow of conquering invaders and raiding nomads, the rise and fall of empires, of khanates, of ephemeral dynasties and of princely states often obscured but never destroyed the underlying cultural unity of Iran. The desert Arabs brought with them their language as well as their religion. Islam, of course, was more than a religion: it was a way of life, a complete culture and civilization which erased the past and began history anew with the Prophet Mohammad, consigning all that had gone before to an era of ignorance. In Iran, unlike Arabia, what had gone before was a high and sophisticated culture. As Zoroastrianism crumbled, bereft of the protection of the centralized state of which it had been the official ideology, Iran embraced Islam by Iranicizing it. In the process, Islam was transformed from an Arab religion into an international religion and culture.[50]

The collapse of Sassanian military and political power did not cause another Iranian institution to disappear. Like that of China, the bureaucracy created by Darius the Great and his descendents contrived not only to survive but to propagate itself. Its influence on the militarily superior but culturally less sophisticated Muslim Arabs was tremendous.

At the same time, Islam's message of equality before God was transforming Iran, and the entire Near East, more than any other single event before or since. Paradoxically, the supreme accomplishment of the Arab conquerors was to unite all Iranians under the banner of Islam, whose cultural vector was Arabic. But within several hundred years Persian gradually supplanted Arabic as the common language[51] while at the same time the Iranian intellectual and artistic elite found a superb tool in Arabic, which remained the international language of religion and culture. Many of the outstanding names in Arabic literature in the first Abbassid century are, in fact Persian.[52]

Attempts by the Zoroastrians to rescue the ancient religion failed; the old belief was almost totally swept away by the flood tide of Islam. Today, only a few tens of thousands of believers in cities of the desert like Yazd and Kerman, and smaller pockets in Tehran and Shiraz, worship fire as a symbol of an invisible, omnipotent God. A few derelict fire temples still dot the desert landscape. The towers of silence, where the Zoroastrians would expose their dead to the cleansing vultures, are no longer. More effective was the struggle waged by the poet Ferdowsi to rescue the ancient literature with its heroic tales of warlike kings and chivalrous deeds before they, too, vanished. Fearing that the Persian language would disappear along with the heritage of the pre-Islamic age, Ferdowsi — a Shi'ite Muslim — set himself, in the last years of the tenth century of the Western era, to the creation of his masterpiece, the Shahnameh, the Book of Kings.

The centre of the new Iranian culture during the first centuries of the Islamic era was not Persia proper, the western part of Iran where the vestiges of Zoroastrianism and the entrenched remains of the Sassanian state slowed the process of cultural regeneration, but the east: the provinces of Khorassan, Transoxiana and what is present-day Afghanistan. Ferdowsi, himself a native of Khorassan, found a powerful protector — a necessity for any poet — in Sultan Mahmoud, the Seljuq ruler of Ghazna, in Afghanistan. Mahmoud had assembled at his court the most brilliant creative spirits of the age, including the poets Farrukhi, Sistani and Manouchiri, and men of science like al-Biruni. Ferdowsi believed that in Mahmoud the Turk he had finally come upon the man who would bring about the unification and rebirth of Iran. The poet began to dispatch at intervals portions of his poem to the ruler, each time accompanied by panegyric verses as was the custom of the day. In them Ferdowsi sings the praises of Mahmoud and, in the same breath, complains of his own financial distress.

After several decades of work Ferdowsi completed his epic in 1009-10 (AH 400). It chronicles the history of Iran, from the first mythical kings to the downfall of the Sassanians. As well as being a rousing tale of battles and heroic exploits, the poem embodies the three fundamental precepts of traditional Iranian morality: the contrast between Good and Evil, the necessity of a legitimate line of succession and the unconditional honour, loyalty and duty of the vassal to his liege-lord. Ferdowsi's Iranian protagonist-heroes are boastful, loquacious and courageous, in contrast with the Arab invaders who overturned the last great dynasty. The poet could certainly not be accused of excessive fondness for things Arab; fewer than 1,000 Arabic words appear in his *Shahnameh* which, in addition to being a chronicle of chivalrous virtue, almost singlehandedly created a new Persian language. The conquest of Iran in the seventh century is the focus of one of the lengthy sections of the poem. The claim of "commoners" — the newly converted Arab Muslims — to the Crown of Kings represents, in the poet's eyes, a violation of universal order, a tragic breakdown of order and the beginning of chaos.

All our labors will be in vain,
And our kingdom the unworthy will gain;
Nor throne, nor crown, nor city will survive;
The stars say only the Arabs will thrive.
When that day comes, we'll suffer a time
Of long decline before our climb.
Some shall be in black arrayed,
Upon their heads hats of brocade —
No golden shoes, no crown, no throne,
No jewels, no diadem, no standards flown.

———

Honor and truth shall be rejected;
Lies and baseness shall be respected.
True warriors shall they dismount,
And the boastful and vain will surmount.
The fighting gentry shall be cut from the root;
The artful race will bring forth no fruit.
This one shall rob that, the other this;
'Tween curse and praise they will judge amiss.

———

The son shall wish his father undone,
The father shall plot against his son.
A worthless slave as king will be brought;
True greatness and lineage will count for naught.
No faith or loyalty in the world will be found;
The tongue and the soul with hatred will be bound.[53]

Ferdowsi took the final version to Ghazna himself, but without success. A violent quarrel between him and the Sultan is said to have broken out, which led the disputatious poet to write a bitter satire, with disastrous consequences for himself. He fled the Sultan's court, and wandered through Iran in penury until he finally obtained pardon and returned to his place of birth, the city of Tus, where he died. The legend goes that as the dead poet was being borne to his grave, a caravan laden with rich gifts from Mahmoud entered the city.[54] But the story, which seems to prefigure the tragic murder of Amir Kabir by the drunken Nasreddin Shah in Kashan eight hundred years later, is more likely apocryphal. For all his pretensions as a protector of culture, the Sultan was a cruel despot. An intransigent Sunnite, he loathed and feared the Shi'ites. His writers and intellectuals in residence had, in fact, been press-ganged into service; a court official controlled poetry. Ferdowsi, for all his panegyrics and anti-Arabism, had almost certainly aroused the Sultan's enmity by his religious beliefs.

THE ISLAMIC GUIDANCE MINISTRY's foreign correspondent bureau on Vali-ye Asr Avenue, the first stop for journalists visiting Iran, is a fetid little room where reporters and television producers fidget impatiently while their interview lists are scrutinized by affably unhurried guides, minders and petty bureaucrats, their programs negotiated and their visas renewed. But the Ministry — familiarly known to its regular clients by its Farsi name, *Ershad* — is much more than an ordeal by petty frustration. It serves as the regime's cultural watchdog, censor and promoter, ultimate bulwark against the Western cultural onslaught which the Islamic revolution may have slowed, but cannot stop.

The strategy and tactics of the cultural war are formulated at the headquarters building overlooking, appropriately, Sa'di Avenue, one of Tehran's noisiest north-south "poet" thoroughfares, named for the author of the *Golestan* (Rose Garden). Early summer of 1988: a pancake of choking pollution sputters on the scorching griddle of the city. Not even the hiss and whine of the air-conditioning system can mask the roar of the street. After a short wait I'm shown into the deputy minister's office, where Abbas Zanganeh awaits me, a frail, studious figure seated behind a large desk. His voice is so soft I must lean forward to hear over the background tumult.

Under the Pahlavis, Iran's 1,350 years of Islamic cultural heritage had been steadily eroded and devalued as a matter of official policy. The Shah preferred instead to glorify a cardboard simulacrum of imperial absolutism's 2,500 year-old legacy. The Islamic era's heritage of great thinkers, artists, poets, scientists and philosophers all but vanished, or subsisted as street names or remote exotics. The net effect, contends Mr. Zanganeh, was to reinforce a feeling of worthlessness among Iranians, to make them feel insignificant in front of foreigners.

The Shah had correctly understood: Western culture was essential to provide the most propitious context for the introduction of Western products, ideology and technique — in short, modernity. Western models in the arts were encouraged as a matter of policy. As Iranian artists could produce only poor imitations, original material had to be imported. He attempted to replace Iranian music with Western music; before the revolution music was at the worst possible level. "It was erotic, sexually exciting," says Mr. Zanganeh, bending forward to stress the point.

In a country with acute historical and cultural sensitivities, this was a recipe for certain disaster. The clergy began to reject the force-fed diet of Western popular culture which directly challenged their moral standards and leadership, but there was more to the *mollahs'* resistance than free-floating resentment of pleasure or the will to puritanical domination, nor were they alone. Beginning in the '60s, Western-educated intellectuals, upon whom the Shah had hoped to rely as vectors of cultural transformation, began to resist — individually at first, often at enormous risk, then collectively — the wholesale dismantling of a nation's heritage. No price, they argued, was high enough to justify this ignominy.

One of the arguments which galvanized secular intellectuals who were to have been the shock-troops of the Shah's New Iran was provided by an essayist named Jalal Al-e Ahmad in a slim volume as explosive as a *plastique* charge entitled *Occidentosis*. In the early '60s, Al-e Ahmad, who had earlier broken with the Tudeh (communist) party over its slavish veneration of the USSR, had identified a fundamental contradiction between traditional Iranian social structures and the forces that were dragging the country toward colonial status. These forces operated in the name of progress and development but were, he claimed, working toward the political and economic subordination of Iran to Europe and the United States.[55]

His diagnosis was implacable: the Occidentosis sufferer, he wrote, "has severed his ties with the depths of society, culture and tradition. He has no link between antiquity and modernity, nor even a dividing line between old and new. He is a thing with no ties to the past and no perception of the future."[56] Al-e Ahmad did more than criticize Iranian passivity before the Westernizing onslaught. He sought national and cultural legitimacy in the country's religious tradition. Alone among the literary intelligentsia of Iran, he perceived that the uprising of 15 Khordad 1342 (6 June 1963) had inaugurated a new and decisive stage in the struggle between what he termed the "secret government of religion" and the Iranian state. The plague of Occidentosis, he thundered, could only be stopped by a religious and national revival, drawing on Iran's contribution to Islam and Islam's decisive shaping of Iran's national identity:

> While being apparently only a part of the Islamic totality, what a totality we bore of Islamic civilization! Was it not we who, in the darkest days of Ommayad domination, relying on our national identity, on what of our Iranian heritage we had conveyed to Islam, carried the black banner of the Abbassids from Khorassan to Baghdad, and so thoroughly imparted the distinctive stamp of our civilization to Islam that even now fledgling Orientalists find it difficult to discern what percentage of Islamic civilization can be traced to extra-Iranian elements.[57]

The sharp sense of self-awareness touched off by Al-e Ahmad's book gathered momentum in the decade following his death, in 1969, and the word — Occidentosis or Westoxication — went on to become one of the rallying cries of the revolutionary upheaval. It remains a part of the Islamic regime's polemic vocabulary — even as the regime slides gradually toward commercial and thus cultural accommodation with the West.

THE EXCITEMENT IS PALPABLE as the crowd mills around in the foyer of Vahdat Hall. Mustachioed men in glasses wearing turtleneck sweaters under tweed sportcoats, accompanied by women in elegantly-cut coats and floral print headscarves, rub elbows with *bazaaris*, whom I recognize by their frayed cuffs and perpetual five-day beards. The war with Iraq is over and the internal armed opposition either exterminated or dormant, but even now, in the winter of 1989, Iran is security-conscious. Armed guards patrol the sidewalks outside, and concert-goers must submit to cursory body searches before entering through separate men's and women's gates. But Tehranis have grown accustomed to the ritual of being frisked by adolescent Revolutionary Guardsmen or stern *Komiteh* ladies. At the sound of a gong the doors swing open and the throng rushes in, jostling politely for seats — this is no working-class bus queue at Enqelab Square, after all. Public concerts are still a relative rarity; concerts of tonight's calibre are rarer still. Iran's great *santur* virtuoso Majid Kiani will join singer Nasrollah Nahsepour for a performance of Iranian traditional music.

After years of clandestine existence, music has suddenly re-emerged into acceptability, if not full respectability. But now Imam Khomeini, the supreme arbiter, is dead. The war is over, and Iran stands poised on the threshold of a the greater challenge: peace, high expectations and a massive reconstruction program. Iranians are thirsty for a taste of prosperity and pleasure, for respite from the years of hardship and Islamic rigour. Now light Western classical music can be heard over hotel sound systems, and Tehran radio regularly broadcasts Iranian music, although never sung by a woman's voice: that would be putting the fox of erotic temptation amongst the chickens of repressed male desire. Of course, music had never entirely disappeared. Iranian television would sign on and off every day with rousing martial choruses extolling the virtues of Islamic revolution, and during the war *Jang jang ta Pirouzi* could be heard at every moment of the day or night, only to vanish without a trace as the war drifted to a bloody, inconclusive and unvictorious end. But it had become impossible to supervise all Iranian cassette players, halt copying of Western rock music cassettes, stop all cars, raid all shops, arrest all itinerant music vendors, prohibit young men and women from dreaming of music, from purchasing instruments, from whistling or humming or singing on the street. The confusion over what to allow, what to prohibit and what to prosecute had become so acute that by early 1989 the deputy commander of the *Komiteh* corps crying out for government or clerical guidance, plaintively admitted: "We don't know what to do about music."

To a torrent of applause, Kiani, whose greying hair and slender fingers are soon belied by the power and energy of his performance, and Nahsepour, a man in his sixties with a short clipped beard, walk on stage and sit down on cushions atop a Persian carpet laid across a low riser. In the perfect silence of anticipation the music begins, the theme stated first by the *santur*, a rectangular stringed instrument played with two small hammers, then taken up and embellished by Nahsepour's richly textured voice. Common across the Islamic world, west through Turkey and Greece and into the Balkans, and east to India and beyond, the *santur* produces a haunting, ethereal sound which creates a perfect counterpoint to the pure, unmannered singing of Nahsepour who, in the rigourous Oriental manner, lets his voice carry all the emotional charge, his body immobile, a human sounding board which resonates with the complex timbres of fine old wood. The rise and fall of the voice set against the soulful percussive drone of the *santur* plunges us back into the country's ancient musical continuum. First used to accompany Zoroastrian religious ceremonies and promote its teachings, Iranian music became more refined, spiritual and unitary in structure with the advent of Islam. The form of music came to reflect the vagaries of life and, at the same time, embody the progression of the soul toward what Muslim aesthetics call the ultimate degree: true happiness and true life in concert with God.

The next afternoon, I meet Majid Kiani after rehearsal at Vahdat Hall. We settle into seats halfway up the auditorium as the stage crew bustles about its preparations for the night's concert. Like every other Iranian artist I've encountered, Kiani is quiet and self-effacing — uncomfortable with the journalistic staples of biography and career, becoming animated when the discussion turns to the methods and the ideas of art. His story could have come straight from the pages of Nikos Kazantzakis' *Zorba the Greek*, whose eponymous hero also falls under the *santur*'s magical spell: "I was twenty. I heard the *santur* for the first time at a village fête, over there at the foot of Olympus. It took my breath away. I couldn't eat anything for three days."[58]

Through the same osmotic process which operates across all cultures the young Kiani felt the attraction and the power of the *santur*, and began to teach himself to play. After sitting at the feet of Iran's greatest living masters, he went off to study oriental musicology at the Sorbonne. Unlike many of his countrymen, he returned to Tehran after the revolution. Less, as I understand him, out of overt political motivation than because he had mastered a method of *santur* playing known by no one else in Iran, a method passed on through many generations, combining the historic and the heroic, yet very delicate. "If I did not come back, this method would eventually have died. Now I'm happy; I've trained five or six students, and the music will live on."

The Islamic revolution has been a positive experience for music, he tells me as the stagehands move up and down the aisles uncoiling cables and doing voice tests. With the cultural offensive of the West blunted, Iranians have been able to learn more about their own culture. Part of the learning process has been the painstaking reconstitution, begun a century ago, of traditional Iranian classical music, a complex and ancient art form. This music, he explains in patent delight at his subject, can be likened to miniature painting. To appreciate its detail and inner beauty, it must be heard from close range, and not through the deforming medium of amplification. The audience, too, must enter into the music. "Our music has simple melodies; what makes it difficult is its emotional content and its abstract form. In fact, our music is like our ceramic design, our architecture and our miniature painting. If the listener pays close attention, he can penetrate deep into its beauty."

§

Great nations write their autobiographies in three manuscripts: the books of their deeds, the book of their words, and the book of their art. Not one of these can be understood unless we read the two others; but of the three, the only quite trustworthy one is the last.

— John Ruskin

THE 1992-93 WINTER EXHIBIT at Tehran's Museum of Modern Art is, unremarkably, a retrospective of works by painters of the Islamic revolution. On each of my visits to the museum, I am continuously fascinated by the juxtaposition of paintings which hew closely to the new cannons of Islamic aesthetics with a setting designed to house the avant-garde art of the West and its Iranian emulators. Founded by her then-Imperial Highness Farah in her role as patroness of the arts, the building overlooks the tree-lined paths of Laleh Park. It is a striking contemporary structure whose configuration is that of a spiral burrowing down into the ground. At the structure's core is a monumental installation consisting of a reflecting pool of crude oil contained in a steel-walled basin — a brutal, yet curiously contemplative expression of Iran's enthrallment to the lubricant force of progress and the fuel of its own alienation. The museum's new administrators would surely have been unenthusiastic about attempting to pump thousands of gallons of oil from the lowest level of their institution, and so decided to let it stay on in ironic counterpoint to the new, anti-materialist subject matter which now dominates the walls.

That paintings of any kind are on display might come as a surprise. Despite powerful countervailing evidence, many Westerners retain the impression that the representation of living things is forbidden in Islam. True, Islam is inflexible on one point: any depiction of the divine is considered a form of idol worship. Mohammad, like his precursor in prophecy Jesus Christ, was a great smasher of idols. But Islamic civilization in its 1,400 year history is far too multiple and various to suggest that Islam is, by its nature, inimical to figural representation, let alone to lock "Islamic" art into a narrow set of definitions.

When the emerging Islamic Empire engulfed most of a world that had been previously Christian, it may well have found itself "tempted" by the visual and representational richness of the lands it had conquered. It was only natural that the conquerors would search out visual symbols of their own. These symbols often included representations of persons and living things. But, for reasons which remain obscure, the search slowed, then ceased. Non-figurative images began to replace the older themes which had been inherited from the Hellenistic and Byzantine tradition. They had iconographic content, but they lacked representation of human beings.[59]

Although there is no direct Qur'anic injunction against representational art, it is as though Islam came to assume that in fashioning the form of a being that has life, the artist usurps the creative function of God.[60] So powerful did this non-figurative thrust become that it emerged as near dogma, culminating in a decree forbidding images promulgated by the Ommayad caliph Yazid II in 721. The decree may have been the culmination of the bitter conflict which pitted the expanding Islamic Empire against its Byzantine adversaries, a conflict which was as ideological as it was military. Perhaps it was coincidence, but the Byzantine iconoclast (icon-smashing) movement may have either been a response or a trigger to Islam's growing rejection of the cultural practices of the Mediterranean Christian tradition it had replaced. Emperor Leo III, who decreed the smashing of images five years later, in 726, was probably acting in response to the Islamic political threat on the empire's southern and eastern marches. In these regions Monophysites, known for their hostility to figural representation (and thus vulnerable to the appeal of Islam), formed a sizeable minority of the Christian population. The Emperor may also have been attempting to bring Christian practices more into line with those of the Jews and Muslims, the better to convert them.

More than a century later, the Byzantine iconoclasts were finally crushed as resolutely as they themselves had crushed images. In the Arabo-Islamic world depiction of living things took much longer to reemerge; to this day, no strong figurative tradition exists, if we are to except the cyclopean portraits of kings, presidents for life, sheiks and dictators. But in Iran, figurative depiction of the human form was reestablished — in broadly schematic terms — from the East, to the hoof-beats of the invading Mongols and Turks, the bearers of a new Islamic culture shaped and dominated by Persian sensibilities.

The resurgence of representational art in Iran cannot be readily explained by the predominance of Shi'ism. Iran, at the time of the Persian Renaissance, was overwhelmingly Sunni and remained so until the violent imposition of Twelver Shi'ism as the state religion by the Safavids in the sixteenth century. Terry Allen's hypothesis is that since Antiquity, Western art has been "fixated" on the human figure. "Islamic art moved away from this classical heritage, leaving artistic narrative to speech rather than displaying it in pictures."[61] Certainly the blossoming of figural art in the Islamic world — in Iran, the Ottoman Empire, Moghul India — had an intimate connection with manuscript illustration, and an organic relationship to texts.[62] The function of this figural art was not to narrate, but to convey in visual terms the mental images of which the metaphors in poetry and prose are the written expression.[63]

Where does "national" consciousness begin and "Islamic" consciousness end? The question has plagued Western art history, itself a reflection of the traditional Western image of the Islamic Orient now embedded in Western culture, as well as Muslims themselves, ironically influenced by the culture-bound Western view. Seen from Iran, it was no coincidence that Persian consciousness overweighed Islamic practice when miniature painting finally returned to Iranian soil. Iranians, faced with the superior military and political power of the Arab, and later Turkish, invaders, reacted by slowly submerging their rulers with their cultural superiority: a slow-ripening admixture of exile and cunning. The miniature technique probably originated in pre-Islamic Manichean times, and sought shelter in China — and to a lesser extent India — to survive the Arab onslaught. Centuries later, enriched with Chinese motifs and technical sophistication, but with a palette dominated by turquoise and gold of purely Iranian sensibility, it emerged transformed as the national style of the Muslims of Persia.

Miniature painting reached a pinnacle under the Turkish descendants of Tamerlane at Herat. The city, now devastated by the war in Afghanistan, was the Athens of its day and a world centre of poetry and the visual arts, particularly with the great master Bezhad's illustrations of a manuscript of Ferdowsi's *Shahnameh*. This was the painting style which went on to flourish in Tabriz, and eventually made its way across Anatolia to Istanbul at the heart of the Ottoman Empire, and is Iran's greatest contribution — along with the art of carpet weaving — to the world's cultural patrimony.

THE TEHRAN ART MUSEUM EXHIBIT traces, in an elliptic and non-linear fashion appropriate to the new — or is it the old? —vision, a path across the spectrum from figurative to semi-abstract, and across the formal evolution of Iranian painting, less in time than in space. The paintings, with a few exceptions, have strong formal similarities with European painting. But these similarities are more apparent than real, claim the proponents of contemporary Islamic aesthetics. Western art has its roots in the humanist tradition which, since the Renaissance, has shaped Western civilization. This humanism, they insist, means not respect for human dignity, but instead places man at the centre of the universe, and assigns Reason the stature of God in theistic thought. Man perceives no reality outside of himself. It is this calamitous descent into the nether regions of Westoxified egoism that new Islamic art seeks to halt, and to replace with new forms and meanings.[64]

The main ground floor gallery displays the work of the first generation of painters of the Islamic Republic, the earliest fruits of the campaign to revitalize form from within by renewing the allegiance with God. It is an eclectic mix of lurid devotional canvasses with overtly religious or social themes, some echoing socialist realism in their ideological rectitude and dolorous intensity. Here the subject matter is martyrdom and self-abnegation, key themes of early revolutionary exhortatory or persuasive depiction. One canvas, the most overtly political, shows well-dressed rats with semi-human faces counting gold coins in a dank cellar while a poor grieving family gathers around its martyred son in the room above. Others recast young soldiers in the Iran-Iraq war as martyrs in the company of Imam Hossein at Karbala, the galvanizing moment in Shi'ism and constant leitmotif of official iconography.

Paintings of more traditional subjects occupy the second level: delicate morning landscapes with the light, incisive brush-strokes of the miniature style alternate with naturalist depictions of peasant life, semi-abstract land- and cityscapes — Iran's razor-edged horizon of mountains and deserts, or the soft, olive-toned feminine domed rooftops of Kashan. Another hall is given over to works directly inspired by the miniature tradition: scenes of pre-historical Persian heroes from the *Shahnameh*, or the application of the technique to modern-day subject matter like old photographs or documents. Further along are examples of calligraphy, the quintessential Islamic abstract art form which seeks to give visual expression to the meaning of the word through the depiction of that word. As I move deeper into the depths of the museum, I encounter contemporary versions of Iranian religious painting, commonly known as the *ghavekhané* (coffeehouse) style for the places where they were displayed, usually painted directly on the walls. These canvasses depict scenes from daily life or, more importantly, of the martyrdom of Imam Hossein.

They breathe with a pictorial richness reminiscent of post-Byzantine art. Imam Ali's son Imam Hossein has the grieving eyes of religious icon, and his head is surrounded by a luminous halo as he leads his small group of followers toward martyrdom at the hands of the superior forces of Yazid. The disposition of the figures, the dynamic tension of their bodies and the pervading sense of purity and religious intensity evokes, in culture transposition, the frescoes of the itinerant Greek hagiographers like Theofilos whose scenes from daily life illuminated the walls of coffeehouses in the Ottoman-ruled Aegean islands during the last decades of the nineteenth century.

Though not painted in the "coffeehouse" style, I sense the same purity and tension in one of the most striking pictures at the exposition, a massive diptych showing on one panel a second-floor balcony in shadow, or perhaps at night, with a piece of clothing — a woman's undergarment? — hanging from an impromptu clothesline. The second panel depicts the sunlit façades of humble two-storey dwellings against a deep turquoise sky. The painting imparts a pulse-quickening sense of tension and resolution in the interplay of light and darkness, melancholy and luminescent spirituality, setting up a vibration that extends into the three-dimensional space between the painting and the viewer. The stillness is charged with the infinitesimal yet palpable atmospheric vibrations which herald electrical storms. Absence and presence.

Several days after my first visit a meeting with the diptych's painter, Habibollah Sadeqi, has been arranged in an empty office at the museum. As we talk, winter sunlight streams through the leafless plane trees bordering the pathways of the adjoining park. An elderly attendant serves tea and sweets. "For us, as Muslim painters, our beliefs and desires must be in harmony," he says through an unusually alert interpreter from the Islamic Guidance Ministry. Her excitement about meeting the painter is a refreshing change from the customary boredom of the functionary interpreting the same official position for the tenth or one-hundredth time. "To reach this harmony, we need three things, three essential elements: beauty, honour and what we call 'the ultimate degree' — the presence of God in the work."

Sadeqi, a soft-spoken man in his thirties with a wispy beard and lively brown eyes, describes his travels in Europe — I pick up the catalogue of cities in Farsi — and his visits to its major museums. Which European painter does he feel closest to? I ask. El Greco, he responds, because of the Greek's tumultuous and forboding skies. (There may be more to this affinity than Mr. Sadeqi realizes, I speculate. El Greco was, after all, born in Crete, then part of what we now call the Orient, and brought to Spain the exalted breath of post-Byzantine mysticism, itself powerfully though indirectly influenced by the aesthetic of Islam.)

Western painters however, El Greco included, have reduced the artist's three cardinal points to two, which for Islamic artists are only stepping stones to the ultimate. "Please don't misunderstand me," he adds, with a reassuring smile. "I admire the work of your great artists, but my own approach is a different one. I believe Western artists are as capable of searching for God as we are, but they seem caught up in the search for technique, system and form. They cannot see the essence for the apparatus."

Art in the West, I venture, is now facing a post-modernist crisis. Aesthetic canons — to the extent they survived the rise of the non-figurative to dominant orthodoxy — have collapsed. The proliferating micro-heresies which quickly solidify into new, ephemeral dogmas have become a function of personal, sexual or racial identity, caught up in an ever-accelerating thrust toward an infinitely receding, mirage-like progress-horizon. Is this the art which, in its most digitalized and vulgar forms, will soon become part of the discourse of imported culture as Iran abandons its isolation? (As my question takes shape it suddenly reminds me of Philip Roth's complex, essay-length interrogations of Eastern European dissident writers, which would elicit answers of yes, no or maybe.)

Sadeqi listens via our interpreter who is struggling to recast unfamiliar concepts into Farsi, listens intently, a faintly ironic smile playing at the corners of his mouth. But from his response, I realize that some, perhaps all of my *question-fleuve* may have been lost in translation. Question and answer have passed like two brightly lighted ships in the night. "How can we then explain that we can't agree with much of Western culture?" he asks rhetorically. "Still, in spite of our disagreements, we don't go imposing our ideas and our cultural norms on the West. We are not imposing our films or our satellite TV programs on anyone. Strange, isn't it? The West claims it believes in democracy, yet it seems prepared to impose its views, either by force or by cultural means. Can you really do that and be democrats at the same time? But of course this has to do with much more than just culture."

What is Mr. Sadeqi's advice for his fellow artists in the West? "Listen to your heart, to your soul. Search for the third step, for the ultimate degree. That is the only way to combat mass culture, to deal with the satellites and what they stand for. Sure, your scientists can create babies in test-tubes. But science is one thing, forcing people to live in laboratories is another. People should be left to live in their own nature. Maybe the West can change, but I'm not optimistic. Like the pharaohs of ancient Egypt, its rulers will be destroyed. They are powerful and cruel, but they are doomed. And they will be resisted. We can overcome the New World Order."

OF ALL THE VISUAL ARTS practised in Iran, calligraphy hews closest to the Islamic ideal of perfect unity of form and content in the striving toward God. Drawing on the plasticity, stenographic terseness and ornamental quality of the Arabic script which was introduced into Iran with the Arab conquest, Iranian artists raised fine penmanship to the rank of a major art form.[65] Calligraphy, explains Olam-Hossein Amirkhani, is the art form which actually displays the system, the rules and the technical regulations which liberate its practitioners in the pursuit of perfection in their art. In the deepest and most intimate sense the written word, whether the name of God, Qur'anic or profane verse, *is* the content of the work: the visible shape of revelation, visual equivalent of the melodious chant of the Qur'an. Mr. Amirkhani, a lean man with angular features, speaks with the authority of one of Iran's most eminent practitioners of this ancient and exacting art, his tapered fingers playing absentmindedly with the silver mounted agate ring that he wears, like most Iranian men, on the fourth finger of his right hand.

"Historically, all the great thinkers, poets and artists of Iran have been inseparable from Islam," he says. "As their modern counterparts, we are striving to preserve a common heritage, carry it forward into the present and transmit it to future generations. My task is to transmit the spirit of beauty, which is how God reveals his existence to us, through calligraphy. If the work is not beautiful, the spirit cannot be transmitted. This is precisely the role of calligraphy in Iranian culture, and in other cultures as well. Our responsibility as calligraphers is to transmit these ideas, this spirit, to the Iranian people, and through them to all peoples."

Lovingly he speaks of the artist's pen, the kalam, and of the basic building block of Islamic calligraphy, the lozenge shape which is used to determine the length and breadth of letters. As the poet once associated the ideas expressed in his poem with the form of the letter itself, so calligraphic artists must shape their ideas with the tools of art: "Of course we must have talent, and acquire technical skill. But more important, we must attend the school of moral rectitude and practical discipline. Only then can we attain the summit."

THE WIZENED OLD WOMAN attempts once more to thread the needle. The audience of peasants and poor folk is growing restive. They are guests at an outdoor film showing — a kind of late nineteenth-century Persian drive-in theatre where the viewers arrive in donkey carts — staged by Nasreddin Shah who, surrounded by his courtiers and his harem, has fallen asleep. Again and again the old woman, eyes squinting, mouth contorted, tries to thread her needle. Now people in the crowd get up to leave, making rude gestures and shouting insults. Still the old woman on the screen is attempting to thread her needle. In desperation the Shah's personal cinematographer rushes from his makeshift outdoor projection platform in the palace court, leaps into the flickering image and grasps the old woman's hand in an attempt to wrest the needle from her. She resists, and the screen begins to topple. Panic-stricken, the audience scatters as a lyrical montage of scenes from seventy years of Iranian cinema unfurls across the real screen of the real Atlantic theatre on a snowy January day in downtown Tehran. The real audience is on its feet, whistling and clapping for Mohsen Makhmalbaf's latest — and most audacious — film: *I, Shah Nasreddin, Cinematographer.*

Makhmalbaf's film, a convoluted, multi-layered evocation of the history of Iranian cinema, of recent Iranian history and a wry, often caustic examination of the corruption and self-delusion of power, has been slow to appear in Tehran's first-run theatres. The filmmaker himself is said to be in seclusion, depressed by the Islamic Guidance Ministry's insistence that he remove offending scenes from the final cut. He is, I am told, "unavailable" for interviews. Having seen the film, even in its censored version, I understand why. *Nasreddin Shah* teems with winks at American films, from *The Purple Rose of Cairo* to *Don't*

Shoot the Piano Player. It sets up a counter-world, rich in fantasy and evocative power, holds up a deforming mirror to itself and beams, by ricochet, a stark beam of light into the darkest recesses of the repressed present.

Viewers guffaw at the *folies de grandeur* of the Shah who almost single-handedly sold Iran off to the Western powers. When scenes of early Tehran flash across the screen, showing women without *hijab* strolling insouciantly along the sidewalk, the collective intake of breath hits you like a punch in the stomach. Nothing escapes Makhmalbaf's penetrating eye: he intercuts a notorious bathhouse murder scene from a popular film of the pre-revolutionary era with the murder of reformer Amir Kabir in the baths of the Baq-e Fin gardens in Kashan on orders from Nasreddin Shah. And when the vengeance-bound protagonist of a violent *film noir* series from the Pahlavi era comes lumbering toward us, fists clenched and eyes flashing, the audience roars and whistles in delight. "See that actor," whispers my friend Mohsen who's keeping me abreast of the subtleties of the script. "He runs a sweet shop in north Tehran now; people still go there just to see him."

To a Westerner's eye — what Westerner would presume to pretend to see the world with an Iranian eye? — the new Iranian cinema is an unalloyed success story. A corps of bright, creative homegrown filmmakers and skilled technical crews have produced dozens of challenging and often visually stunning films, several of which have gone on to distinguished international festival careers; some have even achieved modest recognition at the box office.

Before the overthrow of the imperial regime, 80% of the films shown in Iran were foreign-made, most of them in the United States. Iranian films were of the cheapest lowest type of film that could be made, designed for uneducated audiences. Imported films would also be modified to cater to the crudest local tastes. *High Noon*, for example. In the Iranian version Gary Cooper strides down the dusty main street of the town to the twanging strains of *Do Not Forsake Me O My Darling*, heads for the doors of the saloon, looks inside. What does he see? A Persian cabaret scene, with scantily-clad belly dancers gyrating in front of a traditional orchestra. Twenty minutes of real time later, refreshed, he stalks back onto main street for his appointment with destiny. Five minutes have passed on the station clock.

The man who is telling me this has enough classical Persian presence — the flashing dark eyes, luxuriant mustache and finely chiselled features — to step in front of the camera. Which is precisely how Ali-

Reza Shoja Nouri made his living before being appointed head of international relations at the Farabi Cinema Foundation, a government-funded agency that supports and promotes Iranian cinema and stages well-attended international film festivals in Isfahan and Tehran. After the revolution, explains Mr. Shoja Nouri, the government became the sole importer of foreign films. "It was the only thing we could do. We didn't want our industry to be destroyed, so our first task was to strengthen home production."

Most Iranian films are of the consciously artistic variety, he admits. Such films get the strongest financial support, are projected at the best times of the year, and in the best theatres. In fact, foreign films cannot be projected if a finished Iranian film is waiting. Iran currently produces at least sixty feature-length films every year.

In our interview at the Islamic Guidance Ministry, Abbas Zanganeh assured me that there were no government rules or regulations governing film production. Filmmakers, he added, are free to select their own subjects and make their films, while at the same time protecting their own personality and the values of society as a whole. Rakhshan Bani-Etemad's answer to the same question made it clear that matters were not quite so simple. After a script is written the director must submit it to the Ministry for approval. Financing is provided only when scripts are approved. And, she adds with a wry smile, "I don't know of any filmmaker who hasn't had at least one script rejected." Still, she adds, filmmakers can negotiate with the authorities, and "correct" the offending parts of their scripts, a process familiar to Hollywood directors who must take care not to offend the laws of the marketplace. In recent years a certification system has been developed, meaning that those in the top three categories need no longer submit their scripts. "The director's skills and talent are the deciding factor."

Certain things Iranian filmmakers may not show. A woman's exposed body, let alone her bare head, heads the list; women must not be depicted as commodities or used to arouse sexual desire. Sexually explicit or violent scenes are out — though historical films like *The Stone Lions* depict epic shoot-outs in a stylized hybrid style derived from the classic Hollywood western and the Japanese sword epic. Modern Iranian films have a unique flavour of their own, a provocative blend of purity, visual sophistication and psychological complexity which Ms. Bani-Etemad explains as a result of the limitations on subject matter. "Filmmakers in Europe and North America," she says, "have tremendous technical resources but lack ideas."

The golden age of the new Iranian cinema, protected like a sensitive crop behind the glass walls of greenhouses, may be drawing to an end. Fascinated by the new orthodoxy of privatization, the government is dismantling the support structure which allowed the country's filmmakers to thrive, and to create a distinctive voice. Iranian film already has a culturally sensitive audience abroad, but Ms. Bani-Etemad despairs of ever being able to compete with the mass-market products churned out by the American majors. "For us, the main question is, if we allow foreign films onto our screens, will foreign countries allow ours on theirs?" Given the workings of American cultural policy, to ask the question is to answer it.

IRANIAN TELEVISION'S principal function as mouthpiece for the regime quickly transformed it into an exemplar of the manipulator so brilliant that he succeeds only in deceiving himself. Official pronouncements are greeted with stony silence or hoots of derision, depending on the company one keeps. Most citizens automatically assume the authorized version is a lie; denial of a rumour by a government spokesperson is taken as its confirmation. After the extraordinary intellectual ferment of the immediate post-revolutionary period had been absorbed or suppressed by the religious leadership, the drab self-seriousness and oppressive piety of state television drove viewers either to sleep or frustration. Iranians wickedly, but accurately, described the country's two television services as the birds and beasts channel and the turban channel. While the first broadcast enough nature documentaries to turn every regular viewer into a zoologist or a wildlife biologist, the second offered an unrelieved tedium of *mollahs* lecturing on public morals, elucidating the Qur'an or preaching interminable exhortatory sermons. As people switched off their television sets the market for clandestine video cassette recorders and cassettes soared.

Things began to improve in the late '80s. The ancient science documentaries produced for American high school students in the 1950s vanished. Long-running, sumptuously mounted historical series exploring recent Iranian history fascinated audiences for months on end. Powerful and technically commanding documentaries told the story of the war from the viewpoint of the soldier, full of mud, horror and death. I recall extraordinary sequences showing drivers of heavy military transport trucks reading their own poetry as they wrestled their huge vehicles along the muddy roads to the Iraqi front. In another program, journalists interviewed Tehran's sidewalk money-changers, some of whom candidly admitted giving up teaching or civil service jobs in order to make enough money to feed their families. Then came children's game shows, and live broadcasts of Qur'anic recitation competitions displaying the vocal mastery and phenomenal memory of contestants from age ten to seventy-five. Political criticism, oblique and implicit, began to surface. Perhaps it was all coincidence. But the country's cultural authorities had concluded that the West, fresh from its victory over the USSR, was also winning its cultural war of attrition against Iran. Exhortation and prohibition, the standard weapons in the purist's cultural arsenal, were no longer effective. In fact, they were having the opposite, negative effect.

In late December, 1992, Ali Larijani, then Iran's minister of culture and Islamic guidance, appeared before the Majlis to announce a radical shift in cultural policy. His message was as simple and direct as it was striking in its admission of failure. Iranian officials were being naïve, he suggested, if they thought "yesterday's cultural policies" could continue. At best they were erasing the visible evidence of something that would come back to haunt them. Iran, Mr. Larijani told the parliamentarians, must understand what characterizes the age of communication in order for it to withstand cultural encroachment.

After the Islamic Revolution triumphed, said the minister, it was somehow assumed that all state institutions were Islamic and that this fact alone would be enough to deter cultural invasion. As it turned out, state institutions were far from Islamic, and deterrence alone was not enough. Responsibility for defense of Iranian culture should be placed on the fundamental institution in society: the family. "We cannot provide answers to all things by preventing or challenging all activities — cultural immunity in society must be achieved through the family institution because it commands and enjoys respect. We must have proper means of resistance. Yesterday's tools cannot be effectively employed today."

Medical metaphors suddenly became popular with Iranian officials. Ayatollah Ahmad Janati, the diminutive seventy-year-old clergyman who heads the Islamic Republic's Cultural Revolution Committee, publicly compared the Western cultural invasion to an epidemic for which a vaccine must be found — the same argument used by Mr. Larijani. Vaccination, announced the minister, would take the form of state-funded video production and distribution facilities, the intention being to neutralize the powerful clandestine operators who currently control 100% of the country's video market. Iran would also use the regional satellite network to broadcast its Islamic tidings beyond its borders, particularly toward the newly semi-independent countries of former Soviet Central Asia. But a painful question remains: Can a generation alienated from the official Islam with which it was force-fed be brought back to the fold by locally-produced Islamic videos? The assurances of Iran's cultural establishment are unlikely to convince increasingly skeptical young people of the clerical establishment's ability to do more than issue anathemas and prohibitions, while it secretly indulges, nay, revels — so go the dark whispers — in the selfsame vices it professes to abominate.

IRAN'S MOST DIRE CULTURAL ENEMY, though, is not the ubiquitous video cassette. Insidious and invisible, a telecommunications satellite floating in orbit high above the Middle East will soon be beaming television signals directly into the homes of the Islamic Republic's loyal and pious citizens. The signal may carry CNN or one of a new generation of competing European all-news vehicles, or simply tap into the unquenchable effluvium of generic programming flushed into the electronic environment by the image-mills of Europe and North America. But whatever the content, the sudden availability of satellite transmission may well prove to be as subversive of the structures and standards of public morality in the Islamic Revolution as the clandestine tape cassettes distributed by Imam Khomeini's followers and supporters were of the Shah's regime. Iranians call it — half-facetiously, half-seriously — the War of the Air-Waves. The regime calls it a Cultural Invasion. But no one misses the metaphor. Suddenly, perhaps opportunely — for what is publicly discussed in Iran almost always reflects official concern — the debate over cultural sovereignty and national culture has been rekindled. Not far behind, comes another question, one with which the authorities are less comfortable: the compatibility of Western technoscience with Islamic values. It does not pass unnoticed in Tehran that these are virtually the same themes that helped rally both intellectuals and religious citizens to the revolutionary cause in the late '70s, as the imperial regime wheeled out the heavy artillery of Western culture to attack what it scornfully called "Islamic obscurantism."

HERBERT MARCUSE, a Tehran intellectual reminds me with a slightly malicious smile, postulated a fifteen-year life span for revolutions. As Iran reaches the fifteen-year mark, the third and fourth post-revolutionary generations are beginning to make their presence felt, less with new ideas and ideals — difficult to express publicly in the restrictive intellectual atmosphere — than in their stubborn reluctance to see things precisely according to the views of the hierocracy. How the country's well-entrenched custodians of approved and certified traditional values respond will have as strong an impact on the course of Iran's cultural development as will satellite broadcast technology. Some Iranian cultural critics affirm, off the record of course, that the regime's "Do as I say, not as I do" approach to issues of culture and public morality have long since cost it its credibility among the young. No amount of youth clubs, uplifting official videos and lip-service to what Islamic Guidance Minister Larijani calls the "marriage problems" of Iranian youth can now bridge the gap, they claim. The third generation is a "lost generation."

A teacher I encountered one afternoon at a Tehran school for the performing arts was grim-faced as he gave me his assessment of the future. His name was Mr. Tehrani, and he was disturbed. It was simple enough: The effect of encroaching Western culture would be tragic. If the kind of programming available to young people in Europe or North America is shown in Iran, viewers may become aggressive and violence may be the result. "Our school is just now training people to produce our own programs, just in case people will be watching Iranian television. Maybe we can divert their attention from satellite programs. But what do you think?"

To accept the technical premises of Western culture, I reflected later, is to accept its societal premises. In competition with the cultural agencies of the West, Iran, like any technologically "backward" country, cannot hope to resist the atomization of audience, the undermining of social solidarity and the shaping of perception — the morbid fascination for the direct, real-time transmission of actuality as against the knowledge of history — that modern televisual technique boasts as its sovereign achievement. Iran's cultural authorities are indifferent to the inherent, terminally debilitating syndrome of self-referentiality which relativizes and reduces all events and human discourse to flashes of "perception." Overwhelmed by a burden of superfluous, redundant and irrelevant information, consumers of media culture are reduced to passivity, content to evaluate what has come to be known as "choices." They are then offered interactivity, identification of preferences among a small number of predetermined alternatives, as a substitute for participation. The result is then offered as liberty; it is, on the contrary, the death of memory.

Yet, this assessment of what the future may bring in Iran rests on a series of assumptions. Not the least of these is the alleged inevitability of cultural transformation. Western culture as forbidden fruit may, in the long run, prove less powerful than its opponents fear, its effect less devastating. Iran is not the former Soviet Bloc, where the possible attractions — and the power — of the Western cultural model were hotly denied for decades. Nor is it an ephemeral, ersatz culture, as was that engendered by Real Socialism in Our Time. Islam, as ideology, does not share the productivist core which made applied Marxism so vulnerable to the attacks of its better entrenched capitalist dominant. (The same productivist core will also render the culture engendered by capitalism equally vulnerable to a critique drawn from the moral dimension of human life.) Persian culture is one of the world's oldest and most deeply rooted. It successfully absorbed the Arab conquest, revitalized Islam, transformed the Islamic arts, gave birth to a new language and literature and, over the tumultuous last 200 years, breathed new vitality into a world religion. It reaches deep into the Persian psyche, as deep as language itself, perpetuating an identity which has little to do with borders, and much to do with a shared history of resistance to assimilation, and of ultimately assimilating or repulsing the invader.

Iran may well bend under the Western cultural assault, but it is unlikely to break. Even wide availability of miniaturized antennas for capturing satellite signals is unlikely to result in massive disaffection for religion, particularly among the country's devout, non-Westernized majority. For all its failures, the Islamic Revolution endowed this majority with a voice, gave it expression, a sense of belonging and a fleeting taste of power. Iranians are legendary in their stubbornness and in their attachment to their religion — though not necessarily as interpreted by the dominant faction of relatively junior *mollahs*.

Of course, the Islamic Revolution may prove to have been an ephemeral upsurge, an historical anomaly, a combination of American fumbling and malfeasance (the "How we lost Iran" syndrome in its many permutations) and Iranian imperial cupidity. It may also be what its creators claim for it (and who is the outside observer to grant them less than to take their premises seriously?): the realization of an almost 1,400-year-old vision of an Islamic state modelled on that founded by the Prophet Mohammad when he migrated from Mecca to Medina to begin the Islamic era.

HAMID AND FARIDEH live in a comfortable flat in north-central Tehran. He commutes to work at the foreign ministry, while she minds their first baby and presides over a complex web of family relations, celebrations, comings and goings, shared happiness or frustration, and day-to-day small talk. Farideh's father is a moderately successful dry goods merchant at the bazaar, a good-humoured, modest man who prefers sitting cross-legged on the floor to using a chair, and who is equally at home in Azeri, the Turkish dialect spoken by nearly one-third of all Iranians, and Farsi.

His two sons, Farideh's brothers, are husky, bright young men in their late twenties — on the leading edge of the third post-revolutionary generation. After a staggering dinner with a spicy Azerbaijani accent, the brothers contrive to entertain me. But unlike uptown parties, whose idea of chic can be defined as alcohol, dancing and contraband video cassettes, on this evening the two young men pull out their musical instruments and stage an impromptu recital on the *tar*, a three-stringed relative of the bouzouki, and the *santur*. Why learn traditional instruments like these instead of, say, the electric guitar? I ask the eldest. "The electric guitar has no soul," he answers with a shy grin, as his fingers play across the strings.

February 11, 1985: the sixth anniversary of the Islamic Revolution, Tehran.
Photo © Michael Coyne / The Image Bank.

8

Ending a Revolution

REVOLUTIONS RUN a certain, predictable course, says conventional wisdom. First comes the exaltation, the sense that everything is possible. The world is fresh clay to be thrown and turned. Then follows compromise accompanied by its dissolute relative, disillusionment. Solemn promises are hedged, tactical considerations become paramount, attacks from without must be repulsed; enemies from within, real and imaginary, must be eliminated. Then comes counter-revolutionary return to a variant of the *status quo ante*. The once plastic raw material hardens into social and political organization obsessed with self-perpetuation. Such, in near-parodical brevity, is the classic schema.

But no. Revolutions can be more convincingly understood as epileptic fits, as outbursts of mass ecstasy and pain. The upheavals which wracked France, Russia or China are, metaphorically, the tongue-biting, thrashing and writhing of the body politic seized by the countervailing powers of despair and hope. Though revolutions are no more lacking in their own internal logic than are natural disasters like volcanic eruptions, typhoons and earthquakes, their supreme mystery is the unpredictability of their advent, intensity, course and duration.

What has gone before becomes clear only in hindsight: the victors revel in the absolute freedom to interpret events and the vanquished, if they still live, fulminate, plot revenge and make mental notes for the revisionist histories they or their survivors may one day write.

The Islamic revolution which swept Iran in the late '70s and early '80s was *sui generis*. It shared little, except for its fury and sweep, with the variants familiar to most Westerners, and offers immense scope for *ex post facto* interpretation. Conflicting voices are legion. The defeated monarchists, many of whom sought refuge in the West, as well as the Western and particularly the American supporters of the *ancien régime*, have devoted their life's work to showing how a little more "firmness" on the part of the Shah could have averted the catastrophe. A few more thousand dead would have done the trick, they hypothesize. Marxists, a rare breed now, claim clerical reactionaries hijacked a democratic uprising staged by workers and peasants. Iranologists less in thrall to ideology analyzed the upheaval as a typical Third World revolution of which religion was merely the vector.[66] The vanquished, like deposed President Abol-Hassan Bani-Sadr, now living in Paris, trumpet a "conspiracy of the *mollahs*." The ruling clerical establishment proclaims its triumph as the victory of the forces of righteousness over the dark powers of corruption. I have decided to accept all these interpretations at face value, for elements of each are present in events as they unfolded. The evidence itself is inescapable: a powerful revolution wracked Iran, created an ostensibly Islamic state on the ruins of an ephemeral dictatorship disguised as an ancient monarchy, and has now consolidated itself as a relatively stable regional power whose popular support, though diminished, remains substantial. For stabilization to occur, however, the revolutionary ferment had to end. This chapter will offer a version of how it ended, as seen from several Iranian perspectives, ever mindful of the dangers of wisdom in hindsight — whether that of the author, the victors or the vanquished. Like its onset, the end of the Islamic Revolution could just as well be ascribed to fortune as to misfortune. The events themselves, part the product of human volition, part the machinations of fate and happenstance — not to exclude divine intervention — possess only the relative truth of their physical occurrence. But this truth is the best we have to work with. And as for the events, they compel scrutiny.

IN LATE EIGHTEENTH-CENTURY France, the revolutionaries saw themselves as the vanguard of a new, secular ruling class swept into power by the ideology of Enlightenment humanism. In the early years of the twentieth century, the conspiratorial Russian Bolsheviks, self-proclaimed agents of social and economic inevitability, cast themselves as the vanguard of the international proletariat. Iran's victorious religious revolutionaries had no such social or economic pretensions. They fought not in the name of the principles of liberty, equality and fraternity, nor of economic determinism, but in the name of an Islamic society which would somehow resolve social conflict and bring about economic justice. For the best of doctrinal reasons they promoted no all-embracing vision of an earthly paradise, condemned Marxism, abjured humanism. "Islam is neither a theory of society nor a philosophy of history," wrote Ayatollah Murtada Motahhari, one of the Islamic revolution's leading theoreticians. "In the sacred book of Islam, no social or historical problem is dealt with in the technical jargon of sociology and philosophy of history. In the same way, no other problem, ethical, legal or philosophical is discussed in the Qur'an, either in current terms or according to the traditional classifications of sciences. However, these and other problems related with various sciences can be deduced from the book."[67]

Westerners living in the late twentieth century, force-fed with the disjointed, sweetly addictive ephemera of the information culture like so many *foie-gras* producing geese, saw Ayatollah Khomeini and his followers as incomprehensible throwbacks to what, we were told, was a medieval belief system just short of barbarous; as living anachronisms. These people were ahistorical anomalies, members of an unscrupulous fundamentalist cult not unlike the Bible-thumping Evangelicals who flourish so luxuriantly on the fringes of North American society, or the secretive ultra-orthodox Hassidim of Crown Heights and Outremont. In Iran itself, where it counted, a significant number of people saw him as a man inspired by divine wisdom, and illuminated by the flame of righteousness and justice. Some even whispered that Khomeini was the vanished Imam whose coming all faithful Shi'ites yearned and prayed for, the harbinger of a new realm of justice.

History — our civilization instructs us — is a constantly rising curve of progress guided by the twin secular gods of Reason and Technique, its wars and atrocities merely exceptions which prove the rule. Suddenly, in Iran, dark forces had been released, forces which seemed to fly in the face of this most precious myth. For Iranians, however, these forces seemed to bubble up, unchecked at last, from the deepest reaches of the Islamic past and from a people's long struggle for emancipation. The West looked on stupefied as God, long certified dead, suddenly reasserted Himself, tormenting evil-doers through the hands of the believers, as the Qur'an enjoins.

A favourite reason for the suddenness of the Shah's collapse was that in their obsession with the spectre of the putative International Communist Conspiracy, Americans, as tutelary power, and, to a lesser extent, Europeans, failed to allow even the possibility that religion had become the prime mover in the increasingly insurrectionary social and political protest movement which flooded through Iran in the '70s. Many Iranians, too, were accustomed to Western ways and trained in the inevitability — even the desirability — of the Western cultural and political model. They, no less than the Shah's admirers, were stunned by the sudden fury which whirled out of the poverty, destitution and humiliation of the urban slums of Tehran and Isfahan, Shiraz and Tabriz and Mashhad, and dozens — hundreds — of smaller cities and towns. The faceless, sullen, stooped-back wretched of the earth — the urban mob — had suddenly emerged onto the stage of history, responding to the simply-worded commands of an octogenarian leader who was as familiar to them as he was foreign to the Westernized intelligentsia.

The Shah and his entourage, isolated at the pinnacle of a pyramid of arrogance, wealth and power, saw and heard little of the coming storm. Lavishly entertained foreign sycophants and allies believed the Shah's assurances that the people would always love him, despite the warnings of a handful of Farsi-speaking Western scholars who had caught the distant rumble, as the vibration of the rail signals the approach of the train long before it can be seen or heard. Iran's intellectuals, poets and writers, long in the forefront of the struggle against the dictatorship, ignored or loathed as anti-modern the clerical establishment. Many Iranians could not tolerate the vainglorious despotism of the imperial regime, but could not imagine that a religious movement would ever succeed in overthrowing it, let alone be able to rule the country.

Meanwhile, the influence of the hierocracy on Iranian politics had been growing in inverse proportion to the stability of a secular political leadership which over the course of a century the *mollahs* had come to consider as inherently illegitimate. In 1892, a religious boycott of tobacco products forced the Qajar regime to cancel the tobacco monopoly which it had conceded to British interests. The constitutional revolution, from 1905 until 1912, pitted a coalition of Western-educated democrats and two of the leading *mujtahids* of the day, Ayatollahs Bihbihani and Tabatabai, against the monarchy and its competing foreign supporters, England and Russia. While the secularists sought representative institutions for their own sake, on the Western model, representative democracy, for the *ulama*, remained only an interim solution.

Coming at the height of the Pahlavi dictatorship's power, the uprising of 15 Khordad foreshadowed, in its sudden violence and insurrectionary form, the country-wide convulsion which would burst out fifteen years later. Since March of that year, Ayatollah Khomeini had begun speaking out on political issues from his position at the Qom theological seminary. His attack on the Shah's "white revolution" brought police raids, his arrest and subsequent release. But when, in June he attacked the laws which granted extraterritorial immunity to Americans in Iran as contrary to the Qur'an, and called upon the people no longer to tolerate the tyranny of the Pahlavi regime, violent rioting erupted in most of Iran's major cities. The Shah's security forces and elite army units shot to kill; at least 15,000 protestors died in the upheaval. Khomeini was arrested again, exiled first to Turkey then to Iraq.[68]

When we met in December, 1990, Abdullah Zandieh was chancellor of Az-Zahra University for Women in Vanak, once a village north of Tehran, today engulfed by the sprawling metropolis. Like many members of the anti-Shah intelligentsia, Dr. Zandieh dates his awareness of the nascent revolutionary movement to the uprising and its bloody repression. "One of the clearest memories I have was the uprising on the fifteenth of Khordad, where villagers and low-paid workers in southern Tehran began confronting the Shah's regime and thousands of people were killed by the secret police and by the Shah's troops. We saw that less educated people, people deprived of minimum standards of living, took this bold step and we intellectuals took a very limited share in it. And this was a shame. I still feel the responsibility, even today."

Intellectuals like Dr. Zandieh who went on to join the religious movement and hold high positions in the Islamic regime today, were galvanized by the events of June, 1963. But, such was the distance between the rarified intellectual atmosphere of north Tehran and the brutal existence of the slum-dwellers who had fought and died, that they were as startled as were the combined intelligence-gathering forces of the CIA and SAVAK by the speed and power of the revolutionary onslaught which ripped across Iran fifteen years later. Demonstration followed demonstration, memorial ceremonies flowed into pitched street battles, thousands were martyred at the call of Ayatollah Khomeini, climaxing in the flight of the Shah and the triumphal return from Paris of the man they now called the Imam.

With its deep, organic roots in Iranian society, the hierocracy was a reasonable facsimile, in microcosm, of social reality in all its complexity, its intertwining, shifting interests, and in its singular admixture of conflict and convergence. Its ranks were far from monolithic; they included a minority of socially committed clerics whose interpretation of the Qur'an embodied a powerful element of distributive economic justice; militant Third Worldists dedicated to the spread of Islamic revolutionary ideas throughout the Muslim world; a large number of apolitical moderates who believed that men of religion should restrict their activities to the realm of the spirit; influential Ayatollahs close to the bazaar; and conservatives like the Hojjatiyeh Society, an anti-Bahai group which favoured a free market economy and opposed the doctrine of the Rule of the Jurisconsult, the innovation which ultimately allowed Khomeini to wield power.

It was not unusual for men of religion to hold views on economic issues which might be considered "radical," while maintaining extremely conservative social positions. Only under the leadership of Ayatollah Khomeini were these differences sublimated and channelled into the struggle against the Shah. But if the revolution would have to make do without a vanguard party, it could not succeed without "cadre" — these were the clerics who trained under Khomeini during the years he taught at Qom, and later at Najaf in Iraq. One of the most eminent among them was Grand Ayatollah Hossein Ali Montazeri, Khomeini's first designated successor as *faqih* (Jurisconsult), a tragic figure whose rise, then fall from grace — and power — closely parallels the rise and fall of the Islamic revolution.

According to the official biography published on his appointment as future leader in 1985, Ayatollah Montazeri was born in 1922 in Najaf-Abad village, some thirty kilometres southwest of Isfahan, into a poor religious family. He later studied theology under Ayatollahs Borujerdi and Khomeini, and assumed internal leadership of the religious resistance to the Shah's regime after the expulsion of Khomeini in 1963. First arrested in 1967 and imprisoned, Montazeri spent the next fifteen years either in prison, where he was a cell-mate of Ayatollah Taleqani as well as of non-religious student revolutionaries, or in exile in remote and desolate places like Kurdistan and the desert town of Tabas. But, notes the biography, "the regime's efforts to isolate and silence the Ayatollah only strengthened the people's desire to hear his message." After several years of internal exile he was re-arrested in 1975, and subjected to severe torture of which he still bears the "mental and physical scars," and refused an offer of release on condition of silence. Finally, after this last three and one-half year ordeal, he was released in November, 1978.

Though his direct manner of speech and lack of political finesse were often mocked by sophisticated Tehranis and the foreign journalists they cultivated (*Time* magazine once described him as the "Gabby Hayes" of Iranian politics), Montazeri maintained a strong base of support among the *mostazafin*, and was outspoken in his criticism of the errors and arrogance of the new regime. "It is incumbent upon Islamic scholars and the committed *ulama* to put the high status given by Islam to the deprived class and the ways to combat poverty, cruelty and exploitation at the disposal of the downtrodden nations who are thirsty for Islamic justice," he declared in May, 1985, as he criticized the regime's flagging concern for the fate of those who had first rallied to the revolutionary cause.

The press, he frequently argued, should be independent rather than the semi-official institution it had become. One of the main obstacles to the success of the Islamic revolution he identified as the holier-than-thou attitude of Islamic students which "may deter people from Islam and the revolution" with high-handed and arbitrary behaviour. Another was the "rude and untactful behaviour" of members of committees dealing with violations of Islamic ethical codes. This kind of behaviour, warned Montazeri, would remind people of the former regime and create ill-feeling among potential supporters. There was a danger of recreating an atmosphere reminiscent of the former regime's SAVAK. Seen in retrospect, his injunctions were far from abstract statements of lofty principle. Unlike many of the leading *ulama*, who were only too content to speed about in armour-plated Mercedes Benz limousines and live in luxurious north Tehran villas surrounded by fawning lackeys, Montazeri kept his door open to the common people, and his fingertips on the pulse of grass-roots discontent. His manner was modest and his life simple; during the war, he and his family used ration coupons like any normal citizen. Though he was as approachable as a village *mollah*, he also enjoyed a broad range of political connections, from the lay nationalists around Mehdi Bazargan to the fiercest Islamic internationalists. It was his close connections with these groups that led first to his isolation from the centre of power in the conflict over the rapprochement with the United States, and then to his dismissal three years later.

"Whether in or out of power, he has not changed his outlook," said a University of Tehran political scientist and life-long supporter of

Montazeri whom I agreed to identify as Hassan N. "This is one of the main reasons he could not compromise with the power lovers who rule the country today, despite their repeated attempts to compromise him. He always told people 'I have no pocket for myself' and never tried to establish himself as an 'official' clergyman."

In November, 1985, Ayatollah Montazeri was confirmed by the Assembly of Experts as successor to Imam Khomeini. The appointment, announced by Majlis Speaker Hashemi Rafsanjani himself, corresponded with the period of strongest "radical" influence in post-revolutionary politics. By endorsing Montazeri, the panel of high-ranking *mollahs* and lay dignitaries whose function was to rule on the Islamic suitability of legislation, were seemingly endorsing his stinging judgement of the weaknesses of the regime. When the same panel voted to dismiss him less than four years later, they withdrew their sanction. What had happened?

For some Iranians, the rise and fall of Montazeri more than epitomizes the matching curve of the revolution. The undoing of Montazeri, says Hassan N., was also a plot against the founding principals of the Islamic revolution itself. While most of the documentary evidence required to support these allegations — as opposed to abundant rumour and hearsay — is inaccessible to all but high-ranking members of the ruling establishment, there exists enough circumstantial evidence to allow us to sketch a schematic account. It also reveals points of convergence — if not a direct cause and effect relationship — between Montazeri's fall, the abortive attempt to purchase arms from the United States (what we know as the Iran-Contra affair) and the consolidation of power by the faction led by President Ali Akbar Hashemi Rafsanjani.

DEMONSTRATIONS AND DISTRIBUTIONS of leaflets not approved by the authorities or not in support of official policy are not an everyday occurrence in post-revolutionary Iran. Former Prime Minister Mehdi Bazargan's Iran Liberation Movement, though barely tolerated, was able to circulate open letters critical of the war among a small number of intellectuals, businessmen and religious dignitaries; mourners who congregated at funerals of opposition political figures sometimes transformed these events into brief demonstrations of discreet protest. So when, on October 15, 1986, groups of Tehran University students distributed tens of thousands of unauthorized leaflets in the city streets, the effect was explosive. The leaflet contained allegations which shocked the regime's supporters and would soon shake two governments to their foundations. A delegation of US officials led by Ronald Reagan's ex-National Security Adviser Robert McFarlane had earlier visited Iran, it claimed; while in Tehran, the visitors held high-level talks with key members of the Islamic government, and concluded an agreement to release hostages held by pro-Iranian groups in Lebanon in exchange for arms and guided missile spare parts.

Within three weeks the governments of both countries were exposed as having surreptitiously done precisely what the leaflets alleged: the unthinkable. The Reagan administration, unbending in its doctrinaire public refusal to "deal with terrorists," had in fact provided arms to a state it had long defined as a breeding ground of world terrorism and an international pariah — ostensibly to gain the release of American hostages. The Iranian regime's moderate wing, led by Hashemi Rafsanjani, had welcomed representatives of the Great Satan into its own house and discussed opening up relations. Ironically, in 1979, at the height of the revolution, Mehdi Bazargan's provisional government had been forced to resign when it was revealed that he had met while in Algiers with President Carter's National Security Adviser Zbigniew Brzezinski. In a twist of double irony, during the so-called "hostage crisis" following the seizure of the American Embassy in Tehran, leading members of the hierocracy concluded secretly with the then-opposition Republicans that the captive Americans would only be released after the defeat of the Carter administration. Though still taken as inconclusive in official Washington, the "October Surprise" is accepted as fact in Tehran.

Two weeks before the leaflet distribution, on October 2, a bizarre incident had occurred in central Tehran, where little escapes the close scrutiny of the information ministry. Syria's *chargé d'affaires* Ayad Mahmoud was kidnapped by armed men in broad daylight. State radio initially claimed that the abduction of a diplomat representing one of Iran's few allies in the Arab world was the work of CIA agents, a story so wildly implausible that it rapidly evaporated. Several days later it was revealed that the kidnappers of Mr. Mahmoud belonged to a group headed by a man named Mehdi Hashemi, one of Iran's best known Islamic agitators.

Hashemi ran the World Islamic Organization, a group dedicated to the spread of militant Islamic ideology throughout the Muslim world, out of the office of Ayatollah Montazeri, himself a long-time advocate of Islamic internationalism. Hashemi, whose brother Hadi was Montazeri's son-in-law, had been active in the revolutionary movement since 1961, and had been involved in the capture of the US Embassy in Tehran on December 4, 1979 — an action which had been quickly endorsed by Khomeini. He also, wrote the usually well-informed Patrick Seale, ran an Islamic publishing house in Zurich that functioned as a front for European arms purchases for Iran's Revolutionary Guards; the 10% commission he charged was used to finance radical Shi'a groups in Lebanon. This gave him, concluded Seale, influence over the hostage-takers and, ultimately, the fate of the hostages.[69] While Hashemi's precise motivation in abducting the Syrian diplomat remained unclear, observers in Tehran surmised it was connected with statements by President Hafez al-Assad that Syria would not allow any country to occupy Iraq. He meant, of course, Syria's ally Iran, whose military operations against the forces of Iraqi dictator Saddam Hussein had suddenly become brilliantly successful, thanks in part to the influx of sophisticated American-made arms. By late August, Iranian officials had begun to exude confidence about the outcome of the war, and in early September Iran's massive Karbala III operation led to significant territorial gains along the southern front. The offensive reached its peak with the daring capture by Iranian amphibious commandos of Iraq's Al-Omyyan Persian Gulf drilling platform, hailed by Speaker Rafsanjani as a "turning point in the war."

August and September, 1986, marked a "turning point" of another kind for Rafsanjani. Ali Hashemi Bahramani, a close relative of the Speaker — either a nephew or his eldest son — had taken over as chief Iranian negotiator in the ongoing talks with representatives of President Ronald Reagan's National Security Council, led by US Marine Corps Lieutenant Colonel Oliver North. An exploratory meeting had been held in Brussels on August 25, which prepared the ground for a visit to Washington by Bahramani in mid-September.

In Iran, opponents of the opening of the doors to the United States could not publicly oppose the initiative. Enjoying as it did the tacit support of Imam Khomeini, the still-secret policy was politically untouchable. However the opponents — one of whom was Ayatollah Montazeri — had been able to suggest indirectly that Iran was receiving military supplies not only from the Great Satan, but also from the Little Satan, Israel. In a press conference held on August 30, the Majlis Speaker responded to rumours of arms sales to Iran by the Zionist regime saying: "If we were compelled to ask for something from Israel, we would prefer to stop the war."

Strictly speaking, Iran may not have "asked for" anything from Israel, since virtually all sensitive arms shipments were arranged not by the government's procurement agencies but by a variety of arm's-length intermediaries, including such colourful characters as Manucher Ghorbanifar, the Iranian-born international arms broker who enjoyed the confidence of the conservative *mollahs* and excellent links with the remnants of the Shah's regime. Israeli arms shipments to Iran's hard-pressed military were a fact, however, an arrangement of mutual benefit to the former allies turned ostensibly bitter adversaries. They were also substantial: worth more than $5 billion, some sources claim. The Israeli shipments began as early as 1982. Though official American policy throughout the early '80s sought to block arms supplies to Iran from other, primarily European, countries, the absence of United States condemnation of its surrogate's lucrative ventures could only have been interpreted in Tel Aviv as approval. By providing high technology, American-made weapons and spare parts to Iran, Israel was able to weaken its main Arab enemy. By dealing through middlemen and arms dealers with the "Zionist usurpers," Iran's new rulers could maintain the war effort which provided it with political leverage against its domestic opponents, the better to consolidate the regime. Besides, sniffed the cynics, whoever rules Iran becomes an ally of whoever rules Jerusalem: thus it has ever been since the days of Cyrus the Great.[70]

After stalling the Iraqi invasion on the battlefield, then pushing the aggressors out of Iranian territory, Iran went over to the offensive, determined to drive Saddam Hussein from power. The Islamic regime had inherited a military establishment which depended on American-made weapons and systems. Deprived of replacements and spare parts, Iran's armed forces, though better motivated, were unable to match Iraq's formidable defensive firepower in positional warfare. In one of the first Val Fajr (Dawn) operations, which Iran had hoped would decide the outcome of the war, "human wave" assaults on well-defended Iraqi positions failed, at an enormous cost in lives.[71]

As early as the summer of 1984 Ghorbanifar had discussed the mechanics of a possible arms-for-hostages deal with Saudi billionaire Adnan Khashoggi. Iran desperately needed a weapon to counter Iraq's Soviet-built tanks. The heroics of motorcycle-mounted daredevil tank-hunters armed with hand-held RPG launchers were not enough. Iran knew what it wanted: US-made TOW (Tube-launched, optically tracked, wire guided) anti-tank missiles. It was not long before Washington was aware of the discussions. In late August, National Security Adviser McFarlane coincidentally requested a formal inter-agency review of America's Iran policy. Six weeks later, the review board's report concluded that the United States had no high-level contacts and could not influence events in Iran. Still, one month later, on November 20, a meeting took place in Hamburg, West Germany, at which Americans were introduced to Ghorbanifar in the presence of representatives of the Iranian government and a former SAVAK general.

In March, 1985, an operation code named Badr succeeded in breaking through to the Basra-Baghdad highway, Iran's deepest penetration of the war on the southern front, before being repulsed. While the daring Iranian offensive set alarm bells ringing in Western capitals, it also touched off a fierce controversy in Tehran over the merits of massive infantry assaults against fortified Iraqi positions. Shortly after the battle, the pace of contact between Israelis, Iranian arms dealers and Americans picked up, and on July 16, after a series of meetings involving intermediaries, McFarlane obtained approval from Ronald Reagan to proceed with an attempt to negotiate an arms-for-hostages deal. The key had been Iran's intervention to end the hijacking of TWA flight 847, diverted to Beirut in June, which the United States correctly interpreted as a signal of Iran's willingness to seek new arrangements. For Iran, the overriding consideration was the prosecution and eventual outcome of the war.

A first shipment of 100 TOWs was delivered to Tehran from Israel on August 30, followed two weeks later by a second shipment of 408 of the missiles. One day after the cargo arrived, one of the hostages — the Reverend Benjamin Weir — was released by his Lebanese captors, to demonstrate Iran's good faith. (The United States' first choice, CIA Middle East station chief William Buckley, was dead, having been tortured and killed by his captors.) A discordant note disturbed the relative harmony when Iran rejected a shipment of 18 HAWK anti-aircraft missiles which had been shipped to the city of Tabriz in exchange for an anticipated five hostages. Iran, which had deposited $18 million for the missiles, was dismayed to find that the models delivered were not only obsolescent, but that they bore Israeli markings. The flourishing relationship seemed compromised, but the Reagan administration's determination to release American hostages was undiminished.

The bare bones of this determination were fleshed out on January 17, 1986, when Ronald Reagan signed a Presidential Finding authorizing the sale of arms and spare parts to Iran. On the following day, Reagan's new National Security Adviser, Admiral John Poindexter, ordered the United States Defense Department to release 4,000 TOWs to the CIA for direct sale to Iran. This brought the total to 4,508, including those which replaced the 508 missiles sold by Israel the previous August. One week later, American officials released limited battle-front intelligence to Iran.

The information, regarding troop concentrations and defensive positions, proved immediately useful when Iran launched one of its most spectacular offensives. Code named Val Fajr VIII, the operation was designed to surround the port city of Basra. After a diversionary attack through the marshes to the northeast, Iranian forces captured the Fao peninsula to the south, cutting Iraq off from the Persian Gulf. Within the ensuing two weeks, another 1,000 TOWs were delivered, to Tehran and to the southern port of Bandar Abbas, at close proximity to the front. When no hostages were released, American suspicions were aroused, but North, who by then had assumed primary responsibility for carrying out Reagan's policy, claimed that Iranian officials had proposed direct meetings between the United States and Iran. Iran may not have proposed such meetings, but was receptive to the US initiative.

Capping several months of preparation involving Israeli gunrunners, the omnipresent Ghorbanifar and Oliver North, an American delegation made up of McFarlane, North, George Cave, Howard J. Teicher, the Israeli freebooter Amiram Nir and a CIA communicator touched down in Tehran on May 26, 1986, after a flight from Israel. They bore as gift a set of matched pistols and a chocolate cake from a Tel Aviv kosher bakery. The black, unmarked aircraft, which carried a pallet of HAWK missile spares, reached Mehrabad airport ahead of schedule: No official welcoming party was on hand to greet the unlikely visitors.

Throughout the strangely choreographed ballet of attraction and repulsion which climaxed in the Tehran visit, the Americans maintained the fiction that they were dealing with anti-Khomeini moderates. From the beginning, however, their true interlocutors were high-ranking members of the Iranian government, including the putatively anti-American Prime Minister Mir Hossein Mousavi, a personal friend of Ghorbanifar, and the powerful, enigmatic then-Speaker of the Majlis, Hashemi Rafsanjani. And all were operating with the approval — or non-disapproval — of the Imam himself. Without at least tacit acceptance from Khomeini, who justified the initiative in terms of sustaining Iran's bitter struggle against Iraq, the opening to the United States would have been unthinkable. Although the dialogue between the two countries was dominated by hard-nosed bargaining for the weapons and spare parts Iran so desperately needed in its bitter war, and for the release of the hostages which had become an obsession with the single-minded American president, it had an intriguing sub-text, one much better understood by Iran than by the impulsive, action-obsessed Americans.

Few were better qualified to understand the complexities of this sub-text than Mohammad-Javad Larijani, then deputy foreign minister. Mr. Larijani, a mathematician who did postgraduate work at the University of California, today heads Iran's Institute for Studies in Theoretical Physics and Mathematics and sits in the Majlis, where he is closely associated with the Rafsanjani group. In a wide-ranging interview held in the winter of 1990 at the Institute's headquarters in Niavaran, a northern Tehran suburb, Mr. Larijani told me that when the American delegation arrived, the Iranian authorities were expecting not Robert McFarlane but "an arms dealer with some of his companions. Then when we discovered that they are McFarlane, a group has been sent to go and to see what they want to say."

"There was no high-level contact with them," he went on, "partly because we were not prepared, and partly we did not know exactly what they wanted. When I say that I did not meet them, or that any high-level delegation did not meet them, it's not because somebody is afraid to meet them, but because we were not prepared for that."

Larijani, a self-avowed member of Iran's peace lobby, said that the Americans had "reached this conclusion, that the relation with Iran should be opened up. And they were thinking that everything is ripe for that. It was so important for them that they were ready to take the first step. They thought that at that time Iran was in real need of weapons, for Iran to be successful in the war was very important and dear to the Iranians and Iranian politicians. And they said if we tried to help Iran in this war, both the people will be happy of that because we help them in an issue which is the most dear one to them. And the politicians will be thankful because we help them in a thing which is very decisive for them. So they have chosen the area of military help. But during the action, I think a lot of other external things had been included in it. While I think the Contra affair and the connection with the Israelis, they already were detrimental [sic] in undermining the whole policy."

"I should add another factor which is more important," he continued. "I think the Americans also said, if this does not go in that way, even if it goes, we can have a strong leverage politically inside Iran against the present regime, because we can kind of expose the whole affair at the proper time. If the regime collapses because of that exposure, then it's fine, the regime has collapsed. If it did not collapse and then the relation with the United States is coming to the surface, it means that they should defend the relation with the United States. So this is also fine."

"I think these calculations were a mistake. My personal judgement is this: Their policy of trying to open the relation with Iran was fine. I think it was a correct one. To choose the issue of the war to enter, it was also a right one. But they missed to understand that there was not the confidence needed for this rapprochement. They tried to pick the fruit before it's getting ripe. In order that two countries with this kind of animosity among them, to get closer, they should gradually build a kind of confidence. There should be confidence-building measures, an attempt before they get to that position. Thirdly, their view that to exploit the vulnerability of exposure of the relations of the United States internally, I think it was unfair. It shows that they were not totally sincere in their approach to us. This was also what the Iranians thought. The whole affair was going in a very normal way, and perhaps it was getting its fruits in due course, but the Americans tried to exploit that. They brought it to the surface and thought it will be the Iranian government that will suffer from that exposure. It was not correct. The result of that premature exposure was that the whole relation with the United States suffered and the situation became much harder for the resumption of relations."

The incident showed that there were "radicals" as well as "moderates" within the American political establishment on the Iran issue. "Perhaps those in the stronger position in the United States are those who do not favour any action against Iran. But the idea of containing Iran, or moderating Iran, I think these are ideas in the minds of the Americans."

Ideally, the Americans should have "taken us as we are," he said. "Trying to change the Iranian government, or pushing them to moderation will have a very contrary effect in Iran. There are groups in Iran who think we can never trust the Americans, so there is no rationale for relations with the United States. As a result, they are opposing relations with the United States very harshly and severely. There are other groups who think the American policy was not correct, but that through dialogue we can reach a common agreement. In Iran, the issue of relations with the United States is a sensitive one. In both governments, that of Iran and that of America, there are difficulties in respect to policy making and public opinion in order to reach a common workable agenda for that relation."

Given his influential position and close ties with the moderates in the hierocracy, Mohammad-Javad Larijani's personal views can be taken as an accurate expression of the thinking of proponents of *rapprochement* with the United States. But his explanation that while Iran was expecting an arms dealer and his companions and instead got McFarlane was more a reflection of the political sensitivity of the issue than of the desire on both sides to strike a bargain. At the Tehran meeting, and later in Germany and Washington, the Iranians took considerable pains to alert their American counterparts to the political dangers they faced from the radical opposition. The dangers were substantial and visible. Even as the McFarlane group was making its way to its top-floor suite in the north Tehran Esteqlal Hotel (former Hilton), the escort group exchanged shots in the parking lot with a group of Revolutionary Guards.

Ali Akbar Mohtashemi who, as minister of the interior at the time was responsible for the police, insists he and his fellow radicals knew nothing about the deal: "The visit," he told me in an interview at his Tehran home in early 1993, "was arranged by opportunists and non-revolutionary people, and done surreptitiously. If the revolutionary forces had known of it, they would have arrested him. He and his group were responsible for crimes in Iran and throughout the region." There is, however, every reason to conclude that the parking lot shoot-out was in fact a failed attempt, either by Mr. Mohtashemi's men or people loyal to Mehdi Hashemi, to arrest McFarlane and his cohorts.

Throughout the negotiating process, Iranian policy makers never wavered in their determination both to improve relations with the United States and to obtain a satisfactory price for doing so. The key was to be precisely the kind of confidence-building measures Mr. Larijani alluded to: delivery of weapons, particularly spare parts for Hawk surface-to-air missiles and TOWs, which would allow the Iranian government to regain the battlefield initiative and thus improve its public image in the face of growing war-weariness on the home front. What Mr. Larijani does not mention, but what underlay the talks — and could certainly be viewed, along with the release of American hostages, as a confidence-building measure — was his government's intention to bring to heel the fractious radicals. If they could be curtailed, the Lebanese groups alleged to have carried out the kidnapping of American citizens could then be brought under direct control.

IRANIAN JOURNALISTS had early on become aware of their government's dealings with both Israel and the United States but were unable to make the story public. Their frustration had moved Ayatollah Montazeri to issue another public appeal for greater press freedom in mid-August. This time, however, Montazeri drew a pointed rebuke from the Jurisconsult himself on August 31: "Some people tend to concentrate only on the weak points of the government in their speeches and writings without giving any credit to the government for the good things it has done," thundered Khomeini. The admonition had the effect of deflecting criticism away from the lack of press freedom which made it impossible to debate the contentious policy and onto the critics themselves — a tactic quite in keeping with Khomeini's style.

Meanwhile, the pace of contact between American and Iranian officials was quickening. On October 6, 1986, Oliver North, George Cave, a Farsi-speaking former CIA-agent, and Iranian-born American businessman Albert Hakim met in Frankfurt with Bahramani and an Iranian named Ali Samii, identified as a senior Islamic Revolutionary Guard Corps (IRCG) intelligence officer. At the meeting, the United States delegation handed the Iranians a Bible inscribed by President Reagan with a passage from Galatians 3:8 ("And the Scripture, foreseeing that God would justify the Gentiles by faith, preached the gospel beforehand to Abraham, saying 'All the nations shall be blessed in you'"). North presented a seven-point proposal for provision of weapons in return for the release of the remaining hostages. The Iranian delegation countered with its own six-point scheme promising the release of one hostage. As connoisseurs of the Iran-Contra hearings know, the American delegation decamped precipitously. They did so partly in frustration, partly out of panic at the shooting down of CIA operative Eugene Hasenfus over Nicaragua, the event that started the unravelling of the Nicaraguan end of what was to become the Iran-Contra scandal. Their departure left Hakim, a private citizen, to negotiate on behalf of the United States government. Hakim and the Iranians quickly hammered out a nine-point deal which committed the United States to work for the release of seventeen Islamic activists held in Kuwait, provide more arms shipments and transmit military intelligence. Iran agreed to release one hostage, and to work for the release of the others.

Mehdi Hashemi, the man the Iranian delegation had identified as the most dangerous — but not the highest ranking — opponent of resumed relations between Iran and the United States, was arrested in mid-October on orders from Information Minister Hojjatoleslam

Mohammad Reyshahri, who was later to play a crucial role in the dismissal of Montazeri. Also arrested were two Majlis members and several leading members of the IRCG. More than forty arrests were made, indicating the breadth of internal opposition.[72]

On October 28, the same day that a shipment of 500 TOW missiles was delivered to Iran, the Mehdi Hashemi case was discussed for the first time in the Tehran English-language daily *Kayhan International*. The paper quoted Imam Khomeini, in a letter to the intelligence minister, as recommending that "judicial scrutiny be made with utmost care and impartiality, without regard to sensational and provocative polemics by persons and groups affiliated to the defendant." The same article detailed the charges brought against Hashemi and his associates. The list was a long one, and included murder, kidnapping, illegal possession of firearms, forging of government documents, unconstitutional underground activities and collaboration with SAVAK dating back to before the revolution. Now that the government's dealings with the Americans were an open secret, connections began to be drawn between them and the arrests.

One day later, as an editorial in the conservative daily *Resaalat* attacked the "mysterious and dangerous" Mehdi Hashemi group as a second MKO (People's Mujaheddin, the Iraq-based armed opposition movement), Americans and Iranians were meeting again in Mainz, West Germany, in an atmosphere of incipient panic. While back in Tehran, President Ali Khamene'i, who had been silent on the issue, stated on November 1 that a "slander campaign" against Ayatollah Montazeri had failed. The President suggested "rumours" were designed to promote the idea that there existed "chasms within the leadership of the State for which purpose they exploit the entire world's media...." The following day, American hostage David Jacobsen was released in Lebanon.

USUALLY IN IRAN, the stronger the official denial, the more accurate the rumour. Chasms had indeed opened up within the leadership. On November 3, an obscure Lebanese weekly called *Al-Shiraa* published a semi-accurate account of McFarlane's May visit to Tehran. The story had been provided by Mehdi Hashemi's group, with the backing of Ayatollah Montazeri's office, according to the magazine's publisher Hassan Sabra. Sabra also revealed that Montazeri and Hashemi had planned to release the information before the latter's arrest, and not, as is commonly believed, after he had been arrested by SAVAMAH, the

Islamic regime's secret police. The *Al-Shiraa* story was initially obscured — perhaps intentionally — by Jacobsen's release. But the jealously guarded secret of Iranian-American complicity soon began to unravel with dizzying rapidity. Two days after the release of Jacobsen and one day after the publication of the *Al-Shiraa* revelations Hashemi Rafsanjani, at a gathering marking the anniversary of the seizure of the US Embassy, admitted rather offhandedly that an American delegation had, in fact, visited Iran.

Rafsanjani referred cryptically to "proof of American goodwill" at Mehrabad airport, by which he almost certainly meant the pallet of HAWK missile spare parts. "The US is stretching its hand toward us through various ways and is admitting its desperation," he told an audience which would have included many influential opponents of the policy, and would certainly have been aware of the October 15 leaflet. Both Mr. Rafsanjani's tone and the content of his remarks assumed knowledge among his audience that certain things had taken place. It was a typical Iranian public event: a high official reveals information already known to his listeners, who must however feign surprise at the staged revelation and be seen to agree with the official version.

In a speech to the Majlis the next day, he expanded on the story, admitting that the plane carried "parts of our sophisticated requirements" and presents, including a cake in the form of a cross. The cake, he joked, was eaten by airport security men. After noting Imam Khomeini's ruling that no talks should take place, he revealed that the visitors' objective was to break the ice between the United States and Iran, and to secure Iran's help in the release of American hostages held in Lebanon. The visitors, said Mr. Rafsanjani, threatened that the US Rapid Deployment Force was on alert. They were also forced to call home using the hotel telephones, which were naturally tapped. "We will give them a copy later if they like it," he joked. "This is the US, the big giant of the world. This is the superpower the Westoxicated and their ilk have illusions about...."

While in Washington the Reagan administration was hotly denying any meeting had taken place, Iranian journalists were asking questions which, while vague, assumed a certain knowledge of events. In an interview with the conservative daily *Abrar*, Prime Minister Mousavi was asked to what extent the pressure from "certain factions" would have been effective in breaking the news. He replied: "When the ground is not appropriate to break news, analyses are different. And when there is another ground, all equations change accordingly." All bets, in other words, were off. Meanwhile, the Israel connection continued to haunt the Tehran authorities. Speaker Rafsanjani, on November 6, hotly denied rumours that arms had been shipped from Israel, quoting Iran's arms purchase budget: "The arms we are purchasing are not the monopoly of the US or any other seller. There is no need for disregarding any principle of ours to buy arms from Israel." But the principle had been disregarded; Iran had bought arms essential to its war effort from the Zionist arch-enemy.

The Persian-language daily *Kayhan*, in its November 8 edition, listed two reasons for the American approach to Iran. The West had "grown," it editorialized, in grasping some dimensions of Islamic Republic foreign policy and diplomacy. The United States thus calculated that it stood to gain from backing "conservatives supporting economic growth and industrialization" against "fundamentalists" supporting revolution. Although the editorial ascribed this analysis to American officials, it was in fact an accurate description of the conflict within Iranian ruling circles.

Under increasing public pressure at home, the American president addressed the nation on November 14 in an attempt to defuse the politically explosive story of dealings with Iran. In Tehran, Speaker Rafsanjani, quoted in *Jomhouri Eslami* (Islamic Republic), a particularly virulent regime mouthpiece, noted that Reagan had been forced to admit the truth about Iran: "The revolution is a reality; the Americans do not like this reality, which is very bitter to them. But they have to accept it." But he rejected Reagan's assertion that talks had begun eighteen months previously. There may have been contact with international arms dealers, but "not even with junior Islamic Republic officials" he said, and denied that McFarlane, when in Tehran, had met anyone higher than security people. "We don't want arms from the US," he explained. "Only the spare parts that are legally ours."

(Immediately prior to the victory of the Islamic revolution Shahpour Bahktiar, the last prime minister appointed by the Shah, had cancelled all Iranian arms purchases from the United States. Arms bought and paid for before that date had been held in American warehouses ever since.)

On the banks of the Potomac, a whiff of scandal and gunpowder filled the air, while in Iran confusion was the dominant mode. After a cabinet meeting Prime Minister Mousavi, theoretically higher in authority than Speaker Rafsanjani, denied relations with what he termed the "criminal US." But the next day, November 17, *Kayhan*

International quoted the prime minister as saying: "Washington is trying to resume relations with the powerful Iran in order to secure its interests in the region [...] because the Iraqi regime is now nearer than ever to the verge of collapse." Meanwhile, at the Majlis, eight deputies — including Seyyed Mohammad Khamene'i, brother of the then-President — presented on November 18 a motion questioning Foreign Minister Velayati on relations between Iran and the United States. The eight asserted that individuals outside the foreign ministry had both contacted and held talks with the Americans. And what, they asked, was the form of the United States delegation? The allegations of the eight were a serious blow to the regime's façade of unanimity. What had previously been nothing but journalists' rumours had now emerged on the floor of the legislature, where proceedings were broadcast live every day on state radio. Quick corrective action was needed. From his Niavaran residence Imam Khomeini lashed out at people who dared criticize officials of the Islamic government instead of the US "Black House." "Your tone in what you presented to the Majlis," he complained, "was harsher than that of Israel. What has made you become like that? I know some of you, and you weren't like that. You must not create division, as it is contrary to Islam, faith and justice." *Jomhouri Eslami*, in an editorial the same day, took a characteristically harsher line: "...some, who might be overlooking the 'blind spot' in which the US might place the country, or some, whom because of the damage they have suffered as a result of recent arrests, prefer to doubt the steps taken by the officials. [They] suggest that an act of treason has been committed. But more regrettable is the signing of a letter by eight Islamic Majlis deputies...." Predictably, the Imam's intervention, as befitted a *deus ex machina*, brought the incident to a rapid close. The chastened eight withdrew their motion and the controversy once again disappeared behind the curtain. But not for long.

The other shoe dropped on December 10, when Mehdi Hashemi's trial concluded. The defendant confessed on state television to all charges, agreeing with Imam Khomeini's description of him as a "deviated conspirator."[73] Hashemi admitted collaborating with SAVAK prior to the revolution, and later, as a member of the IRGC Command Council, to involvement in the theft of documents and munitions when the Liberation Movements' office was separated from the Revolutionary Guards. He also confessed to sowing discord under the guise of criticizing the government, and to opposing the political, economic and social policies of the theologians. The most politically explosive part of the confession came when he revealed how he had used Ayatollah Montazeri's office as a base for his actions, and admitted to abusing the designated successor's trust by feeding him information which reflected his own ideas about current issues. The office promptly issued a blanket denial. Though Montazeri could not publicly support his erstwhile protegé, he maintained up to the end that he should not be executed.[74]

(There was, of course, no public speculation on how the confession was obtained. Such matters are never discussed in public. But it reminded me of a press conference organized by the Islamic Guidance Ministry I once attended. On exhibit was a minor MKO official eager to announce his repentance. Though the man's face showed no traces of abuse it was puffy and wan. He was sweating profusely as he struggled to answer all questions properly, and his eyes had the blank, terrorized look of a tormented animal's. What had they done to break a hardened revolutionary like Mehdi Hashemi?)

His position buttressed by the guilty verdict and by Khomeini's timely silencing of the parliamentary opposition, Majlis Speaker Rafsanjani could now admit that Iran had, in fact, been purchasing US-made spare parts through brokers for the last five or six years. "Recently I learned these supplies came from US warehouses," he told the Majlis. "We did not know this." Iran, he revealed, had actually obtained US-manufactured F-4 and F-5 fighter aircraft, and would purchase arms from any source "except Israel." Ongoing contacts between the United States and Iran were useful, he said, but not at the top level. By then, however, the arms-for-hostages deal had been eclipsed, in Washington, by the scandal of the funds diversion to the Nicaraguan Contras. On the same day that the Iranian government, having either arrested or terrorized the internal opposition into silence, came out in favour of relations, the two countries met once again in Frankfurt. But now officials of the State Department and the CIA, and not Oliver North and his free-booters, met the Iranian delegation. It was to be the last such meeting between the two would-be partners.

On December 15, more details of Mehdi Hashemi's confession were released. A point had been overlooked in the television spectacular: He had also admitted to spreading "corrupt ideas" at the theological schools. Whatever public doubts may have remained about the motives for Hashemi's arrest vanished when Information Minister Reyshahri categorically denied any connection between the arrest and trial of Hashemi, the veiled but unmistakable public embarrassment of Ayatollah Montazeri, and the clandestine dealings between the

American and Iranian governments. When Mehdi Hashemi and two associates were executed in October, 1987, the issue had all but vanished as the United States, stung by the scandal, reversed itself and rallied to the side of Saddam Hussein. In May of that year, the USS Stark was attacked by Iraqi missiles. The incident was promptly labelled a "tragic mistake" by Washington. Within two months reflagging of Kuwaiti tankers by the United States began, and in September, American helicopters attacked an Iranian ship claimed to be laying mines in the Persian Gulf.

THE AMERICAN WEAPONS shipped to Iran from the summer of 1985 to the winter of 1986 had a dramatic effect on the Islamic Republic's ability to mount offensive operations, neutralize Iraq's superiority in tanks and lessen its earlier mastery of the skies. Even though North Korea, by 1986, supplied 70% of all Iranian military supplies, the battlefield impact of the TOW and HAWK missiles was particularly evident in the attacks which saw Iranian forces capture the Fao peninsula and break through the outer defensive lines of the besieged city of Basra. Emboldened by the newfound firepower of their military, the leadership once again began to talk of the final offensive, though carefully presenting it as a response to Iraqi aggression. "If Iranian forces should advance and seize Baghdad," declared President Khamene'i on November 18, "it would be a defensive measure."

The optimism of the clerical establishment masked a serious dilemma: the arrival of large quantities of American arms on the battle-front could not be concealed, nor could the rumours of secret dealings with the United States and Israel be stopped. The regime had concluded a Faustian bargain. In exchange for sophisticated, battlefield-effective weapons it had traded the zeal and death-defying courage of its revolutionary guards and highly motivated young *bassijis* (volunteers). To maintain their faith, the government had to maintain the fierce devotion that had brought down the Shah, staved off the Iraqi invasion and driven the aggressors out of Iran. The compromise with the West, however, undermined the identity of Iran's Islamic combatants as soldiers of God. By tampering with deeply held beliefs in the revolutionary virtues of self-reliance and self-sacrifice, the hierocracy created a crisis of credibility and sincerity which spread through the ranks faster than the whisper of defeat. Both the rank and file, as well as the religiously and ideologically committed front-line commanders were shocked and disoriented by the revelations. By dealing with Satan against the archfiend Saddam, the regime had, in effect, traded on the ideals of its most devoted followers. Doubt and uncertainty gradually eroded their convictions, and paralyzed their fighting spirit. Quite uncoincidently, Iranian mobilization problems began in late 1986 and increased through the following year. So powerful was the impact of the revelations on volunteers and conscripts that officials began to complain openly about the lessening popular fervour for war.[75]

IRAN'S RAPPROCHEMENT WITH THE GREAT SATAN touched off a rapid-fire succession of developments. The Islamic regime's hard-pressed armed forces' new-found fire-power briefly shifted the strategic balance in the Gulf War. At the same time morale, both on the battle front and on the home front was fatally undermined. The failure of Ronald Reagan's Iran initiative sent the United States hurrying back to embrace Saddam Hussein. The end was near. Throughout February and March, 1988, Tehran came under fierce attack from Iraqi Scud missiles whose range and accuracy had been upgraded by Soviet technicians. Tens of thousands fled, fearing that Iraq would use chemical warheads — a threat Iraqi leaders never attempted to temper. Then in April, in coordinated operations, the US navy destroyed Iran's Persian Gulf oil platforms of Sassan and Sirri, while Iraqi forces, using new and deadlier chemical weapons, drove demoralized Iranian troops from Fao. After another major reverse, in which Iran was driven from Iraqi territory around Shalamcheh, Hojjatoleslam Rafsanjani was appointed commander in chief of the Islamic Republic's armed forces on July 2. The move was followed by a string of retreats, withdrawals and defeats unprecedented since the early weeks of the war.

A month later, and only five days after the capture by Iraq of the Majnoun Islands, the Supreme War Council, meeting in Tehran, announced that the war would continue until Saddam's downfall. *Jomhouri Eslami*, in another of its long-winded denials, editorialized: "In the last couple of months the world oppression and its mercenaries, in a widespread psychological warfare, have been trying to pretend that the Islamic Republic of Iran has changed its mind as to continuing a war policy, has begun to lean toward diplomatic efforts only and has acceded to the fallacious argument that the war is at a military impasse and should be solved by a political settlement while the war front is forsaken...." The essence of the matter was exposed when President Khamene'i addressed the issue of low morale at the war front: "Part of the problem," he said, "also involves the home front. Don't assume that it cannot affect the war effort. I say a nation could leave adverse effects on the fronts by its disagreements, politickery, corruption, indulgence in luxury, individual affairs, profiteering and injustice." The president's picture of the home front, while unflattering, was devastatingly accurate. It had also come too late, less a warning than post-mortem.

On July 3, an Iran Air Airbus A-300 airliner carrying 298 passengers and crew was shot down by the USS Vincennes, a missile cruiser operating in Iranian territorial waters in the Strait of Hormuz. Flight 665 had taken off from Bandar Abbas on a scheduled flight to Dubai; there were no survivors. The next day, the official organ of the Islamic Republic Broadcasting service, *Soroush*, editorialized that "time is apparently running in Iraq's favour." *Jomhouri Eslami* struck back quickly, quoting Khomeini: "Today, doubt in any form is treason to Islam." And, as if to convince doubters, the General Command called for a general mobilization of all able-bodied civilians. Iranian ground forces, meanwhile, were withdrawing from Halabja, the town in Iraqi Kurdistan where Iraq had used combat chemical weapons against its own citizens, killing an estimated 5,000 non-combatants.

While Foreign Minister Velayati met United Nations Secretary General Perez de Cuellar in New York, *Jomhouri Eslami*, in its July 14 edition, trumpeted: "The enemy and its patrons have launched a war of adverse publicity to spread demoralization on the war and home fronts..." while *Kayhan International*, allowed that "developments in the past few months" — the downing of the Iran Air Airbus, Iraqi use of chemical weapons and Iran's military defeats — "have raised questions for the people which must be answered precisely and clearly." An answer of sorts came when Deputy Prime Minister Mo'ayyeri, commenting on "peace rumours rife in the country" declared: "Recent developments on the front have created ground for foreign radios to spread their venomous adverse publicity. That is why we tell our people that we are going to continue our holy defense until we have achieved justice. Under the present circumstances, peace will not lead to security...."

But Radio Tehran listeners were probably more interested in the news that a Canadian delegation led by Marc Brault had arrived on July 16, to "discuss normalization of relations and promotion of bilateral relations." And residents of the area around the president's office were undoubtedly more interested in the sudden quickening of activity as members of the Experts Assembly, the Constitution Protection Council and the Supreme Judicial Council met to discuss what were described as "important issues."

One day later the war was over. Iran announced its decision to accept United Nations Resolution 598. The General Command Headquarters, which barely two weeks earlier had called for all-out mobilization, declared: "Today, new conditions have emerged and the continuation of the holy defense and efforts to protect Islam and the Islamic Republic call for adopting a new stand." The communiqué went on to describe the silence of the international community in the face of "extensive and unprecedented development of chemical weapons." Hashemi Rafsanjani, speaking to a press conference the next day, confirmed by rejecting rumours that Iran's withdrawal from Fao and Halabcheh had been, in fact, part of the agreement. "These are the absurd words of the counter-revolution. There is no semblance of weakness or incompetence in our position." Iran's acceptance of the Resolution was in the best interest of Islam, he said. There remained only one voice unheard — that of Khomeini himself. On July 20, he spoke:

> About the acceptance of the resolution — which indeed was a very bitter and distasteful thing for everyone, and especially for myself — until a few days ago I believed that very policy of defence and stands already declared. [...] I was considering the interest of the system, the country and the revolution.... But because of developments and factors which I am not going to discuss here — and with the hope in God will become clear in the future — and in view of the opinion of all the high-ranking political and military experts of the country whose dedication and care and sincerity I trust, I agreed to the acceptance of the resolution and cease-fire. [...]
>
> Blessed is the nation. Blessed are the women and men. Blessed are the disabled and the prisoners of war and the missing-in-action and the great families of the martyrs. And woe is me upon who still remains, has drunk the hemlock of acceptance of the resolution and feel shameful before the greatness and selflessness of this great nation.... I repeat that for me the acceptance of this is more lethal than poison. But I am satisfied with God's satisfaction. And I drunk this hemlock for his satisfaction.

So spoke Khomeini. The Socratic metaphor was well-chosen: The hemlock-bearers — Iran's real rulers — had shunted the Imam aside. Now they were free to turn against their final adversary: Montazeri.

FEBRUARY 11, 1989: the tenth anniversary of the Islamic Revolution. Under a lowering grey sky, millions thronged the streets of Tehran leading to Azadi (Freedom) Square, as air force helicopters showered them with flowers and pedlars did a brisk business hawking hot steamed sugar beets, Islamic trinkets and revolutionary memorabilia. Along with the usual "Death to the United States" and "Down with Israel" placards, marchers carried printed signs calling for harsh measures against drug dealers as the war against Iraq was supplanted by the war against drugs. Highlight of the ceremony was a long speech by President Khamene'i, who cautioned that reconstruction of the country would take at least a decade, and strongly denied what he called "foreign-propagated rumours" of bitter conflict within the hierocracy. "Human beings always have different tastes," he told the crowd. "But there is no such thing as a power struggle in Iran." As usual, the stronger and more high-level the denial, the better-founded the rumour.

That same day in dreary Qom, Ayatollah Montazeri was speaking on the same subject to a group of visitors. His tone was starkly at odds with the bombastic excess of the official celebration. It also gave the lie to President Khamene'i's assurances of unity. The Islamic revolution, he said, belonged to every Iranian; it was not enough "to come together and praise one another and deliver speeches declaiming this and that as our feats and accomplishments and thus pretend to fool ourselves. We cannot, however, deceive the world."

There was more:

> We ought to calculate our invaluable losses of manpower, of towns and cities destroyed, and see if we have erred. If we have, we can atone for them and, at least, prevent their recurrence. We must realize that we have voiced slogans, many of which have contributed to our isolation in the world; slogans for which there were wiser ways, but we closed our eyes and ears and cried: "It is as we say!", and later found out we were wrong. We must understand our mistakes and admit our errors before God and the nation.

"Our society" continued Montazeri, "should be maintained as a free society open to all people for criticism and comment. People should be able to speak up via the mass media of communication. [...] The newspapers should not be the monopoly of a few individuals to censor things things as they please. When we get to the point where they censor the words of a theological student such as myself, who has been in and for the revolution all along, you can imagine what treatment is meted out to the words of others."

In a detailed interview published the same week, Montazeri addressed an even more sensitive issue, and in so doing, did the unthinkable: criticize the small group who now surrounded and controlled Khomeini. The leader must, Montazeri argued, refer to and obtain the views of specialists on all issues, since the issues themselves are so diverse and complex. But, he added, this can only come about if specialists are guaranteed the freedom to express their ideas candidly. "Such expressed views or opinions are then to be relayed to the *faqih*, enabling him to arrive at sound views about issues by considering all the comments made available to him. Otherwise, there will be a danger of committing errors, of being removed from the realities of the society, thus inflicting losses on the people and generating pessimism toward Islam and the clergy."

Khomeini, terminally ill by now and isolated from all but a few advisors who could be relied upon to provide suitable information, would have none of it. Two weeks later, in a message to the nation, the Imam aggressively defended his policies over the previous decade. "The Iranian people," he thundered, "succeeded in fulfilling most of their slogans. We practically observed the slogan of the Shah's fall, we trimmed with our action the slogan of freedom and independence, we watched the slogan of 'Death to America' in the action of enthusiastic, heroic and Muslim youths when capturing America's den of corruption and espionage. We have accomplished all our slogans." He lashed out at critics of the war, accusing with "narrow-mindedness" those who assumed that because Iran did not reach its ultimate goal of the war fronts, martyrdom, bravery, self-sacrifice and devotion were all of no significance. "I formally apologize to mothers, fathers, sisters, brothers, wives and children of martyrs and disabled combatants for such wrong analyses made nowadays."

One month later, Ayatollah Montazeri's photograph disappeared overnight from all public buildings. Few Iranians, ears attuned to the high-pitched whine of rumour, were taken aback. The power struggle which President Khamene'i had publicly denied in his tenth anniversary address had claimed its most important victim.

MONTAZERI'S ADVERSARIES RULE Iran today, asserts Hassan N., a life-long supporter of the disgraced Ayatollah. He is convinced that President Rafsanjani, Seyyed Ahmad Khomeini, son of the Imam and self-appointed guardian of Khomeinite orthodoxy, and, through his "positive silence," the current *faqih* Ayatollah Khamene'i — the three dominant members of the country's power club — coalesced against him. And, he adds, they were joined by a close ally of Ahmad Khomeini, Information Minister Mohammad Reyshahri, who had become the key channel for secret information designed to convince the Imam that, by his constant criticism, Montazeri was weakening the Islamic Republic. There was also another factor, added Hassan N.: the leader-designate's oft-repeated, public insistence that post-war reconstruction should begin at the highest levels of society — meaning those who held power and made wrong decisions. These people, Montazeri said, should either be reconstructed or set aside. Clearly the intractable Ayatollah had not changed his mind, nor was he likely to do so.

The rapprochement with the United States could not have come about without the support of then-Speaker Rafsanjani, Hassan N. said. It coincided with the American desire to approach Iran, and much more than hostages were at stake. "The Americans wanted to see Iran cave in in the face of pressure, and so to penetrate our society. If they could do that, they could denigrate the Islamic movement, show that not only can such movements not succeed, but that they can be corrupted. What better a way to put an end to Islamic 'fundamentalism'? Ultimately the price of the deal was the elimination by Iran of radical elements."

Imam Khomeini's role was to protect the achievements of the Islamic Republic, he explained. As designated successor, Montazeri was to preserve our society for the future. But Khomeini had become his son's "captive," and was being fed fabricated information designed to show that Montazeri was connected with the outlaw MKO, and thus "in rebellion" against the Islamic state itself. "The Ayatollah knew this was going on, and complained to Khomeini. He was also well aware of the maltreatment of prisoners, because they knew they could turn to him for a fair hearing, and for redress. This is what led him to claim that the information ministry had become worse than SAVAK — which is true."

Another source in Tehran confirmed this view. Though this man, whom I shall call Reza, a policy analyst at a government research institute, does not share the visceral anti-Americanism of radicals like Hassan N., his political career has been in limbo since he made public statements of support for Ayatollah Montazeri. Prior to the Ayatollah's dismissal, explained Reza, he regularly discussed the problems of government with Khomeini, and suggested the Imam obtain first-hand information. Khomeini asked his successor-designate to report, which he did. But the reports were, in Khomeini's eyes, negative. "However," he continued, "they were factual and true. The Information Minister, Mohammad Reyshahri, was able to use the Mehdi Hashemi connection for political leverage. Khomeini was led to conclude that Montazeri was behaving irresponsibly, that he had been surrounded by negative elements."

It was elaborately staged theatre, snorted my informant Hassan N. A "peace meeting" was set up, he said, at which the Imam recommended to Montazeri not to let "liberals and counter-revolutionaries" approach him. Montazeri agreed, but protested he had never done any such thing in the first place. Meanwhile, Reyshahri had already provided Khomeini with the necessary disinformation to link the successor with such people. In his memoirs, the former information minister himself attributes the matter to an anonymous telephone tip.

Montazeri's resignation took the form of a response to a letter from Khomeini. In it the former successor asked to be allowed to teach "as in the past, as a small, humble seminarist at this [Qom] school and be engaged in scientific activities, and serving Islam and the revolution" and called on his supporters to take no action, not even to raise their voices, in his support. The Imam's acceptance termed Montazeri the "fruit of my life" but warned: "In order that past mistakes are not repeated, I advise you to purge your household of dishonest persons and seriously prevent the comings and goings of the opponents of the system who pass themselves off as being interested in Islam and the Islamic Republic. I did give you this advice in the case of Mehdi Hashemi."

The Tehran dailies were quick to pick up on the point. In its March 30 editorial *Kayhan* pinpointed Montazeri's tolerance of Hashemi as the underlying reason for his downfall. The conservative *Abrar* on April 5 concluded that the deputy leader could be too easily influenced, and claimed that the Mehdi Hashemi group was prepared to murder Montazeri himself when and if necessary. Few, if any, could believe the assertion, particularly since the Hashemi incident had shown that the country's highest-ranking leaders themselves were prepared to eliminate people who disagreed with them "when and if necessary." But the issue continued to dog the footsteps of government officials, who were repeatedly forced to spell out to inquisitive student groups the precise nature of the crimes committed by the "counter-revolutionaries."

THE OUSTER OF MONTAZERI continues to haunt Iran's rulers. One of the lessons of the affair, observed Hassan N., is the inherent weakness of the pragmatic policies of the clergy and their readiness to compromise with power at the expense of righteousness and justice. "When, overnight, Montazeri fell, his admirers suddenly became his accusers. The whole story taught ordinary people that their leaders may be fine talkers, but that they had been utterly corrupted by power, and in a very short time at that. They had lost whatever interest they had in establishing justice and defending the rights of the people. It was a costly experience for the clerical establishment. After it, they were broken, but it was the result of their own behaviour. Their true nature stood revealed for all to see."

"The effect of [his] dismissal was devastating," concurs Reza. "Not only did it demoralize clergymen and *bassijis* in Iran. It had an impact in other Islamic countries as well." This may well have been the part of the grand design of the moderate clerics who now manage the Khomeini legacy. Montazeri was a maverick, a man who fit neatly into no categories, whose only badge was his honesty. My friend Mohammad Ja'far put it more bluntly: "People couldn't tolerate Montazeri because he criticized the *mollahs* and the *mollahs* have tried to give the impression that they are above criticism. In fact, they not only try to give you that impression but they've taken it for granted. If you criticize them, you pay a price. And if you're a public figure, if you criticize, on that day your career ends. So somehow Montazeri got on the wrong side of things, got on the wrong side of people. He had to go."

Ali Akbar Hashemi Rafsanjani in his office while in the position of Speaker of the Majlis.
Photo © Michael Coyne / The Image Bank.

9

More than the Price
of Watermelons

IN THE LATE DUSK I can barely make out the cluster of thatch-roofed, mud-brick houses nestled on a terraced platform at the foot of the stony hillside. Rain falls infrequently in these deep-cut valleys cut off from the moist air of the Caspian by the jagged peaks of the Gilan mountains, and when it does the water rushes in a roiling, mud-filled flood into the Shahrud. Centuries of overgrazing have stripped the hillsides bare of undergrowth, leaving only clumps of scrawny poplars, thorn-bushes and thistles. The landscape is elemental, brutal, unforgiving.

As we clamber from the Toyota four-wheel drive onto the hard-packed soil the villagers come out to meet us. The little girls shelter coyly behind their mothers' skirts; the boys, shaved heads gleaming like billiard balls, stare at us with wide-eyed defiance. What manner of unlikely motorized visitors must these be, I imagine them wondering. But my pastoral musings are several years out of date. Though no electric lines lead to these primitive dwellings, they have already been visited by modernity. Kanishdou, the name of this place, is the site of a rural recon-struction mini-project, the kind of initiative which has made the Reconstruction Crusade, the *Jihad-e Sazandegui*, Iran's most— some say only — successful post-revolutionary organization.

As demonstration projects go, the cistern at Kanishdou is the soul of modesty. There are no local officials to meet us, no engineers, no del-egations of model peasants, no toasts or speeches. This is the antithesis of the kind of rural development that, in the once-socialist countries, was usually accomplished by forced labour, perhaps by reeducated city folk or anti-social elements. There are no terraced fields at Kanishdou, no irrigation ditches.

Declining an invitation to take tea — darkness is coming on fast — we walk quickly around behind the houses and up a short path. Here is what we have come to see: a humble, leaky cistern roughly built of split rock held together by straw-reinforced mortar. Water is trickling melodiously into the cement-lined tank from a small pipe which seems to emerge from the depths of the hillside. Tufts of green grass have sprouted around the base of the cistern walls; over the tinkling of water we hear the whine of mosquitoes. "This is one of the small springs we build in the high mountains," my guide Mr. Mahmoud-Nejad tells me. "It can keep five families in this valley. They can continue their agricul-ture, and not leave the land like the others who left and went to the big cities. This place is called Kanishdou, here in the Loushan district of Gilan province."

For Westerners *jihad* is synonymous with "Holy War," and its shop-worn images of scimitar-wielding desert horsemen or, latterly, "Arab terrorists," the kind of people broadly defined as anyone bold enough to challenge Western interests or, graver still, Israel. By linking the concept of *jihad* to rural reconstruction, Iran's religious revolutionaries were re-investing it with its wider, deeper sense: that of endeavour and sacrifice for the cause of Allah.[76]

Mr. Mahmoud-Nejad, a middle-aged gentleman with the devout Shi'ite's five-day stubble and a courtly, punctilious manner, is a walking compendium of *Jihad* facts and figures, stories and anecdotes, and a source of information and insight I found to be both evenhanded and compassionate. After graduating from Tehran University in English Literature, he worked with Iran's nomadic tribespeople as a United Nations specialist until 1979, when the revolutionary torrent swept him into the world of rural reconstruction. When not in the field surveying projects, he shares office space atop the organization's dusty, echoing Tehran headquarters building — a requisitioned, reconverted hotel —

with five colleagues, bookcases full of documents, a tattered National Geographic world map, and a hectoring, wild-eyed Iraqi deserter named Adib whose precise function I could never determine. Mr. Mahmoud-Nejad seemed helpless to stop the Iraqi from breaking into one of his virulent anti-West tirades whenever I would appear. He would gaze mournfully at his thumbs, or out the window across the rooftops toward the mountains, while Adib ranted and enjoined me with a pointing finger to convey messages of truth about perfidious Saddam Hussein and his backers to the people of Canada and America. Eventually, though, the outburst would run its course. I promised to convey the message, the Iraqi would drift off mumbling, tugging at his *tasbi*, and we would return to our discussion.

Keeping people on the land was the main objective of the *Jihad*, he explained when we first met on a tour of water control projects near Tehran in 1986. The Shah's "White revolution," launched in the early 1960s, had been trumpeted as an ambitious land reform program. The reform, ostensibly intended to break up the great estates and distribute land to the peasants, had the effect of accelerating migration from the rural areas. Peasants, their holdings often too small to be viable, sold their land to Iranian or foreign agribusiness conglomerates and fled to the cities. By the early 1970s, the government estimated that more than half the population of Tehran was made up of landless peasants and farm labourers. As agricultural prices plummeted, as markets dried up during the economic upheavals brought on by revolution and war, the constant bleeding of internal migration became a hemorrhage.

The *Jihad* was founded in June, 1979, by a coalition of idealistic young professionals and students eager to place their skills and knowledge at the service of their countrymen. It quickly caught the attention of Imam Khomeini, whose endorsement sent enrollment soaring. The *Jihad* would attempt to revitalize the rural economy, and in the process develop a model for rural development applicable in Third World countries like Tanzania and Burkina Faso, places so destitute that even this impoverished village in the Gilan mountains seemed rich by comparison.

Welcome to Kanishdou, the poorest, most desolate and isolated place I have ever seen. We'd come here as the last leg of a whirlwind tour of *Jihad* projects in the countryside 200 kilometres west of Tehran. Earlier in the day we had inspected a road-building project near Takestan, a region famous for its grapes. Earth-movers roared back and forth and dump trucks pirouetted in ponderous ballet as what seemed like the entire adolescent male population of the village looked on. The idea, we learned, was to widen the roads so that farmers could park their pick-ups and farm machinery inside their compounds, in town. Progress, here in the countryside, was driven by cheap and abundant gasoline.

Then we watched dump-trucks loading grain at an elevator which had been abandoned by its Soviet builders halfway through construction in 1979, and completed by the *Jihad's* own technicians only seven years later. It was an enormous structure, rising out of the flat fields against a slate blue overcast sky like some prehistoric megalith.

As the day progressed we'd fallen ever further behind schedule. There were the inevitable invitations for tea with village elders in Takestan, a brief stop at a local mosque for Mr. Mahmoud-Nejad and the driver to say their midday prayers, and then, as the sun began to dis-appear behind the craggy peaks, a heart-stopping slalom down the main highway toward the city of Rasht. Our *Jihad* driver was a craggy-faced man with an immense hawk nose called Ali. Like all Iranian drivers — or so it seemed at the time — Ali was more skillful with steering wheel, accelerator and horn than with brakes. He also had an insatiable appetite, or perhaps the disregard of the frustrated would-be martyr, for danger. Now he was threading the Toyota at full bore through a living obstacle course of cows and donkeys meandering down the middle of the road, in supreme indifference to the traffic roaring around them. (Months later, I learned that this particular stretch of the Rasht road was known as a kind of *kebab* alley. Animals struck down by passing vehicles are quickly scooped up by the drivers, hacked into serviceable chunks for sale at urban meat markets — no questions asked about its *hallal* qualities.)

As we swept into an uphill blind curve, jagged cliff walls on one side and a precipice on the other, we came up behind a heavily-laden transport truck. The greasy diesel fumes belching from its exhaust pipe obscured most of the road. Without an instant's hesitation, Ali swung the Toyota out into the oncoming traffic lane to pass. Suddenly looming out of the smoke appeared an oncoming truck heading straight for us. I clutched the seat back in front of me and shouted in horror. Certain death, with the face of a three-tipped Mercedes Benz star and two squinting headlights, stared us in the face. At the last possible instant, with a wrench of the wheel, Ali yanked us out of the path of the oncoming behemoth. I watched, shaken, as battered fenders roared by at eye level centimetres away, while its horn blast wailed mournfully, the sudden pitch drop of the Doppler effect echoing the mournful sinking of my stomach. Ali, never slowing, threw a glance over his shoulder, caught my eye and burst into laughter. A few moments later, when my thumping heart had subsided I apologized, through Mr. Mahmoud-

Nejad, for having impugned his qualities as a driver, for having demeaned an Iranian where it hurt most. Again he turned, and smiled a smile as sweet as jasmine. Mr. Mahmoud-Nejad, arm thrown casually over the seat back, was chuckling.

Below us, on the right, the Shahrud opens out into the Loushan valley, flowing wide, swift and shallow among gravel bars tufted with pale willow trunks. Hardly reducing speed, we swing left off the highway and careen up a steep, bumpy gravel road leading to a small windswept plateau. Ali pulls the Toyota to a skidding halt in a cloud of dust at a complex of low-lying buildings surrounded by a wire fence. "And this," Mr. Mahmoud-Nejad exclaims with a proud flourish, "is the Loushan Poultry Breeding Station." We clamber through a rough gateway and enter one of the buildings, where we are met by the fluttering and beating of 20,000 chicken wings, the cackling and crowing of 10,000 chickens and the pungent heat of the chickenhouse. "Our specialists are working on a native race of poultry which is very resistant to the climate of Iran's villages," he says. "Foreign breeds may produce more eggs, but they just can't survive in the Iranian climate. Now the *Jihad* runs stations like this all over Iran. We keep the birds for two months, then sell them to the villagers. These are, what do you call them? Ah yes, free-of-the-range birds."

After dusting the chicken feathers off our clothing, we climb back into the Toyota and head down the highway toward Kanishdou, our last destination. To get there, Ali veers off the pavement and, all four drive wheels churning, drives us lurching and plunging through the shallow riffles of the Shahrud. Two hours later, our visit to the cistern ended, we're on our way back toward Tehran, the car's knobbly tires whining on the pavement. Ali the driver, exhausted from his day behind the wheel, is crouched in the back seat, devouring chunks of boiled chicken wrapped in Iranian bread. Mr. Mahmoud-Nejad has taken over behind the wheel.

The *Jihad-e Sazandegui* was established to get around the bureaucracy and the bottlenecks of the traditional ministries left over from the old government, he tells me, as he squints into the oncoming headlights. "People from the ministries used to go to the villages with their noses in the air, and the villagers wouldn't listen to them. But since most of our young volunteers are from the villages themselves, they know how to communicate."

The *Jihad* promoted small-scale projects and micro-industries which would employ from eight to twelve people, and encourage self-sufficiency in rural areas. But the war all but destroyed these plans.

While about 10% of personnel in traditional ministries like agriculture went off to the front, more than 80% of all *jihadis* ended up fighting Iraq, either in the trenches or at the controls of a bulldozer. "We had to concentrate our reconstruction work in the war-affected areas first, but we can't stop village improvement and development," he says.

In Iran's hot, arid climate water means survival. One of the *Jihad's* proudest and least appreciated accomplishments was the revitalization of the ancient network of underground irrigation canals, called *qanats*, in many parts of the country. These canals were dug by traditional craftsmen operating by dead reckoning. Using a technology at least 2,000 years old, they link natural springs or melting snow in the mountains with settlements tens, even hundreds of kilometres away, with none of the evaporation losses common to open-air irrigation canals. When Genghis Khan's armies invaded Iran in 1218, they not only devastated great cities and replaced cultural monuments with pyramids of human skulls. The Mongol herdsmen who had, in the space of a generation, been transformed into hard-riding archers with a disdain for sedentary farming, destroyed the infrastructure of oasis agriculture, the *qanat* system. In most parts of Iran the subterranean channels were blocked or ripped open, leaving the desert to reconquer once green and cultivated fields and orchards. The technique of *qanat* construction did not die out, however. Indigenous craftsmen continued to burrow mole-like through the ground, while their assistants hauled buckets of damp clay to the surface at regular intervals to mark the path of the underground conduit. These round heaps of earth laid out along imaginary lines and visible from the air around any settlement, are the signature of *qanat* builders at work.

Considering the *Jihad-e Sazandegui's* bias in favour of small, locally-based projects, it comes as no surprise to hear Mr. Mahmoud-Nejad praise self-reliance. "I think we have about 45,000 personnel all over Iran, most of them young people. They used to come to Tehran and the other big cities but now they are working for their own families and villages and towns. We in the *Jihad-e Sazandegui* believe that all things could be done with the people of Iran. It all depends on the authorities of the country and the political point of view, of course. But for us, in *Jihad*, we believe we can do all of them ourselves, without any interfering by the foreign experts or foreign funds."

Islamic Iran's rulers, however, believed otherwise. A few months after my trip to the hinterland, the *Jihad* was incorporated into the agriculture ministry. The ministry's slickly landscaped, glass-clad high-rise headquarters overlooking Laleh Park stood in stark contrast to the revolutionary agency's grimy makeshift downtown offices. Several years before, Mr. Mahmoud-Nejad had warned me about the possibility. As a loyal civil servant, he didn't think comment was appropriate. But his skeptical look told me what his own feelings were.[77]

In one of those tragic metaphors which seem to haunt Iran's history, the administrative death of the *Jihad* was replicated by its physical destruction in those same craggy mountain valleys I had visited in November, 1990. Seven months later, in June 1991, a massive earthquake roared through the densely populated Loushan region. More than 50,000 died, hundreds of thousands were left homeless. The *Jihad's* micro-projects, the chicken-breeding stations and the up-country cisterns, the technicians and the peasant families, and the organization's hopes for revitalizing the rural economy, were forever obliterated beneath millions of tons of rock.

IN THE SUNLIT COURTYARD of the Modern Art Museum, classes of elementary school pupils wait their turn to visit an exhibition of children's book illustration. While they wait, they recite nursery rhymes in bright sing-song. Their teacher, a young woman in a light gray *chador*, has modified the refrain to throw in the word "potato." When they sing it, the kids squeal with mirth. The same day, a few streets over, on Enqelab Avenue, I spot intense Revolutionary Guardsmen with bristling beards, automatic rifles at the ready, supervising the unloading of sacks of potatoes at a government food distribution centre. Knots of curious pedestrians have quickly congregated on the sidewalk to watch, kibbitz and offer acid comments *sotto voce*. A few days earlier, my visit with a professor of economics is cut short when his wife rushes into his office. There are potatoes for sale at a neighbourhood fruit store, she blurts out breathlessly. "If we leave now, they may still have some left when we get there." Together they rush out the door, bidding me a hasty goodbye. Officials claim the potato shortage is the work of speculators holding back the precious tubers from the market until prices soar. The government, now in the hands of the technocrats, and the self-proclaimed free market moderates led by President Rafsanjani, are eager to take on the hoarders. But few Tehranis believe a word of the government's version; instead they mutter darkly about *mollah* connections and corruption. Besides, as a friend drily observed, if people could afford rice — the Iranian national staple — they wouldn't even have to buy potatoes as a substitute. It's December, 1989. Now that the bombs and missile attacks of the "War of the Cities" are over, the "War of the Potatoes" is on everyone's lips. The new war has immersed normally cautious citizens in a craze of potato hunting: even the blasé uptowners who never liked the real war, and even less the new regime, are caught up in tuber madness.

The potato crisis was the last gasp of Iran's brief experiment with a guided economy. The end was hastened by a quick-march Islamic pere-stroika (minus the glasnost) which wound up in unmethodical haste as the Soviet Union crumbled, then collapsed. The presence of a powerful neighbour to the north had once given the Islamic Republic, as it had so many non-aligned countries, a certain manoeuvrability in international affairs, and had lent some legitimacy to schemes for centrally planned development and government control of industry and trade. No more. Now, determined to avoid the fate of the former East Bloc satellite states (the sudden overthrow of Iran's erstwhile ally, Romanian dictator Nicolae Ceaucescu while on a state visit to Iran panicked government strategists), Tehran rapidly moved to reduce centralized planning, pro-claimed the virtues of the free market and sought the favours of the International Monetary Fund and the World Bank. The radicals fulmi-nated, but after twelve years of "war communism" Iranian style, they had been revealed as inept, not to say corrupt, managers, and worse, as poor politicians unable to rally a majority of the clerical establishment to their views. Imam Khomeini, the supreme arbiter between feuding factions, was no longer alive. Ayatollah Montazeri, no friend of econo-mic radicalism despite his anti-Western sympathies, was in disgrace. No one could stop Iran's inexorable and rapid drift toward the free market.

The revolution is not, Imam Khomeini used to say, about the price of watermelons. But even for the devout Muslims and Iranian patriots who fought at the Imam's behest, endured hardships, suffered indignities and who turned out in their millions to bury him, the price of water-melons did matter.

The imperial regime's development schemes — trickle-down eco-nomics with a vengeance — had accentuated disparities between city and country, and helped create both a nascent industrial working class and a much larger, rootless urban underclass which, were Marxism still credible, might be described as a reserve army of labour. As it turned out, they were a reserve army of the Islamic revolution. These were the *mostazafin* — the disinherited, the oppressed — in whose name the Islamic Revolution legitimized itself and who became its driving force. While Khomeini and the lesser leaders of the religious movement had defined the people's goals in primarily spiritual terms, there was never any doubt that revolution was also a worldly thing. It offered, as all revolutions must, the hope of escape from poverty and hopelessness not only in the hereafter but in the here-and-now. Governments, whether they are Islamic or not, must provide specific solutions to the specific problems of society, a friend told me. "In the early years of the revolution it was easy; we blamed everything on the Shah. But this had the effect of increasing expectations."

Expectations were fuelled by a powerful religious impulse which the conservative traditional *mollahs*, whom many Iranians regard as obscurantists, were reluctant to encourage. They met their match in Ali Shariati, the protean European-trained charismatic whose bold reinterpretation of Islamic doctrine brought Iran's intellectuals, high school and university students into the fray, and undermined the influence of the traditionalists. The *mostazafin*, proclaimed Shariati, would inherit the earth. Identifying himself with the nameless, faceless slaves who built the great monuments of human history, he wrote: "They rope us now like four-legged animals. They use us for gaining interest for themselves and have done so even before your time and your generation. We turn with our skin, flesh, blood, pain, bewilderment and deprivation against all of these powers whose essence is mechanization, the building of great palaces of the world, all this rich capital and wealth of production. Our value to them extends to our ability to work the next day."[78] The incendiary tone notwithstanding, Shariati was no Marxist. His social credo was drawn from the Islam of Imam Ali, which he presented as a challenge to all vested interests, a call to combat for the establishment of an equitable social system.

The first Imam, in a letter of instruction to his Egyptian lieutenant Malik al-Ashtar, had warned: "Let me remind you once again that your responsibility is to guard the rights of the poor and to look after their welfare. Fear God about their condition and your attitude toward them."[79] Allah, he wrote, has charged the sovereign and his officers with responsibility for their welfare — though neither he nor Shariati, who invokes Imam Ali's example thirteen centuries later, ever suggested that the ruler surrender sovereignty to the poor. He did proclaim that the poor, should their rights and welfare be neglected, remove the sovereign.

Shariati was not alone in his view of Shi'ite Islam as a radical social and economic order. Ayatollah Mahmoud Taleqani, a figure instrumental in breaking down the stereotype of the *mollah* as hidebound traditionalist, believed that by correctly interpreting, then applying Islamic rules, a harmonious society based on equality, social justice and fraternity would arise.[80] Shariati rehabilitated the *mostazafin* — whom orthodox Marxists had long dismissed as an urban mob for hire — and gave Iran's thirsting young intellectuals a counter-vision to the Shah's oil-bloated dream of pseudo-Western prosperity. Taleqani held out a vision of Islamic equality. Both men, however, died before the consolidation of power by the hierocracy, leaving their legacies to be defended by lesser minds or discredited by desperados like the MKO. Several of Shariati's books, particularly those critical of the clergy, are still banned in Iran. As the vision of a new Islamic social order has been superseded by the dogma of free market inevitability, the views of Shariati, the "Great Teacher," and "father" Taleqani, have been inexorably pushed to the fringes by the resurgence of the conservatives.

Islamic writ and law, when rigourously interpreted, can only only be interpreted as broadly capitalist in form. Islam, a religion of shopkeepers and traders, opposes economic abuse and outlaws interest but encourages well-gotten gain and productive self-enrichment. Power and wealth should be used as a means of securing the high and noble objectives of life, argue Ayatollahs Beheshti and Bahonar in their handbook on Islamic philosophy.[81] But the basic economic institutions approved by Islamic law, particularly those regarding the legitimacy of private ownership and the primacy of market transactions, leave little room for doubt. The influential *mollahs* of the Council of Guardians who systematically blocked land reform were as well-grounded in Islamic economics as Shariati and Taleqani. Perhaps more important, they had the ear and the support of the bazaar. In the mind of the ascetic Imam, the price of watermelons was beneath contempt. For his followers — and for his opponents — it furnished the most tangible daily evidence of the success, or failure, of the Islamic revolution.

IRAN SEETHES with private initiatives, currency speculation, smuggling, risk ventures, financial scams, family favouritism and insider trading, all pursued by fiercely competitive religious factions. The real business of Islamic Iran, to paraphrase Calvin Coolidge, is business — and most business in the country still gets done at the Tehran bazaar. The bazaar is more than a sprawling labyrinth of dark corridors lined with tens of thousands of shops; it is a state of mind and a social institution rolled into one. The bazaar, having bankrolled the victorious coalition of *mollahs*, is now pressing its claim to a share of the spoils. The Shah's ambitious, US-inspired program of top-down economic and political reform, the "White Revolution," was a dagger pointed at the bazaar's heart. Huge state-fostered conglomerates, supermarkets and Japanese-style combines were to take over from the bazaar's tradition of modesty, Islamic piety and deals sealed with a handshake.

Though the bazaar has regained some of its former health, it has come under criticism from the Islamic radicals, from a population increasingly impatient with the halting (not to say backward) pace of economic development and, paradoxically, from the efforts of its closest ally, President Rafsanjani, to haul Iran into the world marketplace. In the summer of 1991, a series of fires destroyed large sections of its labyrinthine central section. Although the authorities rejected suggestions of politically motivated arson, public opinion took undisguised glee in the discomfiture of the arrogant *bazaaris* who are viewed as greedy speculators grown fat on foreign exchange manipulation while an entire generation was making the ultimate sacrifice in defense of country and religion. Nonsense, said the realists: The fires were set by bankrupt merchants in order to collect insurance.

One cold day in January, 1993, just as an Iranian friend and I were about to abandon our search for a teahouse somewhere in the bowels of the bazaar, we heard cries of invitation. A door on the second floor had opened and a head popped out: "Come up and join us for tea." Squeezing between bales of merchandise we clamber up a dank staircase and into the minuscule office, where a samovar is steaming contentedly atop a portable kerosene heater. The shopkeeper, a certain Hushang, swears that he recognized my friend from high school. Wrong, in the event. But in the bazaar, on a frigid day, any excuse for hot tea and conversation will do, and we're soon sipping and chattering away.

Hushang, who is a wholesaler of cheap, locally-produced plastic toys, plies us with more tea, and information, solicited and not. We are particularly amused by his tale of Abbas Banki — Abbas the banker — a mysterious individual who, Hushang claims, appears on the sidewalk just outside the bazaar where most of Tehran's ambulant money changers ply their semi-legal trade. This Abbas strolls back and forth silently until mid-afternoon, at which point he announces the day's free market exchange rate in a loud voice, then disappears until the morrow. "No one knows where the rate comes from, but everybody believes it must be the Central Bank," he says. But the Central Bank is supposed to buy and sell foreign currency at the insanely low "official rate," we protest.

"You figure it out," he sighs. "This is Iran."

A few months later, the "official rate" was abolished. The rial became fully convertible. And Iranians faced another round of price increases. I never heard of Abbas Banki again; he may never have existed.

"THE CONTROLLED ECONOMY was not a product of the Islamic revolution, it's as simple as that." The man telling me this speaks with the urgency of ignored authority. Morteza Alviri is a former Majlis member and economist who manipulates the international techno-jargon of gross national products, exchange rates and deficits with quiet assurance. After being disbarred from standing for re-election because of deficient religious credentials (his transgression: defending the now non-person Ayatollah Montazeri from the rostrum of parliament), Mr. Alviri works as a deputy in one of Iran's key industrial ministries. We meet in his smartly revamped downtown Tehran offices one Thursday morning, the equivalent of Saturday in Iran. The office, tastefully done in green and white with Western-style cubicles, dividers and potted plants, is deserted except for the concierge, who brings us hot tea and replenishes the brimming bowl of fresh fruit. Crypto-socialist centralized planning never had the support of the religious establishment, he argues as I nibble on pistachios and sip tea while jotting down notes.

Iran's constitution specifies a free market economy, Mr. Alviri explains, but things didn't go exactly as planned. Just after the revolution the US Embassy hostage crisis broke out, leading to problems with the United States. The Iraqi invasion was not far behind. Iran could not pursue a reconstruction program at the same time its infrastructure was being destroyed. In the circumstances, there was no alternative but to adopt a state-run economy. During the war Imam Khomeini and then-Prime Minister Mousavi encountered sharp opposition to their emergency economic measures from men like Ayatollahs Yazdi and Qomi, elderly and influential conservatives who rallied much of the Qom-based clergy behind them. Only Khomeini's support for the policy allowed it to proceed, but it could not stop the passive resistance of the conservative *mollahs* or reign in the speculators. "This was not our first choice, but we were facing war and an economic embargo. Due to the scarcity we had to ration basic commodities like rice, sugar and cooking oil. As the war went on our GNP fell drastically. We admitted millions of refugees from Iraq and from Afghanistan, plus we had very high population growth of our own. The clergy encouraged people to have large families to support the war effort. We had no choice; we had to spend precious foreign exchange to buy arms on the world black market."

The state-run economy put decision-making power in the hands of officials, some of whom were only too human. The government took over production, distribution and sale of goods and services. Rationing led to hoarding; a black market thrived. Low civil service wages led to endemic corruption which the authorities seemed helpless to stop. "Doing business became a bureaucratic nightmare. We simply could not deal with the corruption," he admits.

As surely as the death of Imam Khomeini sealed the fate of Iran's short-lived flirtation with "Islamic socialism," the rise of Hashemi Rafsanjani to the presidency signalled the turn toward a free market economy. Predictably, adds Mr. Alviri, the move has been accompanied by a widening of the gap between rich and poor. During the war, inflation remained relatively low, at no more than 10 or 15% annually. But when hostilities ended it more than doubled, to around 30%. "Such a high rate of inflation is politically dangerous. The poorest 20% of the population — which was precisely the government's base of support — will be under extreme pressure. These are the same people who fought the Shah's regime, and in the war against Iraq. But we have no other choice."

In fairness, it must be admitted that the Islamic regime inherited a single-resource economic structure — the poisoned heritage of the Shah. Prior to the 1960s, oil had not been the major source of the country's income. The Iranian economy may have been underdeveloped, but it was diversified. As the Shah consolidated his rule following the overthrow of the Mossadegh government in 1953, oil revenues soared while other exports languished, then evaporated. As recently as 1959-60, more than 80% of Iran's exports were non-petroleum products. Two years later oil had risen to become the single, dominant item, accounting for 54% of exports. By 1978, the eve of the revolution, non-petroleum exports had fallen to a puny 3.8% of the total. Iran could neither choose nor set oil prices; this was done by the American and European companies, Mr. Alviri explains. "Our industrial and agricultural economy was destroyed. People from the rural areas flocked to the towns looking for oil-generated dollars. Our GNP may have been high, but it was entirely based on oil. The economy was a parasitical one. Take oil out of the equation and Iran would have been a very poor country."

In its forced march toward economic orthodoxy the Rafsanjani government has created another set of problems for Iran, Mr. Alviri continues. The country's financial reserves are wholly inadequate to the monumental task of reconstruction, which some observers estimate at more than $50 billion. Foreign borrowing has become inescapable. But funds from the International Monetary Fund and the World Bank are contingent on recipient countries applying what the borrowing agencies term structural readjustment measures. Iran, he suggests, will be unable to compete if it is forced to accept the tariff reduction regulations prescribed by international agencies. "Our technological level is too low, we have a serious unemployment problem. We cannot afford to lay off workers, nor can we compete with cheap, mass-produced imports. If we cannot use protective tariffs our factories will close." And while IMF policy would abolish consumer price supports, he adds, "it simply isn't possible for our country to allow the gap between rich and poor to grow any wider. Take bread; it's the basis of the Iranian diet. We cannot remove subsidies from bread prices."

A foretaste of what might happen if subsidies were removed came in the spring of 1992, when violent rioting swept several large cities. In Shiraz, Islamic Revolutionary Guards fired on protestors, killing several wheel-chair bound war veterans. In Mashhad, security forces remained on the sidelines as demonstrators burned government offices and briefly took over the city. Though the unrest was economically motivated it had a political dimension, Mr. Alviri warns. The topic is a sensitive one: economic criticism of the government is permitted. Political (and religious) objections, however, must be couched in exquisitely cautious tones. "If we tell people the truth, we will not be facing these difficulties. But if the political atmosphere is not suitable then we may find ourselves facing political unrest as well."

I'M SUCKING HALF A SWEET LEMON as I listen to Said Rajai'e Khorassani discourse on his country's economic problems. Iran as a state, he assures me, is still going through a trial period; it is therefore too soon to make a judgement. Of course our situation is imperfect, he says with his wide-eyed smile. "But, providing our theory is correct, it can be improved. My argument is not based on the achievements of my friends in office, but on principle. We should work out models which will widen our freedom. Currently we have too many limitations."

Is it possible, I enquire, that religion itself could become discredited by the economic and social failings of a government which so closely identifies itself with Islam? Now Dr. Rajai'e is not smiling: "Whatever our failings, they are certainly not a result of Islam. When we made the Islamic Revolution, our population was less than forty million; oil revenues were twice their current levels. Now our population is just under sixty million. Whether you pray or not, you're not going to get the dollars. The shortages we face are a result of insufficient resources, not ideology. Can anyone do better? Where are the claimants to alternate solutions? Bazargan had a golden opportunity, but failed as a result of his own inability. Mr. Mousavi, the former prime minister, with his centralized, socialist administration had ten years to test his ideas. He is a lovely man, but there was no miracle. Now another model is being tested, and it seems to be working slightly better."

"IT IS FAR WORSE THAN YOU can imagine," the stocky, intense man with the gruff yet suave manner and the booming voice blurts out as he gulps down a mouthful of boiled chicken. "The government cannot pay its bills. Oil revenue plus total export revenue from all other sources cannot make up the $18 billion shortfall. No wonder Iranian bank drafts and cheques are bouncing all over Europe." What am I to make of Sadeq Sami'i? Mr. Sami'i is a rarity in a country whose prim and proper national persona is assumed to reflect religious rectitude: an outspoken, even virulent critic of the regime; a man who walks the streets and listens to conversations in the bus queues, hobnobs with foreign diplomats and — the sceptre touch of media "credibility" — is frequently interviewed by the BBC. The Sami'i name still opens doors, I was told. The extended family was one of Iran's most powerful and influential during the Shah's regime, though its leading members kept a discreet critical distance between themselves and the monarch. Hardly surprising that he generates rumour as surely as a *mollah* generates sanctimoniousness.

Mr. Sami'i speaks with the brusquely self-assured tone of the man who knows. He is a master of the pithy quote, the kind that causes journalists to surrender their critical faculties at the door. Here, I find myself musing, is a man to dares to say aloud what everyone whispers behind closed doors: "These new breed Iranian capitalists are nothing but wheeler-dealers, commission agents, fast-buck artists. The people's purchasing power is low. Privatize heavy industry? Hah. The post-revolutionary organizations, the big foundations which manage confiscated property...they're nothing but machines for organized thievery. Are they going to let go?"

Our interview takes place over a low-fat lunch in the offices of Mr. Sami'i's thriving publishing house on a quiet side street just off Vali-ye Asr Avenue. Where, I wonder, does my charming host obtains his information. Government statistics are notoriously inaccurate, often cooked, say critics. The rate of suicide and emotional illness is soaring, he affirms, as he bites off a chunk of radish. People simply aren't coping.

But how can people who endured eight years of war, including missile attacks and chemical warfare, be suddenly so helpless? Could Sadeq Sami'i be part of a brilliantly crafted strategy to create the illusion of "dissidence" in a state which does not believe that a free market of ideas need accompany a free market of goods and services. Or is his frankness tolerated because he has the kind of connections and know-how which the *mollahs* lack and may find useful? Perhaps he is a kind of Manucher Ghorbanifar figure, feet firmly planted in all camps, existing in a kind of politico-economic-ideological free zone of his own. Rumours connect him with high-level banking circles, key regime figures whom he advises on economic and fiscal matters. Sounds plausible. Behind the curtain, as the Iranians say, everything is possible. The closer I approach the Islamic Republic, the more it resembles an immense hall of mirrors, something straight out of the final scene of Orson Welles' *The Lady from Shanghai*. Or perhaps a huge kaleidoscope of fragmented images forming, dissolving and reforming. Or the light reflected from the complex mirror-work of an Islamic shrine, as from a multifaceted prism.

The "golden revolution" — the phrase drips from Mr. Sami'i's tongue with honeyed rhetorical irony — is, he affirms, hardly more than a creation of the international oil market. What has happened to world oil prices since 1979-80? Answer: they've held steady at around $17 per barrel in constant dollars. Not coincidentally, the remaining world superpower is controlled by the very same two dozen or so leading families who, via their banks and interlocking directorates, run five of the "seven sisters." Jimmy Carter once said, he tells me between mouthfuls of cucumber and yogurt, that the United States could not sit by idly while a Middle Eastern Japan emerged under its very nose. "That was precisely the Shah's objective," he says. "The Shah, who created OPEC, always contended that oil should be treated as a commodity, like any finished manufactured product."

"Mind you, I wouldn't have believed a word of this five years ago," he says. (A few days later a high-ranking official of a conservative bent who works at a government-sponsored policy research institute told me, on condition his name not be used: "There is no doubt in my mind that the oil companies reaped enormous benefits from the Islamic revolution.") For those who lamented the demise of the Shah, the theory is an attractive one. Since the earliest days of the revolution, disgruntled monarchists have claimed that Khomeini was working, if not for the CIA, then for Britain's Intelligence Service — both agencies assumed, in the minds of some Iranians, to possess an almost supernatural knowledge of and influence over Iranian affairs.

Did the Shah seal his fate when he took the lead in raising world oil prices? A few weeks after my chat with Sadeq Sami'i, I asked Morteza Alviri the question. "I don't think the Shah was alone in raising prices. Oil company profits were quite low at the time," he said. "I think he had the support of the majors, even though Japan, and to a lesser extent Europe, were hard hit. As an economist I can tell you this: The Shah's policies destroyed the country. If we had continued at such a pace for another ten years, we would have had nothing left."

The seductive charm of conspiracy theories! How they flatter the powerful while consoling the weak, and mask the chaos of the universe beneath a crust of verisimilitude. In Iran, where all important decisions are arrived at far from the prying eyes and ears of the press and the view of the citizens, the idea that foreign intelligence services are powerful and influential enough to make and unmake governments still retains a certain justifiable currency. Many older Iranians can still recall the spectacle of wads of US cash being openly distributed by CIA operatives to anti-Mossadeq goons on the streets of Tehran in 1953.

A deep opinion shift may be underway, however. Even though the regime stills pays lip service to an incantatory anti-Americanism designed to mollify its radical wing, President Rafsanjani is known to favour reestablishment of relations with the Global Arrogance. A mid-rank official told me, speaking confidentially: "The fight against America should not be an obsession; I don't see American power and influence everywhere. Too many people in Iran blame all our problems on outsiders. But most of these problems are of our own making."

KAYHAN INSTITUTE, on a side street off Ferdowsi Avenue hard by the foreign ministry and only a few moments' fast walk from the Majlis, is home to Iran's largest media conglomerate, a stable of newspapers including the flagship daily *Kayhan*, with a 500,000 circulation and the "radical" English-language *Kayhan International*, weeklies in Farsi, Turkish and Urdu, and monthlies whose subjects range from women through sports to humour and satire. Islamic Iran's newspapers are owned and operated by financial groups with close ties to the country's dominant politico-religious factions, and express a limited range of opinion, running from the ultra-liberal supply-side pro-*bazaari* economics of *Etalaat* to the radical Islamic populism of *Salaam*, or the strictly news-oriented, boosterish four-colour *Hamshahri* (The Citizen) published by the Tehran mayor's office. Though officials assert there is no press censorship in Iran, events often have a curious way of going unreported — or of being alluded to only through official rebuttal of rumours. Reading the Iranian press can often be an exercise in textual exegesis, or more simply, an attempt to interpret an unwritten subtext. So when *Kayhan's* workers took labour action in July, 1992, the fact was ignored by everyone except spoilsport *Salaam*, which dispatched a reporter and a photographer.

The dispute, I learned from an inside source, turned on refusal by management to pay employees their customary year-end bonuses in the form of an "Azadi" gold coin. After several weeks of fruitless efforts to negotiate, the employees stopped work for the first time since the strike wave which sealed the fate of the Shah in 1978. Printers, pressmen and journalists congregated in the courtyard of the Institute building brandishing hastily produced placards and shouted slogans castigating management for its stinginess. Soon the demonstration was joined by the institute's contract employees, and production quickly ground to a halt. A rapid-fire exchange of proposals and counter-proposals quickly flared up into a demand by employees for a face-to-face meeting with management. When this was refused the crowd, now over a thousand strong, voted to march straight through Tehran's downtown core to present its grievances to the Leader, Ayatollah Khamene'i. Miraculously, noted my source with a touch of irony, the company changed its mind, agreed to direct talks with a large employees' delegation, and promised to pay the overdue bonus. While the protest appeared spontaneous, tradition may have played a role. *Kayhan*, the same source told me, had been a stronghold of the pro-Soviet Tudeh party until the organization was dissolved in 1983.

The one-day work stoppage had not fallen from the sky. It was, in fact, the first attempt by the Institute's newly-formed Islamic Labour Council to flex its muscles. The councils, which were set up shortly after the revolution to replace the country's conventional trade unions, were not formally established by law until 1985, while six more years of heated debate between radicals and moderates went by before a much-amended version of Iran's new Labour Code was finally approved in 1991. The legislation gave workers the right to elect their own representatives, explains Mohammad Bakhshali, General Director of Iran's Labour Council Federation, in an interview in his office on one of the upper floors of the labour ministry — a logical enough place for an organization which is less concerned with protecting the interests of workers than with reconciling labour and capital. The General Director's quarters are Spartan: a desk, a few filing cabinets and a large conference table. But the bowl of fruit and the plate of honeyed sweets on the table are staggering in their quantity and variety, despite the fact that our rendezvous had been arranged only earlier that day. Speaking through an Islamic Guidance interpreter, Mr. Bakhshali explains that the Federation's main responsibility is to help workers set up labour councils in factories and workshops. "Workers elect their own representatives, but they must register local chapter rules with us. Elections have to conform to national standards, and candidates have to meet the requirements of the law."

To be eligible for election, reads the act, workers must show "faith and practical allegiance to Islam and the Jurisprudential authority," while for members of the Jewish, Christian and Zoroastrian minorities, "loyalty to the Constitutional Law shall suffice." Candidates must also show an "absence of tendencies towards unlawful parties, organizations, groups" and demonstrate "probity, integrity and good moral reputation," provisions designed to weed out "sleepers" from organizations like the officially disbanded and outlawed Tudeh and the better entrenched terrorist opposition MKO. The councils handle grievances, deal with production problems and address health and safety issues. At the beginning, he says with a grin, they made life difficult for workers and employers alike. "Now everything is much clearer, for both sides."

Ideological restrictions notwithstanding, the labour councils are models of enlightened paternalism...on paper. Workers are required to sit on the employer's board of directors, something few Western trade unions have been able to achieve. What's more, failure to appoint a representative is a violation, Mr. Bakhshali adds. The councils are responsible for raising all work-related problems with management, and for finding solutions. Disputes are referred to a complex conciliation and arbitration mechanism. In the event one party does not accept the decision of the arbitrator, industrial action — though not specifically mentioned in the legislation — can occur. "We have three or four strikes a year," he admits when I press the issue. What was the longest strike? "Last year, in a textile mill, we had one that lasted four days. That was the longest. We also had work stoppages at an automobile assembly plant."

Minimum wages in Islamic Iran begin at 85,000 rials (less than $60) per month for married workers, 60,000 for single people [1993 figures]. But even though discrimination is prohibited by the Code, working women are ineligible for the dependent children premium, the reasoning being that men, as the sole support of their families, must assume the greater burden. It comes as no surprise to find that wages are the main source of disharmony. "Employers are reluctant to pay the workers what they want," says Mr. Bakhshali, in a concise masterwork of understatement. What he does not, and cannot, say is that statutory minimum wage levels are absolutely inadequate to the basic needs of a family, and that even the wages of skilled workers have not kept pace with Iran's soaring inflation rates.

Government workers, those long-suffering beasts of burden who keep the Islamic regime afloat, are not protected by the Labour Councils Act. As in many Middle Eastern countries, the Iranian civil service has long acted as a surplus labour sponge, absorbing dangerously high unemployment in the major cities and creating spin-off opportunities for political favouritism and corruption. Public sector wages are so low — well below those of industrial workers — that civil servants are obliged to hold second or even third jobs to make ends meet. (One of my most edifying insights into wage structures in the Islamic Republic was a cross-town journey in a taxi driven by a courteous, articulate active-duty colonel in the Iranian army, double moonlighting in order to feed his family.)

Though the government brooks no challenge to its control of the streets, in 1991 teachers in the provincial towns of Yazd, Oroumieh and Kashan took to the streets, pockets turned inside out, chanting slogans comparing recent pay increases for the military with their own wages, unchanged since the 1979 revolution. Some carried hand-lettered signs quoting Imam Khomeini's admonition that the work of teachers is comparable to that of the Prophet of Islam. Shamed, the authorities relented and raised teachers' wages. But a teacher's monthly pay cheque still won't pay the rent.

MY FRIEND MR. JAMSHID is a capitalist. While many wealthy Iranians fled the country after the revolution, and while the Shah's cronies were expropriated, Mr. Jamshid stayed in Iran throughout the war. Today, dressed in a well-cut sports jacket and sporting a paisley print silk ascot, he radiates cautious optimism about the future. After years on the drawing board and in the slow-flowing bureaucratic pipeline, his crockery and glassware factory is scheduled to begin production by 1994. "If you compare our situation with four years ago, confidence is much better," he reassures me as we drive north through Tehran in his dark blue Cadillac on our way to lunch.

The automobile itself reflects a none-too-subtle shift in public attitudes. Assembled in Iran before the revolution, it fits in nicely with Tehran's wide, Los Angeles-style streets and expressways if less so with the city's infernal, fender-bending traffic. At the height of the revolutionary upheaval, when it was unhealthy to be seen on the streets in a Cadillac, my friend drove his wife's Saipa. Now, as deference to wealth has reasserted itself, possession of a luxury vehicle — and an American one at that — may even spare its driver the indignity of a traffic ticket in the no-go zone of the city centre.

The labour councils had to be "reigned in," he explains as we float through traffic as though in an air-tight bubble. They were too often able to thwart with impunity any management decision while imposing strict "Islamic" standards on workers, including compulsory prayers at lunch break, and there were stiff penalties for non-attendance. "As far as I know," he adds, with the merest hint of steely indignation ruffling his cultivated surface, "these people were nothing but communists with a beard and a *tasbi*, pretending to be Muslims."

The restaurant, identified only by a discreet plaque on its massive wooden door, is located on the ground level shopping concourse of a new, high-rise apartment building north of Vanak Square. A group of prosperously dressed, impeccably made-up ladies, their heads barely covered, is chatting at one table, switching back and forth from English to Farsi; at another, a pair of British businessmen are discussing contracts and commissions with their Iranian hosts over substantial quantities of caviar. I order sautéed salmon, my host veal. While we wait, Mr. Jamshid and I talk politics. A supporter of former Prime Minister Bazargan, now he has nothing but praise for President Rafsanjani's decision to keep radicals out of the Majlis. If this leads to uniformity of views, so be it

With a flourish, the waiter wheels up the serving cart, lifts the silver plate covers and sets our plates in front of us: the salmon is appealingly presented in the continental manner, with crisp-tender vegetables and fragrant roast potatoes on the side. We are in another culinary universe, leagues away from the hubbub of the cavernous *kebabi* houses of the bazaar. Between mouthfuls — the food is delicious, and leads to thoughts of forbidden beverages — we continue our conversation. The focus, Mr. Jamshid insists, must be on creating a climate appropriate for industrial development. Iran cannot afford the luxury of high wages, social programs or competing political parties. A firm hand is necessary to guide the country out of the wilderness of economic distress. "Once we've settled the basic question of building up our country and strengthening our industry, then we'll be able to afford the luxury of conflicting political parties and parliamentary debate."

THE JANUARY SUN IS RISING FAINTLY over the Alborz range as I settle in across from Dr. Habib Chini at the conference table in his twelfth-floor office at the Iran Chamber of Commerce. There is a faint symbolism in the location of the building: It overlooks the huge downtown compound of the former United States Embassy — the "nest of spies" whose capture in November, 1979, enabled the radical clergy to tighten its grip on the Iranian revolution and eventually bring down the Bazargan provisional government. These thoughts are running through my mind as I listen to Dr. Chini, a veteran journalist who edited the financial pages of *Kayhan* before the revolution. Now, as director of the Chamber of Commerce's Economic Research and Analysis Centre, he finds himself thrust into a certain prominence at the leading edge of the country's brave new turn toward economic reform.

The background, according to Dr. Chini, is this. It is hard to exaggerate Iran's hardships: a four-month general strike prior to the revolution; a year of violence and extreme social unrest followed by eight years of war and sacrifice; a generation which should have been producers transformed into consumers of military goods. Small wonder that a powerful thirst for relief arose, especially among the country's young people. But by war's end stocks of raw materials and basic commodities were all but exhausted; the government was forced to import massively. All the while, Iran was undergoing a net outflow of capital and manpower. An estimated four million Iranians — almost 10% of the pre-war population — departed, causing some cynics to remark that Iranians had become the country's most successful export commodity. Over the same period, oil prices plummeted from almost $50 to less than $20 per barrel. Iran was broke. The government had no choice but to abandon its role as sole producer and importer, and open up to the private sector, a "positive development which, luckily, did not come about too late."

Dr. Chini is convinced that the election of Hashemi Rafsanjani as president helped, perhaps saved, the nation. Had Prime Minister Mousavi remained in power, the outcome would have been, he says, "dismal." Since then, improvement has been steady; annual growth rates are hovering in the 8-9% range. "Iran's gross national product increased by 11% in real terms for 1990-91, in comparison with a target of 8%," he says. Iran sold its oil for an average price of $16.10 per barrel, "which seems low, but for us, given our production costs, was a good price."

Changes over the last years have been rapid, he explains. As an institution, the bazaar has gained from the revolution. In 1991, $28 billion worth of commodities were imported. Exports have also increased, with the bazaar as the principal beneficiary. Export traffic for the same year was $23 billion, giving a deficit of $5 billion. Despite what Dr. Chini terms "encouraging" economic indicators, the pace of privatization has not been as rapid as it should be. The reluctance of government-appointed managers to forego the attractions of managing without the accompanying responsibilities is, he says, understandable. Still, business is doing well, and expanding. Many previous government managers have become entrepreneurs and are prospering. Only the middle class has failed to grow and has, in fact, lost ground, its purchasing power suffering from inflation. Yet if Iran is to have a future as a prosperous country, it must have a stable middle class. Unlike any other religion, Islam, he notes, deeply emphasizes the importance of the middle class. Islam is against idleness; unproductive activity is discouraged, as is passive, non-productive investment. "These principles are all part of the bedrock of Islam. If they are respected, a middle class will emerge."

IRAN'S PROBLEM IS THAT the principles of Islam have been ignored. Worse, they have been violated. The charge comes from Hossein Raghfar, a specialist in political economy who has devoted the better part of the last decade to drawing connections between the corpus of Islamic thought and modern economic concepts in the search for a balance between social and economic justice and freedom. Mr. Raghfar is more than an academic looking down from his ivory tower; he is a combatant in the political struggle which pits the neo-conservatives of the Rafsanjani government, the Central Bank and the Budget and Plan Organization against the unsteady coalition of radicals who favour an interventionist economic model focused on social needs. His views are those of a partisan and a participant; unfettered by the constraints of power, they offer a beguiling contrast to the nostrums of high government officials. Although most of our discussions take place in his office — a small room crammed with bookshelves and filing cabinets — they often overflow the standard interview format and end in an impassioned freewheeling monologue as, bent over the steering wheel of his Paykan careening through the darkened laneways of downtown Tehran, he lashes out at the high and mighty of the regime, vituperating them as callous and uncaring men who have turned their back on their ideals and on the people who supported them.

Far from drawing its inspiration from Islam, Mr. Raghfar contends, Iran's current economic strategy is based on the Holy Trinity of fundamentalist neo-conservatism: an open economy, monetarism and industrialization. The dogma holds that to function effectively, Iran must be integrated into the global economy, which in turn means foreign investment. The purpose of World Bank loans which, for the moment, are more symbolic than real, is to transmit a message of economic credibility to potential investors. Given Iran's political particularities, however, the president's economic advisors must implement International Monetary Fund and World Bank policy directives while at the same time denying they are doing so, he says. "In fact, no information regarding the amount of loans or guarantees has ever been made public and the officials involved are not available for interview."

Iran, he argues, is adopting radical privatization strategies similar to those applied in Chile and Argentina. In the process, no social or economic infrastructure is being created. Transfer of control and power from the state to the private sector is supposed to create greater efficiency. But when a society lacks human resources, how can such a transfer guarantee the interests of society as whole, let alone create greater efficiency? Because of the massive propaganda onslaught, people have become convinced that this course of action is inevitable. Inevitably, however, the combination of capitalist greed and absence of a social safety net will make people themselves the main victims.

The fundamental aims of the international financial institutions are political, he insists. They will stop at nothing to force the governments of developing countries to show "good faith" by changing the basic structures of their society — what they call structural adjustment. In fact, structural adjustment policies create the basis for, and the probability of, popular uprisings in response to deteriorating standards of living. When this happens, as it must, popular reaction is inevitably directed not against the international institutions, but against the local authorities who must manage crisis after crisis. This gives the great powers all the leverage they need to eliminate governments with which they are not satisfied. Governments in developing countries are left with two alternatives: Either use force against their own people, or give in to popular demand for democracy, more consumer goods and the Western life-style. "These were the mechanisms used in the overthrow of the governments of the former East Bloc. The strategy is to create divisions between the people and the political leadership by any means possible, and create new demands using the democracy virus. It has been effective because of their ability to control and shape perceptions, and to focus on dissatisfied elements in society."

Advanced communication technologies such as satellite television transmission have made it easier for the new world order to fuel local frustrations. And when citizens of a country such as Iran are frustrated and dissatisfied, they can be more easily induced to follow such a lead. Minor events can be transformed into major ones; people's perception of their role, even in events in which they themselves participated, can be changed.

The Rafsanjani government, Mr. Raghfar asserts, is trapped in an insoluble contradiction. It must strive to reduce international hostility toward the Islamic Republic by demonstrating goodwill and a willingness to accept the world order. Endorsement by international financial institutions depends, in turn, on the government's ability to guarantee a social and economic climate which can attract and hold foreign investment. But the structural adjustment policies the government must implement to create such a climate are pouring fuel onto the embers of popular unrest and indignation. The spring 1992 riots were a first indication: "And there will be more to come. People cannot tolerate pressure of this kind."

When, faced with mounting public frustration, the government uses force against its own citizens, the international information establishment will raise the spectre of human rights violations. When East Bloc governments tried to convince people that this was what was happening, they could not face, or handle, "human rights" propaganda. So the same authorities took a defensive position, changed hats, pretended to be liberals, democrats and nationalists, and opened negotiations with the dissatisfied elements in their own societies. Dictators were transformed almost overnight into liberals. "This is the process, the cycle of events," says Mr. Raghfar, "through which the attack against the Islamic Republic will be accelerated. If you examine things in this perspective, you can see that all the pieces are in place either for the overthrow of the regime or the disintegration of society. I believe application of these strategies will mean the end of the Islamic Republic."

Ex-American Embassy, Tehran. Photo © Michael Coyne / The Image Bank.

10

Requiem for a Radical

MEYDAN-E AZADI — FREEDOM SQUARE — SEPTEMBER, 1987.
Back in Shah time, atop the concrete triumphal arch, a colossal statue
of the Light of the Aryans gazed steely-eyed into the radiant future of
the Great Civilization. In the first days of the revolution spontaneous
demolition squads from the city's poor districts pulled it to the ground.
Shah raft, Imam amad — the Shah has gone, the Imam has come. Now,
at the foot of the truncated monument, the armed forces of the Islamic
Republic pass in review. Rifles shouldered and free arms swinging, soldiers, sailors and airmen, revolutionary guards and Islamic committeemen march in close ranks past a canopied reviewing stand. Heads
swivelling right as they stride by, they snap off salutes to an unlikely
group of elderly bearded Ayatollahs and younger Hojjatoleslams (including Majlis Speaker and President-to-be Hashemi Rafsanjani) sheltered
from the noonday sun. Only the uniformed officers seem at home, but
with their Islamic beards and open collars, even they lack the ominous
aura of Middle-Eastern military strongmen plotting pro-Western *coups
d'État* from behind mirrored sunglasses. Into earshot comes the sound of
martial music blaring in an intriguingly Oriental mode to the rattle of

snare drums, followed at close quarters by the marching musicians themselves. They are the spiritual heirs of a certain Monsieur Bousquet, the Frenchman who was lured to Iran in 1856 by Nasreddin Shah to initiate a generation of Iranians into the mysteries of the trumpet, clarinet and tuba, the trombone, flute and E-flat mellophone. Flags snap in rhythmic counterpoint.

A distant rumble. Flying low out of the west swoops the Iranian Air Force: troop carriers, cargo aircraft and, bringing up the rear, the country's few remaining operational American-made F-4 fighters. Why aren't they at the front? a Turkish journalist and I speculate. The war with Iraq may still be raging in the southern deserts and marshes and to the northwest, in the mountains and valleys of Kurdistan, but Iran has been reluctant to commit its precious handful of aircraft to battle operations where they would face deadly fire from Iraq's French- and Soviet-made anti-aircraft missiles. Before we can finish our count of the slow-flying planes — for all we know they have already circled around to overfly the reviewing stand twice — the rhythmic chuff-chuff-chuff of helicopter rotors drowns out our voices as a V-formation of choppers swings into view. As they pass overhead, they release what looks like confetti which, as it flutters to earth, turns out to be flowers. The helicopters have hardly disappeared before a flight of smaller reconnaissance craft drones over. Compact shapes fall free and plummet toward the ground until, suddenly, parachutes in red, green and white — the colours of the national flag — pop open. Manoeuvring skillfully, the parachutists are aiming for the crowd.

But there is no crowd. Behind the ranks of journalists, television crews and security men are a few sparse knots of curious bystanders, gangs of skinny gamins with close-cropped heads, and chador-clad ladies from the poor neighbourhoods to the south of the square, plastic shopping bags in hand. And open space, into which the parachutists glide. The solemn, euphonious voice of the Minister of Slogans booms out over the loudspeakers, but where the public's response is supposed to erupt into a unison roar there are only a few thin shouts, fading quickly to embarrassed silence mixed with the receding clash of cymbals.

The parade, which began at the far end of the square, dissolves just a few hundred metres past the reviewing stand, a media event staged by and for the authorities, self-contained, self-referential and for them, I assume, self-validating. My Turkish colleague, a reporter for an Islamic newspaper in Ankara, is muttering darkly about fascism and militarism. No, I argue. Army Day is an exercise in self-deception; a fiction, a fairy tale requiring suspension of disbelief: an Islamic reworking of the fable of the emperor's new clothes. Unlike the visiting and local journalists, the Iranian public has not agreed to join the charade although in its exquisite sensitivity, it avoids proclaiming the emperor's nakedness. Filling volunteer quotas for the front has become impossible. Young Iranians are fleeing the country. Martyrdom for the sacred cause of Islam is one thing; death as a bargaining chip another. By the fall of 1987, the prestige of the war effort, and of the Iranian military establishment, was sinking rapidly in the west.

ISLAMIC IRAN IS QUICKLY dismissed in our latitudes as a survival from the dark ages guided by obscurantist clerical relics. This description is a vulgar caricature, perfected by a generation of Western experts whose ignorance of Iranian religious specificity was matched only by their fealty to the Shah, that demented absolutist who cloaked himself in the patriotic garb of the reformer. As it swept away the Pahlavi regime, however, the religious class demonstrated its capacity for innovation, and its thoroughly modern grasp of the techniques of communicating with, stimulating and activating a mass audience. Khomeini's men and women had, in the years prior to the fall of the monarch, made brilliant use of audio cassettes with recorded sermons and exhortatory messages. These cassettes, which could be easily copied, hidden and transmitted, gave the revolutionaries a parallel system for the diffusion of news, inspiration and marching orders. Anonymous cassettes would appear mysteriously on rooftops or doorsteps overnight, with scribbled instructions to listen and pass on to a friend. Or handed along surreptitiously at the mosque, or from under the table at a bazaar stall.

The Islamic revolution became the first, and perhaps only, prime time social upheaval. Image followed striking image. Millions of demonstrators sweeping through the streets of Tehran were a nightly feature of televised news bulletins in Europe and North America in 1978 and 1979. When Islamic students who proclaimed their loyalty to Imam Khomeini seized the US Embassy, not unjustifiably describing it as a "nest of spies," frightened, blindfolded Americans with bowed heads paraded across the world's television screens. While the price of humiliated Yankees was American hostility, the benefit was a surge of pride among many Iranians and in the have-not world. Vicarious enjoyment at the spectacle of the puffed up bladders of the mighty being pricked by the lowly was intense and contagious, and transcended religious divisions and national boundaries.

Iran's cultural and media authorities were conscious of the impact of their methods against the Shah. They were also aware that the same tools might one day be turned against them. Given the proper selection of images, they reasoned, the social cohesion and sense of purpose which propelled the revolution could be carried over into the construction of the Islamic regime and the combat which now must be waged against its adversaries. If proper structures of control could be established, subversive, dissident or oppositionist voices could be stilled or muffled. If people did get out of line, charges of corruption on earth would be waiting, or perhaps a visit from representatives of the information ministry. Overly enterprising Iranian journalists might find themselves in jail, or sentenced to a lashing by zealous local officials. And the *Komiteh* was everywhere; vigilant, alert for any telltale signs. Wrong-thinking, even wrong-speaking, as long as they took place in private and in hushed tones, could be tolerated. Wrong-doing, however, could be dangerous to health. Often to life. More later. But first, this.

PIERRE NADEAU is one of the princes of the tiny kingdom of Québec television. A seasoned reporter become TV personality, Nadeau arrived in Tehran in the fall of 1987 to report for Radio-Canada's flagship French-language public affairs program *Le Point* with a travel bag full of preconceptions and a monumental case of ill-humour. Iranian visas remain valid only for a limited period after issue; when Mr. Nadeau arrived at Mehrabad airport his visa had expired. After more than twelve hours in the transit lounge, frenzied pleading by producer Jean-Claude Burger through the Danish Embassy which then represented Canadian interests, and my own efforts through Iranian official channels, Nadeau was finally released, fuming at the Iranians' for their *lèse-majesté*, into the greater maelstrom of wartime Tehran.

"Treat him with kid gloves, humour him; whatever you do, don't get into an argument," Burger pleaded with me before the great man arrived. But I'd hardly sat down to breakfast at Nadeau's table that morning before I caught a broadside of anti-Iranian bile. You wouldn't have known it by the convivial hum and clatter of the hotel restaurant, but tension was peaking. United States warships were cruising the Persian Gulf like drunken gunslingers itching for a shootout. There was ominous talk of Chinese-made Silkworm missiles in the Strait of Hormuz (sure it was the standard Yankee sabre-rattling based on the usual CIA information, but you never knew when these yahoos might start cutting loose). An Iranian ship allegedly laying mines had been attacked by US naval aircraft and was limping toward port. Was there a Persian Gulf-style Gulf of Tonkin incident brewing? Meanwhile, here sat Pierre Nadeau, unamused, straight from being inopportuned by the Iranian authorities, peremptorily declaiming the virtues of an American "surgical strike." Although he didn't say as much, what he really wanted was the scoop, complete with standup against the backdrop of a flaming city, of Yanks administering yet another iron-fisted — or was that ham-fisted? — lesson to terrorists.

(Countries, cities, wars, disasters and famines...all were inter-changeable backdrops for standups by the centurions of an imperial media establishment whose prime content is itself, for whom the event, whatever it may be, has all the veracity of a crudely painted carnival backdrop unrolled and tacked up for the occasion.)

The invasion never took place. Iran in 1987 was not Iraq five years later. Mr. Nadeau eventually did his standups on the roof of the hotel and in the squalor of south Tehran, where he was quickly surrounded by a small mob of youngsters who answered his questions about the war with chants of "Death to America" and "Khomeini is our leader." Four days later the star reporter had decamped, leaving the crew to mop up. By then the putative mine-layer had reached Bandar Abbas, and the injured captain and crew were being flown to Tehran for an official hero's welcome. The scene in the VIP lounge was a surrealist frenzy, with television cameramen hovering like praying mantises over groan-ing, bleeding men laid out in stretchers on the floor. The captain was hovering near the brink of martyrdom. Only the whites of his eyes were visible; but a German TV reporter insisted in pressing his point: "What about the mines, captain? Were you laying mines?" as if the man, despite the officials monitoring the scene, would somehow volunteer that Yes, he had been mining the Persian Gulf, single-handedly provoking the Global Arrogance. "Quick, you've got to stop this, they're killing him," I rasped to a passing foreign ministry official. The man, Deputy Minister Hossein Sheikholeslam, the senior foreign ministry officer present, waded into the fray and brought the macabre interview to a halt.

Unsurprisingly, the news business attracts its share of ghouls, and more than its share of prima donnas, whose haughtiness stands in direct proportion to their expense accounts. Official press conferences in Tehran were held at the Majlis under tight security. Television cameras must be presented a day early for thorough checking by technicians, and all visitors, Iranian and foreign, were thoroughly searched and required to leave such items as watches, pens and keys on deposit. The measures, while perhaps excessive, were understandable: Iran was at war; bomb blasts in the early '80s had wiped out most of the country's first-line religious leadership. They were also applied indiscriminately. But reporters visiting Iran for the first time never failed to turn the security measures into a matter of principle, portraying the temporary removal of their pens and watches as a denial of their rights, and calling on Mr. Rafsanjani for redress. "Are you less able to write the truth with the pencil and paper we provide?" he would fire back. A female reporter, alert for any competitive edge in a competitive trade, tried another gambit. Rather than ask for information, she pleaded openly for a visa extension: "I need more time in order to understand your fascinating country" went the line. Mr. Rafsanjani, never one to disappoint a lady in distress — and, implicitly, to put plenty of distance between himself and his hidebound colleagues — would nod to an adjutant and the matter would quickly be settled. Meanwhile hapless male colleagues, forced to wring their hands abjectly in the Islamic Guidance Ministry offices for a few extra days, muttered about unfair competition.

Of course the mainstream media were interested in the poverty of the south Tehran slums, the instant crowds, the pushing and shoving, the slogans and the shouting. But not for long. You couldn't talk to these people, after all; the adolescents with the motorbikes and the close-cropped hair or the sharp-featured women in dusty *chadors* who wouldn't stop chanting. How much easier it was to get along with uptown folks, people like themselves — suave, moneyed English-speakers who threw parties with rock music, dancing, contraband booze and maybe the odd porno video fresh from the USA. The north Tehran "party" had quickly become a staple, even obligatory, item in most print reports on Islamic Iran — sometimes the only item. No wonder. Alcohol, along with money, is the chief lubricant of the international media machine. And officially dry Iran was a hardship posting. In the luxurious villas of the Iranian elite, amidst the peace and quiet procured from an understanding *mollah* or *Komiteh* officer in exchange for certain considerations, the men and women who bring us the news could assuage their thirst and have their worst fears — or pre-cooked analyses — confirmed.

FOREIGN JOURNALISTS — television crews in particular — applied for Iranian visas, arrived in Tehran and went about their business in full knowledge that they, the masters of image manipulation, were themselves being controlled by the Islamic Guidance Ministry. (If they did not know this, their naïveté was truly boundless.) Iranian missions abroad are staffed primarily by career diplomats from the foreign ministry. They are generally intelligent men with a good grasp of the Western mindset and an ironic though off-the-record sense of the peculiarities of the media establishment at home and abroad. The Islamic Guidance Ministry, which is the ultimate arbitrator of visa applications as well as having full responsibility for journalists, has remained a bastion of Iran's radical faction — a mini-state within a state, a preserve of orthodoxy where behaviour can veer quickly and unpredictably from cordial accommodation into obtuseness. Visiting journalists find it difficult to avoid the Ministry's seedy offices on Vali-ye Asr Avenue, the dog-eared copies of *Tehran Times* with its warmed-over press releases masquerading as news, the long wait for interview applications, the interminable delays, the brief flurries of action. Underpaid "minders" from the Ministry tag along to all official interviews, less to monitor questions and answers (which they've already heard dozens of times over) than to assert, by their presence, the influence of their superiors as the ultimate bastion of Islamic political correctness. These "minders," once their blasé and rather cynical outer shell has been breached, can be sensitive to the special needs of one correspondent or another. One of my most stimulating literary discussions took place one afternoon behind the closed doors of the former deputy director. We had begun by talking about the Rushdie case, and drifted on to the controversy then raging around Martin Scorcese's film of *The Last Temptation of Christ*. Nikos Kazantzakis' novel, he assured me, was far from the blasphemous pamphlet described by its Christian fundamentalist critics. Not only had the deputy director read *The Last Temptation*, he had read several other novels by the great Greek author. "These are ignorant people, Mr. Reed," he said. "If they read this book by Kazantzakis, they will see that it is deeply religious."

Overt censorship hardly exists. Though certain things — food lineups and any military or security-related installations — may not be filmed, and certain non-persons — such as Ayatollah Montazeri — may not be interviewed, the written, audio or visual material produced by foreign correspondents is not subjected to the kind of restrictions that prevail in, for instance, Israel, where army security operatives sit in judgement as a matter of policy. In Iran, self-censorship, extreme caution and the threat of disavowal by superiors has already persuaded interviewees not to stray far beyond the official platitudes. Television coverage of the Islamic Republic all seems to end up looking the same, with the same people saying the same things. Confidences can be gained in private encounters, out of earshot of assistants, drivers and secretaries, in parks or in moving automobiles...providing names are changed and identities disguised — as has frequently been the case in this book.

"ALL FOREIGN CORRESPONDENTS are treated in exactly the same way," a deputy director of the press office once assured me with the fulsome sincerity of high invention. Like truth, equality has, in Iran, a certain elasticity. Some, such as the big American networks, the BBC, and US publications like the New York Times and Time magazine are more equal than others — certainly more than Dutch or Brazilian reporters, or Canadian free-lance writers. This, from the point of view of Iranian media managers, is as it should be. When the Yanks turn up in Tehran, it's because the government has something to show: a successful military operation during the war, the misery of Kurdish refugees fleeing Iraqi chemical attacks, relief efforts after a devastating earthquake, or the launch, with a Time interview, of President Rafsanjani's 1993 re-election campaign.

The correspondents stay at the Laleh Hotel — formerly the Tehran Intercontinental — overlooking Laleh Park on one side, and the snow-clad Alborz range on the other. Phones at the Laleh are conveniently tapped, the in-house security services discreet but thorough, the atmosphere one of threadbare pseudo-luxury, the food in the top floor panoramic restaurants among the best in Tehran, and the staff skilled in dealing with the quirks (and the cash) of foreign correspondents. A large portrait of Imam Khomeini glares across the lobby. The words "Down with USA" are spelled out in what look like the bottoms of fruit-juice tins. When important press "programs" are in full swing the Islamic Guidance office takes up full-time residence in one of the hotel's suites, the better to process the lineup of supplicants for the elusive exclusive. In the lobby reporters and television producers scurry to and fro, arranging satellite feeds; radio reporters dictate their daily dispatches from the house phones, and print journalists dawdle over yet another cup of tea before wandering off to file their stories.

It was on the eleventh floor of the Laleh that I encountered NBC's then-star reporter Arthur Kent, he of erstwhile "Scud stud" fame, standing small, forlorn and unstud-like among crates of equipment. We introduced ourselves and chatted briefly until the elevator arrived with a gang of porters to haul the gear away to the truck waiting downstairs. Kent may not be a humble man. Humility and a successful career as an on-camera journalist never make for a comfortable fit. But, unlike some of the satraps of the US media I'd encountered at various Tehran events, he seemed straightforward, even vulnerable. Refreshing. Maybe the circumstances — riding herd on dozens of packing crates of cables, video-cameras, lights, monitors and God-only-knows-what-else — had an ego-moderating effect. When Kent was sacked by NBC, less for refusing a dangerous assignment in Bosnia than for having spoken harsh on-air truths about the American narcotics trade, then staged a one-man protest demonstration on the sidewalks of Manhattan, he won my sympathy. Perhaps it all came down to the inherent — inbred? — modesty of the proper Canadian. A preposterous notion. Somehow, Kent had kept his journalistic reflexes, and his integrity, intact; he still cared about the story as it revealed itself. Not so most mainstream US reporters, the men and women who truly believe themselves to be purveyors of the National Interest, who speak of the United States in the first person plural. Fresh from high-level government and intelligence agency briefings in Washington they come, armed with contact lists and lavish budgets, radiating the rectitude bred by promiscuity with power. They are high-powered, arrogant, often brilliant, domineering, vain and boastful to their inferiors; abjectly they bend to kiss the jewel-encrusted rings of their masters. "The editorial board decides if President Mitterand gets invited to lunch, not Mitterand," *Time*'s Mideast correspondent confided in early 1993. He had come to Iran to help smooth out relations between the newly elected Clinton administration and the Islamic regime, he continued with no hint of irony. He didn't say who had invited whom for lunch.

The quantity of equipment needed by the television establishment to "cover" a story confirms the axiom that the quality of information is inversely proportional to the complexity of the technology used to gather, process and transmit it. Ostensibly, television goes where the action is. But with logistical problems resembling those of a full-fledged military operation, television becomes first a part of the action, then, functioning as God in a small space, breathes life into corpses and shapes events. Whether the technical crew was large or small — a full-scale Hollywood-inspired location shoot or a two-man video crew — coverage of Iran consisted almost entirely of television's depiction of itself covering Iran, a closed loop which legitimized the few, over-simplified images selected for inclusion and invalidated all others, and banished the complexity of the Islamic Republic (the same mechanism can, of course, be applied to all subjects) to a never-never land of the unspoken, the unseen and, thus, the unknown. Television's tunnel vision evokes a truncated reality which is actually the convincing non-reality of artifice, a sort of reverse and thereby perverse guerilla theatre. Far too cultured and polite to disappoint their guests, Iranians, whether officials or spontaneous demonstrators, had become adept at performing on cue, at striking poses, at gesticulating and shouting and glaring at the lens — all the essential shorthand of fundamentalist wrath. When the red lights were switched off, the tripods folded, the batteries disconnected and the microphones stored away, normal life would resume. People would return to their shopping or their families, officials would smile and joke and sip tea. The television image of Islamic Iran was — and is — an elaborately staged representation, with all the authenticity of a talk show and the sincerity of a rock-video clip. "Iran," not Iran. A case-study in virtual unreality.

WHEN THE IMPERIAL REGIME COLLAPSED the first target of popular outrage was the SAVAK, the Shah's ruthless and ultimately useless secret police. Founded in 1957 with full assistance from the United States and later from Israeli intelligence and interrogation experts, SAVAK quickly earned a worldwide reputation for extreme brutality.[82] By the late '70s, SAVAK and the CIA had so thoroughly interpenetrated one another as to be indistinguishable. Despite the horrors of the agency's torture chambers and prisons and the sophistication of its information gathering methods, neither parent nor offspring foresaw nor could prevent the subterranean rumblings which created the revolutionary wave. As the wave crested and broke over Iran, enraged mobs exacted rough justice against the symbols and the representatives of the hated old order. Even before the Islamic Republic had been proclaimed, the new regime embarked on a draconian policy of revolutionary justice, arresting and summarily executing military and police leaders, SAVAK informers, thugs and torturers. These categories accounted for more than 80% of all documented executions carried out between February 11 and June 11, 1979.[83]

The Islamic revolution did not happen in an international vacuum: Assaults from without were not long in coming. The Revolutionary Guards and Committees which were established by Khomeini's order in May, 1979, acted rapidly to control and defeat die-hard supporters of the Shah and frustrated leftists. They also absorbed the first, punishing Iraqi offensives in September, 1980. However, assassination of much of the Islamic leadership in the early days demonstrated that the new rulers needed more than a corps of loyal and devoted guards; they needed a sophisticated security and intelligence apparatus to provide information on potential opponents at home and abroad, to monitor unreliable elements in the armed forces and the civilian bureaucracy. They needed, above all, a last line of defense.

Iranians are extremely reluctant to talk about the information ministry, also known as SAVAMAH, the Islamic replacement for SAVAK. Those who do, make sure that no one is listening, and speak in low voices. You can't see it, an Iranian friend, who is by no means an opponent of the *mollahs*, cautioned me on my last visit, in early 1993. But it is there. The secret police apparatus, he whispered, is "more violent and deadlier" than that of the previous regime. The number of people summarily executed far exceeds that of the Shah's day. Ayatollah Montazeri, who made it his business to stay well-informed on the maltreatment of prisoners, had made the same claim in letters to Khomeini, and later in public statements. None of this sat well with the then-Information Minister Mr. Reyshahri, who had already earned himself a reputation for ruthlessness in the Mehdi Hashemi case and had a bone to pick with Montazeri.

Unless visitors to Iran show undue interest in military affairs or security matters they may remain oblivious to the existence of the secret police. But over time I obtained insights, fleeting glimpses: more the shadow than the thing itself. As I was walking along the sidewalk near my hotel one morning, the passenger in an unmarked car motioned to me to come over. He identified himself as the *Komiteh*, and demanded to see my passport. One learns early on not to trifle with the *Komiteh*, which has the reputation of being a law unto itself. I complied, but kept a tight grip on my papers. Let me see that, he said, pointing to my shoulder bag, which held my notebook and a wallet containing several hundred dollars in undeclared US bills. I did as told. Turn around, said the man, I am going to search you. I turned around, and the car roared off into Tehran traffic, my bag along with it.

I immediately reported the affair, keeping quiet about the lost funds (though foreign currency had to be declared on entry and exchanged at the derisory official rate, only the naïve did so). Several days later I was taken to police headquarters to identify the miscreants. The police investigator led me into a small room where a group of six terrified men stood against the wall. One spoke English: "I was not mister, I was not!" he blurted out. None of them looked at all like the authoritative type in the white Paykan. Two weeks later the police announced the arrest of a gang of Pakistanis who had been, they stated, preying on foreigner businessmen and journalists. No Iranian would do this kind of thing, they stated. But a friend told me that I may well have been the victim of a *Komiteh* squad involved in extra-curricular activities. Or simply doing their job. Who will watch the watchers?

An acquaintance, a manager in the semi-public sector who shall remain anonymous, related a telephone call requesting that he place certain of his office facilities at the disposition of "government officials." He politely declined, arguing that he would prefer to rent out the space. Several days later he received another call, instructing him to proceed to a large downtown Tehran apartment building. The caller's manner convinced him he should keep the rendezvous. On arrival, he was shown to an empty, unfurnished apartment, ushered in and ordered to stand facing the wall. A voice — another voice — calmly but very firmly asked him to reconsider his refusal to make his space available. If not, the consequences could be unpleasant. He quickly agreed. After all, he reasoned, what's a minor loss of revenue?

MAJID AND I are eating *chelo kebab* in an uptown restaurant. The usual kind. Walk down a flight of stairs beneath a large mirror and a Tehran restaurant owners' association poster enjoining women to wear proper Islamic dress. We're sitting at a table next to the wall; the place is almost empty and the waiters are indifferent. The atmosphere is faintly conspiratorial; perfect for a man like Majid, with a multiplicity of connections and an endless supply of rumours ranging from the wild to the reasonable and, most of the time, with one foot in each extreme. "Fred," he's telling me, "there's this guy, I can't tell you his name but he's a friend of mine from school, seems somebody passed him one of the letters from Ayatollah Montazeri." Hmmm. Plausible. Such letters, highly critical of the regime, are circulated clandestinely though officially they do not exist. I knew too that mentioning Montazeri's name in public is dangerous. I could not dismiss Majid as a crank. To establish his credentials, had he not led me unannounced and with an insouciance bordering on truculence through a rear entrance into the bowels of the foreign ministry one afternoon to meet his protector, an influential *mollah* who now holds a high diplomatic post abroad? He goes on: "So, with no, what do you call it...no search paper or no charges — this is Iran you know — they arrest my friend from his office one afternoon and hold him for many weeks. Nobody knows where; his wife is going crazy, where he is? Finally they let him go. I go to visit him at his place. I don't know what they did to him; he couldn't hear very well anymore. What happened? I ask him but wouldn't talk about it. I'm through with politics, is all he said."

Another day we're drinking tea in the lobby of my hotel. Majid casually drops a bombshell: Another friend of mine, he says in his flattest, most matter-of-fact tone, has told the secret police about his relations with me, resulting in a few days in jail. True or not — and given Majid's propensity for colourful tales, I wasn't convinced — the seeds of doubt were planted. Doubt? Consternation. Was it possible that the man, a person with whom I'd shared bread, laughter and confidence could be an informer? Could it be that, assuming he may have been approached by the police, they might have offered him a choice: cooperation or loss of his job, or worse? A few days later, on a drive across town Majid, even more casually than ever, attempts to offer me some material about the MKO.

The organization is one of the enigmas of the Middle East, more impeccably terrorist than Lebanon's Hezbollah and as patently offshore funded as Jonas Savimbi's UNITA in Angola, as cruel as Pol Pot's Cambodian Khmer Rouge: the ideal group for hire as "freedom fighters," useful destabilizers for later use. After being expelled from Paris following a rapprochement between France and Iran which may have been related, some say, to an outburst of terrorism in the French capital, the organization re-established itself in Iraq under the benevolent co-sponsorship of Saddam Hussein and the CIA. (One of the unsolved riddles of the relationship between the United States and Iraq is continuing American political and financial support for a group which depends entirely on the hospitality and good graces of the Iraqi dictator for its survival.) During the war the organization's network of informants inside Iran helped guide Iraqi air and missile attacks, and the group's well-armed troops, backed by Iraqi armour, actually crossed the border into Iran immediately after the 1988 cease-fire, proclaiming they would march on Tehran. The oppressed masses of Iran would, they boasted, rally to their cause. The opposite occurred. The Revolutionary Guards, aided by war-weary local citizens, needed less than a week to surround and crush the invading force, killing thousands. Meanwhile MKO prisoners at Evin Prison, sure of victory, had mutinied and demanded that the authorities surrender control of the prison to them. When the invasion failed they were summarily executed, perhaps in their hundreds.

Back to Majid: the more off-hand the manner, the more extraordinary the tale being told or the information volunteered. My suspicion

— and confusion — deepened. That wasn't all. Several days later, I asked my friend Abbas about Majid. Abbas ran a grocery store, but he also maintained a lively interest in the affairs of his former government department. "You should keep away from this gentleman, Mr. Reed," he told me. "He is not trustworthy. They say he works for the police. They say he provides them with information." Hurriedly I began to flip through my mental cardex of Iranian acquaintances, especially those who moved in the narrow and high-risk space between officialdom and the foreign press, a space seething with the intrigues of petty jealousy, frustration, rivalry for the favours of the major networks and the substantial attraction of hard US cash. Could they all be connected, no matter how tenuously, with the information ministry? Were some of my tips and leads little more than planted stories designed to discredit one faction while indirectly supporting the other? Or to create the illusion of openness or dissent where neither existed? If this were so, then the individuals I encountered were polished, sophisticated and unscrupulous liars. Grave thoughts, these silent suspicions against people whom I'd known for years.

Though all was nothing but hearsay, though there was no proof, I had thought the thoughts and now have written the words. Slipped into a paranoia of half-ignorance, entertained the unthinkable, ripped the delicate fabric of credulity. Slender consolation: the image that lay revealed was not that of Iran. It was my own reflection against a background of duplicity and cynicism painted in the colours of sincerity. And it was too unsavoury to be wholly inaccurate.

The perils of scrutinizing a strange land through an obscure lens: No matter how extensive, the journalist's familiarity is superficial. He sees moving shapes and shadowy figures, hears whispered voices, muffled words. The shapes may be doing the most commonplace things, the voices speaking the most banal of conversations — or they may be spreading rumours of sedition and opposition. Learning to read the meanings of shapes and sounds is more than the beginning of language; it is the end of illusion and the beginning of wisdom.

BENEATH THE VEIL of institutional stability, is Islamic Iran a police state? As with all things Iranian, a simple, direct answer is impossible. There is no doubt, for instance, that the information ministry's operatives are both thorough and ruthless. Despite their ruthlessness, they were powerless to predict or head off the rioting of May, 1992, although they did claim to apprehend the ringleaders, some of whom were summarily executed. If they alone form the ultimate rampart of a regime whose revolutionary credibility is exhausted, they will be no more effective than the East German Stasi, whose tentacular organization finally collapsed under its own weight, unable to process and digest the mass of information it gathered. In the end, police terror failed as well to protect the Shah; it would likely fail the *mollahs* as well. But the religious establishment, even at its corrupt and venal worst, is not the Shah's malignantly hypertrophied regime, nor is it like the regimes of the defunct East Bloc. The *mollahs* represent, as the Shah did not (and as the socialist one-party states did not), a belief system to which an overwhelming majority of Iranians still subscribe and with which they identify. Having assumed political power they are religiously obliged to rule by the divine precepts of the Qur'an and the immutable laws of the *shari'a*, to administer the appropriate punishments, to defend the faith. Protection of this order is the simple yet ambiguous mandate of the information ministry. A climate of righteous intimidation must be maintained over social, personal and political relations, an atmosphere of suspicion and fear flowing from the religious imperative to foster the good and combat the bad. Still, the information ministry cannot (or will not) entirely stifle the dissent which can be heard with increasing frequency and in increasing volume.

Far removed from the ancient Athenian prototype — although closer to it than any of the sad parodies prevailing throughout the Middle East — the Islamic revolution has given Iranians their first taste of rough democracy in more than two and one half millennia of recorded history. At the same time, the deeply felt grievances of the Muslim world — which includes Iran — over its humiliation at the hands of European colonialism and latterly, the New World Order, have combined to create an explosive complex of alienation from, and resistance to, the political institutions of the West. There is yet a third ingredient of Iranian history, my journalist friend Mohsen would remind me pointedly. "Don't forget, people used to believe the Shah was God," or at least the shadow of God, as the Safavid monarchs styled themselves. The corollary was that the monarch exercised the full prerogatives of life and death over his subjects. Life, Mohsen was politely suggesting, was cheap indeed: worth less than the ruler's dog, and at the disposal of authority. The result was a blend of fatalism and passivity long encouraged by the arcane spiritual disputations of the quietist Shi'ite clergy, what Ali Shariati called Black Shi'ism. The same fatalism, the same passivity remain a component of the national psychology.

OVER THE LAST FIFTEEN YEARS has sprung up a cottage industry which attempts to describe and chart the web of shifting alliances that make up the power structure of the Islamic Republic, harking back to the Kremlinologists of a bygone day who spent their working lives scrutinizing retouched photographs of the dignitaries on the Red Square reviewing stand and analyzing clippings from the official press. Such attempts to grasp the inner workings of the Iranian state and clerical establishment promise to be about as productive as snaring smoke barehanded. In a country where the shifts, realignments and constant play of political and personal alliances take place "behind the curtain," what is seen and reported upon is only that which may be shown, and has only rhetorical or metaphorical weight. The representation is reminiscent of the *Tazieh*, the Ashura passion play, where uni-dimensional figures of absolute virtue (Imam Hossein and his companions) and absolute evil (the forces of Yazid) meet in ritual enactment of the engagement at Karbala.

This is not an attempt to contrast the "darkness" of Iran with the light of Western democracy. Such a comparison would be invidious. Western civilization's openness — its readiness to enfold others in an objectifying embrace — is rarely brought to bear on itself and its own workings. These continue to be obscured by a penumbra of cultural and political myth. We may claim a certain transparency of political debate, but the public limits of debate have been established by a cultural consensus rooted as firmly in our collective mythology as is our self-concept as being of the West in opposition to an imaginary Orient of our projected fantasies.[84]

In Iran, it has become popular to say that a coalition of *mollahs*, *bazaaris* and the urban underclass (the *mostazafin*) wields power. Some Iranians scornfully dismiss even such generalizations: "These people represent only themselves," banker and publisher Sadeq Sami'i says of the inner circle of power. "The men who make up this regime are from modest social circumstances," he says. "They know firsthand how easily any power structure can collapse; they never expected to take power so easily."

This version offers the all the virtues of simplicity — which is why it is far too simple to express the complexity of Iranian politics. Reza H. is an Islamic modernist, a believer in the technocratic method who works as a political analyst at a government research institute. He spent the better part of an hour explaining to me how, after the Islamic revolution, three distinct yet interlocking power centres arose: an overt constitutional and institutional structure, including government ministries and the Majlis; the *Faqih* — the Jurisconsult — who gives religious and revolutionary guidance and who can veto all government measures; and the leading Ayatollahs, the *marjas* (sources of emulation) who guide their devout voluntary followers. Two centres too many, he says. "The only way we can reconstruct the country is to have one centre of power. The duties of the Leader, for instance, are defined in Article 110 of the Constitution — but today, in reality, he can overrule the government. For a country to be governed well, it must be governed by the rule of law."

The law of men or the law of God?

TERRORISM IS ONE of those words visitors to Iran learn to use with caution. Beware, I keep reminding myself, of the temptation to see the Assassins of Alamut as a prefiguring of the Islamic Republic's dealings with its opponents abroad. In Iran the spectrum of religiously motivated political action is broad and ramified, spreading beyond the primary colours into ultraviolets and infrareds well beyond the visual spectrum. Some Iranians claim that the country's international terrorist activities are, as they put it, an open secret. But, I wondered at the same time, wasn't the very outspokenness of such people part of a stratagem to make the regime appear tolerant of dissent, another clever dissimulation. Dissimulation — *taqiye* — is, after all, a fundamental precept of Shi'ism, by which the believer conceals his true beliefs if his survival is at stake.

Officials are quick to stand any insinuation of terrorism on its head. When challenged, they recite long, exhaustively documented catalogues of offenses organized and perpetrated by outsiders — ranging from the proven involvement of foreign legations in overthrowing constitutional governments to the plotting by intelligence services of assassination schemes which usually fail, not for lack of money, but for lack of an executioner of conviction. Yes, they admit, grudgingly and off the record, shadowy "fundamentalist" fanatics inspired by Iran have possibly, probably, even certainly, been encouraged, even funded by low-level functionaries with deniability. Persian versions of Lt-Col. Oliver North operating out of the office of one or another leading Ayatollah, may have been connected with kidnappings, bombings and other reprehensible acts. At the same time Western governments, operating openly or clandestinely, have blown civilian airliners out of the sky, provided chemical warfare technology to Iraqi dictator and former "terrorist" now demoted to "strongman" Saddam Hussein, and later reduced his un-happy land to rubble over a trumped-up territorial dispute designed to reassert control over oil resources. Which came first? Who, indeed, Iranians kept asking, were the terrorists, and whence did they come? They have a point.

"MOST OF THE CRIMES committed in the region during the 1980s were the work of the Reagan-Bush administration. These people were the terrorists. Not us!" I could hardly have expected to hear it stated more succinctly. The man speaking to me across a low table is Hojjatoleslam Ali Akbar Mohtashemi, the cleric who spent twelve years on the interface between the anti-fundamentalist zeal of the United States State Department, National Security Council, CIA and assorted tributary agencies on the one hand, and on the other hand, the Islamic Republic's efforts to promote its chosen proxies in the volatile Near East. Mr. Mohtashemi may rank high on the American hit list of most-wanted world terrorists, but today, with Iran's radical faction on the wane, he lives a quiet life in a large, sparsely-furnished house in north Tehran, not far from one of the Shah's former palaces which now serves as a Revolutionary Guard garrison.

When my interpreter and I ring at the gate on a cold January after-noon his son Ali, barefoot in plastic sandals, opens for us. Inside a fire crackles in the hearth, and a bowl of fresh fruit awaits us on the table where the interview will take place. In the next room I notice a Macintosh computer on Mr. Mohtashemi's work table. So this is the house of the evil genius who single-handedly inspired political kidnap-pings and organized fundamentalist militias in Lebanon and Afghanistan. While we wait, warming our hands in front of the fire, young Ali returns with steaming cups of tea on a tray, and a bowl of pis-tachios. There is no sign of servants, of bodyguards not a trace, although for all we know, heavily armed revolutionary guards loyal to the ex-min-ister may have been poised in the next room. The stillness in the house spoke more of isolation than mystery or menace.

Calling on the former minister of the interior had not been easy. Like most of his fellow radicals, Mr. Mohtashemi is out of favour, and prospects for a comeback seem dim. Arrangements for the meeting had to be made through unofficial channels, in roundabout ways. In early 1993 political tension was building in Tehran, as the two factions drew battle-lines over President Hashemi Rafsanjani's ambitious plans to pri-vatize the economy, while a third group made up of supporters of

Ayatollah Montazeri continued their campaign to undermine the Leader Ayatollah Khamene'i, whom they regard, not inaccurately, as both a theological lightweight and a usurper.

But the radical resurgence seems ephemeral; the "moderates" are too well in control. The true believers of the revolutionary cause now seem stranded like mollusks caught on a steep shore in a fast ebbing tide. When Mr. Mohtashemi enters the room, he seems small, wistful, perhaps — is it my imagination? — bitter. He extends his left hand in greeting; the right hand is an artificial one; the original limb was blown off by a powerful — dare I say "terrorist?" — letter-bomb which also cost him three fingers of his left hand and most of his hearing while he served as Iran's ambassador to Syria in the early '80s. During his tour of duty in Damascus he helped found the Lebanese Hezbollah. He may have been connected, say his critics in Lebanon, with the suicide bombings of the United States and French garrisons in Beirut, which forced both countries to withdraw their expeditionary forces in unseemly haste, and certainly won the ambassador no friends in Washington or Paris.

Despite his close links with Imam Khomeini, Mr. Mohtashemi committed several political errors which hastened his demise. A major tactical blunder was his misreading, in 1988, of Khomeini's willingness to turn away from an exclusively state-controlled economy. He publicly insinuated that those who would accept foreign investment were either ignorant or traitors, a position he has scarcely retreated from. When he advocated that Iran support Iraqi dictator Saddam against the US-led coalition in the Gulf War he eroded even his support among fellow radicals, who could read the mood on the streets. War veterans and martyr families were outraged at the thought of allying with the monster they had fought so desperately.

The violent protest demonstrations of 1992 which rocked several Iranian cities, including Shiraz, Mashhad and the suburbs of Tehran were the result of economic unrest, says Mr. Mohtashemi. "If foreign interference increases and if economic problems are not solved, it is likely that such unrest will be repeated. But even if it is, it would not impair the Islamic Republic's ability to function." Before I can complete my next question, he adds: "Let me make one thing clear: I am not in the business of making advertisements for the government of the Islamic Republic. I speak for the Islamic revolution."

What does Mr. Mohtashemi mean by interference? The structural adjustment measures prescribed by the International Monetary Fund and the World Bank as preconditions for international assistance, of course. "When an international institution provides 'assistance' it does not do so without strings attached. These are not simply recommendations; they are commands to be obeyed. Why should it be any different here? Any such outside commands would of course be interference in our internal affairs. But," he adds, "the free market economy does not correspond with the goals of the Islamic revolution. We believe neither in the Western, free market approach, nor in the former socialist approach. The government should create the conditions for the broadest economic independence, and not foster a return to a privileged class and a wide mass of poor people — a feudal master and serf model."

A telephone rings in another room and we are interrupted by a soft tapping. Mr. Mohtashemi turns his head; in the shadow we see his son Ali beckoning him. When he returns, he carries in the tray with another round of steaming tea, the perfect antidote to the late-afternoon chill creeping into the room.

The Islamic Revolution has been driven off course by two factors, domestic economic pressure from the *bazaaris*, and pressure from outside. "The same forces were brought to bear on us during the Imam's lifetime, but he was able to resist them. When he died, his principles were relaxed. I believe mere lip service is being paid to our original goals, while contrary policies are being pursued," he says.

Mr. Mohtashemi, and Sadeq Khalkali, the notorious "hanging judge" who inhabits a luxurious north Tehran villa not far away and finds little to occupy his idle hours, face a dilemma. The very people who have relaxed the principles of the revolution are those with whom they, the politically outmanoeuvred radicals, previously served. They cannot simply be dismissed as irredeemably compromised. In fact, all they must do, he quickly adds, is return to the genuine values of the revolution. "They are genuine, committed revolutionaries. But today, under domestic and external pressure they believe that if they change, they can better solve economic and political problems. If they understood that these outside forces are against the Islamic revolution, they would certainly change their policy."

These leaders, who include President Hashemi Rafsanjani and Ahmad Khomeini, son of the Imam, are the same people who gave the green light for the visit of then-US National Security Adviser Robert McFarlane to Tehran in May, 1986, and conferred with President Reagan's personal envoys when they arrived. Paradox in Iran is never far from the surface. Mr. Mohtashemi who, as interior minister, controlled the police — which no one in Iran accuses of excessive libertarian convictions — today pleads that President Rafsanjani's administration is now violating the elementary rules of democracy. Let us be just, however. Mr. Mohtashemi is also the man who, while a cabinet member, drafted the law permitting political parties and supported its application. "While I was interior minister I issued permits for eighteen parties and political groups. But even though I drafted the law, because of fears and propaganda against me as a 'radical', these political groups and parties never came forward."

What, I ask, of Mehdi Bazargan, prime minister in revolutionary Iran's provisional government, and the only non-clerical opposition politician never entirely silenced by the *mollahs?* "Bazargan? Hah! He didn't have much of a party, more of an informal grouping or movement. One of the reasons he was made first prime minister was that his organization was not a political party, and he would work outside the party framework." Five years later, only two political parties are recognized: the Militant Clergymen, the group allied with President Rafsanjani, and the Militant Clergy, the "radical" faction. "Other groups apply for recognition, but are denied the right to register," he says. Why? "Ask Mr. President."

Worse, during the 1991 parliamentary election for the fourth Majlis many candidates were ruled ineligible by the Guardian Council, the select body of six high-ranking clergymen and six hand-picked lay experts who evaluate legislation for conformity with Islamic standards. Eighty percent of those were not permitted to stand because they could not meet new criteria, argues Mr. Mohtashemi. "But as far as these 80% are concerned, most supported the Islamic revolution; they did not change their position. Their only problem was that they were not supporters of the current president."

But, he cautions, the packed parliament will narrow the government's base of support and drive it into the hands of outsiders. The government may have thought it could implement its economic policies more effectively, "under present circumstances, but the situation can neither be corrected or reformed. The opening of the political atmosphere and the application of economic policies imported from the West will automatically bring about penetration by Western culture. This cultural introduction will be a by-product; it will occur automatically."

Mr. Mohtashemi is no raving isolationist. Nor does he claim a contradiction between the ideals of the Islamic revolution and the free flow of scientific knowledge. "Our problem is with capitalist economic policies. As far as academic economic studies, there is no problem. But when these policies are used in development, they can focus either on the private sector or on the entire population. Problems arise when the focus is only on the private sector. Such policies become deleterious when they advocate narrow private sector development."

As capitalism swaggers like a plunder-drunk vandal through the ruins of "real, existing socialism" and its now vanished corollary, the Third World, Mr. Mohtashemi's attack has an anachronistic ring. Iran's attempt at an indigenous Islamic path to socialism under the Mousavi government during the war years left few fond memories and created enormous resentments, particularly among the regime's strongest financial supporters, the *bazaaris*. Strong-armed market-based remedies can be counted upon to generate equally strong reactions. But the radicals, themselves architects of the worst excesses of the state-run economy and its leading beneficiaries, are unlikely to be able to profit from Iran's latent economic and social crisis.

Iran's radicals, however, cannot be entirely dismissed. The power structure of the Islamic Republic is now shifting. President Rafsanjani is less a religious man in politician's garb than a politician dressed as a *mollah*. His contradictory policies have unsettled the populace, and at the same time loosened the grip of Iran's established economic power centre, the bazaar, allowing both traditionalists and radicals to channel rising popular dissatisfaction against the neo-conservatives and the technocrats. The alliance between the religious establishment and the bazaar is the key to the strength of the Islamic regime — and simultaneously its weakness. Though the interests of *mollahs* and *bazaaris* have historically converged, the government's commitment to development and modernization, as expressed by its strategic alliance with the IMF and the World Bank, have turned the bazaar against the brain trust which formulates economic policy. A modern banking system, which dissimulates Western banking practices beneath a veneer of euphemism to satisfy the letter of the Qur'anic ban on interest, is emerging as a replacement for long-established *bazaari* traditions. As much of the religious leadership lacks both administrative ability and a solid grasp of economic affairs, the *mollahs* must rely either on their Western-educated technocrat advisors, or maintain their historical alliance with the bazaar. "Without support from the bazaar, they cannot survive, and they know it," says Hassan N. "The paradox is that religion can survive in Iranian society only if it breaks free from the bazaar. Our greatest religious leaders never depended on the bazaar. Each of them had their own constituencies."

The president's opponents, however, have few alternatives and fewer illusions. Should Mr. Rafsanjani fall or be removed from power, Hassan N. told me in one of the wide-ranging analyses of Iranian politics he liked so well, disintegration of the kind seen in former Yugoslavia or the ex-USSR would be almost certain. The opposition radicals themselves are so lacking in popular support that the eventuality could well deal a fatal blow to the clerical class. "The likely effect would be to throw our doors wide open to the Western powers. The US would still like to take revenge on Iran for the overthrow of the Shah and the hostage crisis. The radicals? They have no coherent alternative. Still, in hindsight, their policies during the war seem better and more equitable than those now in effect. Perhaps the radicals have become a bit more rational; they might be able to implement policies more successfully. The regime's current economic measures will certainly push people toward them," he continued. "Inevitably they will gather some of the support they lost. In the process, the current clerical leaders could be pushed aside by a movement led by Muslim intellectuals and nationalists — who are not so far apart as it might seem." From what I could observe, the category seemed perfect for Hassan N.

BENEATH THE DRY STREAM-BED of political speculation flows a subterranean current of bitter realism. No one of Khomeini's stature remains to mobilize the poor, whose lot continues to decline under the dictates of free market dogma. The Grand Ayatollahs are all either dead, or old and infirm. No outstanding spiritual or political leader has emerged from the religious establishment since the victory of the revolution. Islam is what the ruling conservative *mollahs* say it is, and their definition is certain to reinforce their power and interests. Hardly surprising that the malfeasance and incompetence of the ruling establishment has undermined respect not only for the clerical class, but for religion. Perhaps the only surprise was that it happened so fast.

"We are still looking forward to an Islam as evoked by Ali Shariati, where the clergy do not make up a privileged class," whispered a dissident follower of Ayatollah Montazeri. "If they are going to exist at all, the *mollahs* must learn all over again to coexist with people, to work as hard and live as humbly, to forego their privileges and advantages. They should compete with others for positions, and win positions on capacity and merit. Enough of the talking and cheating."

Mohammad Ja'far has no illusions, no expectations. Time has run out. Iran is evolving into a nation state like any other. "If you check the ranks of people who claim to be legatees of Imam Khomeini, you won't find anybody who lives like he did. They've done quite well, with their property, their fine cars, their businesses. The Imam was very far from those kinds of things. He died with nothing. And these ideas of exporting revolution, and these ideas of being a model for oppressed people everywhere in the world.... Let me put it shortly: the Islamic revolution is a thing of history, not a thing of the future."

"THE THING THAT MADE the greatest impact on me," said the man with the white beard as a pugnacious spark flickered, then flared in his sad eyes, "was the personality of the Imam himself. I knew straightaway that here was a leader from outside the mainstream of post-colonial Muslim leaders, people who were really created into leadership roles by the departing or not so departing colonial powers. I thought, surely this man must be the right kind of leader for this time of history because we have tried everything. The Western-educated leaders have been tried and they have failed everywhere in the Muslim world."

The speaker is Kalim Siddiqui, one of Khomeini's most indefatigable supporters. He lives not in Tehran but in a middle-class garden cottage on the southern fringes of the sprawling London conurbation. On a foggy December evening I stand at his front door while the Pakistani cabbie who has proudly brought me to "the Doctor's" home waits in the street. I ring, and reflect on the man I am about to meet. Mr. Siddiqui is not an Iranian, not a *mollah*, and not a Shi'ite Muslim; he is, in fact, a Pakistan-born political scientist in the panislamist tradition of Jamal al-din Assadabadi (the Persian-born religious scholar better known as al-Afghani, "The Afghan"), and the Arab founders of the Muslim Brotherhood — men like Mohammad Abduh, Rashid Rida, al-Bannah and Sayyed Qutb. As director of the London-based Muslim Institute, he has emerged as one of Britain's leading Islamist spokesmen in the campaign against Salman Rushdie's *Satanic Verses* and as founder of the country's controversial Muslim Parliament.

After several minutes, Mr. Siddiqui answers, his round face taut with concern in the dim light of the porch lamp. He escorts me around behind the house to his office, a small, book-lined room adjoining the garage, then excuses himself. Soon he returns, carrying a tray laden with tea and sweets and begs my pardon for his distracted manner. His son, he tells me, is rather ill but his wife is looking after him. We may talk as long as we wish. It was only several weeks later that I learned his son lay dying as we spoke.

Muslims, for the last two centuries, have tried to reconcile Islam with Western ideas about politics, society, economy, he explains. "Imam Khomeini's leadership insisted that there is only one way and that is the Islamic way. The Western way has to be abandoned in totality. This is something that has to be understood very clearly. For the first time, we had a leader who did not speak English, French, German or Russian. The only languages he knew were Arabic and Farsi, and therefore he was informed by Islam and Islam alone. This, I think, is the greatest impact he has made, the personality of the Imam and the source of leadership deep in the root of Islam itself."

ISLAMIC IRAN IS an admixture of purity and corruption, hope and despair, energy and inertia: sometimes repulsive, always compelling, often incomprehensible. Today, after eight years of observing the country at varying degrees of proximity, all of my short-lived certainties have vanished, except one: After 2,500 years of the absolutist rule of Shahs, emperors, tyrants and usurpers, after more than a century of foreign intervention, Iranians have assumed full responsibility for their fate. This they have done under the leadership of their hidden government, in a manner consistent with their hidden history, the shaping of resistance to the tyranny of kings and of Shi'ite millenarianism into a national-religious consciousness which Imam Khomeini and Ali Shariati were able, brilliantly, to shape, then to tap.

The revolution created hope where hope was lost. Fashioned, out of the raw material of Islamic tradition, a new sense of empowerment for women. Placed weapons and knowledge of their use in the hands of the powerless and gave the poor a heady taste of the power of the street. Sent hundreds of thousands of its most devoted followers to a martyr's death in a futile war which at the same time forged the new regime in fire. Generated heroism and cowardice; self-denial and corruption. As in all social upheavals born in turmoil the cost in blood was high. How effective was it in transforming Iranian society? The old order was smashed; a new class of rulers and politicians emerged. Yet the conservative hierocracy outlived the great innovator; the vestiges of the old Persian bureaucracy which once ruled in the name of caliphs and sultans remained intact. Wealth became more concentrated, poverty more widespread.

Imam Khomeini was right: The Islamic revolution was not about the price of watermelons. It was a sea-change, a sudden, wrenching shift, a realignment in the human geography of the Muslim world.

Iranians thirsting to spread their insurrectionary creed among their Sunni Arab brethren encountered incomprehension, hostility and war. No fast-burning powder train of spontaneous uprisings spread across the Islamic world to shouts of *Allah ô-Akbar*. Entrenched Arab secularist regimes saw to that. The war with Iraq pitted Muslim against Muslim, and dashed the hopes of even the most exalted panislamic visionaries for a short-term triumph.

But even if he accomplished nothing else Khomeini brought down the temple of irreligion and immorality. The collapse touched off deeper resonances, long-wave subterranean reverberations. These I encountered in places as diverse as the thresholds of crowded mosques in Istanbul, and in the isolated villages of Muslim Pomaks in northern Greece. The same resonances, with topical variations, are working deep in the bowels of Muslim society from Algeria to Central Asia and beyond. The root of Islam.

The collapse of the structure of ideology in the West has brought with it the rise of a world culture — I use the term in its most superficial sense, as in the oxymoron, "corporate culture" — whose core value is the absence of values, whose deepest expectation is no expectation, a culture free of hope or despair against which no other future is thinkable; no other society imaginable; a culture obsessed with structure. Measured against the socio-historical absolute of the universal civilization, the Islamic revolution is indeed an anachronism. It posits, we are assured, not an ideal future society but a return to an idealized society of the past — that of Mohammad and his companions, of the caliphate of Imam Ali, of the moral example of Hossein at Karbala — all the while insisting on its compatibility with the material forms of Western modernity. If, however, we take Universal Civilization as an emanation of the West, as the Hegelian pinnacle, as a myth-bound historical construct no less finite or ineluctable than other, preceding paradigms of empire, then we should be less hasty to dismiss the dynamic of a resurgent Islam.

Islam may well seem to us an inarticulate cry from the past, adrift and incoherent, condemned to the fringes of an inevitable modernity, hopelessly burdened by its own myths, empty of substance, offering a curious blend of revelation and scientific rationality in a world where today Reason's bastards, Method and Structure, alone stand triumphant. The assessment, from our point of view, may even be accurate. The disparate project to transform Islam into a political ideology has not, in the short term, changed the political structures of the Muslim world except in Iran and Afghanistan, nor has it changed the way Muslims live, as measured by our best analytical indices. But such an analysis would be shortsighted. Iran's Islamic upheaval has irrevocably altered the way Muslims see themselves, the way they understand their religious and cultural heritage. For millions, Islam has reasserted itself as a value structure and a vision of hope: as a vehicle for transforming life and, perhaps fundamentally, as an end in itself. As such, and as nothing else, it can undertake the process of reappropriating its past and its present. The singular merit of the Iranian revolution, and an integral component of its ambiguity, is to have given this process, set in motion more than one hundred years ago, a fierce new impetus.

Notes

1. Thierry Hentsch, *Imagining the Middle East* (Montréal: Black Rose, 1992) xiv.

2. Esmail Kho'i, "*Shomal, Niz*" ["North, Too"] in M.R. Ghanoonparvar, *Prophets of Doom: Literature as a Socio-Political Phenomenon in Modern Iran* (Lanham: University Press of America, 1984) 53.

3. Louise L'Estrange Fawcette, *Iran and the Cold War: The Azerbaijani Crisis of 1946*, reviewed in *Middle East Report* July-August 1993: 46.

4. Bernard Hourcade, *L'Homme vertical: un mythe, une ville, un divorce* in *Téhéran: au dessous du volcan* in *Autrement* (Paris), hors-série n° 27 (nov. 1987): 61

5. Quoted in James F. Bill, *The Eagle and the Lion: The Tragedy of American-Iranian Relations* (New Haven: Yale UP, 1988) 159.

6. Malise Ruthven, *Islam in the World* (New York, Oxford UP, 1984) 178.

7. Jan Rypka, *History of Persian Literature* (Dordrecht: D. Reidel Publishing Co., 1968) 184.

8. Quoted in Bernard Lewis, *The Assassins: A Radical Sect in Islam* (London: Weidenfield and Nicholson, 1967) 44.

9. Edward Burman, *The Assassins: Holy Killers of Islam* (London: Crucible, 1988) 36.

10. Ali Dashti, *In Search of Omar Khayyam*, translated by L.P. Elwell-Sutton (London: George Allen & Unwin, 1971) 62.

11. Vladimir Bartol, *Alamut* (Paris: Phébus, 1988).

12. Ibid. 365.

13. Burman, *Assassins* 157.

14. Forugh Farrokhzad, "*Kasi Keh Mesl-e Hichkas Nist*" ["Someone Who Isn't Like Anyone"], quoted in Ghanoonparvar, *Prophets* 56. Most twentieth-century Iranian writers have been as critical of the Islamic religious institution as practised and perpetuated by the clerics in Iran as they had been of the governing regime. While Farrokhzad's poem, as a whole, does not suggest the possibility of a religious revolution, the lines quoted evoke a presence which was, for intellectuals, as unforeseen as the Islamic revolution itself.

15. Ali Shariati, *Shahadat* [Martyrdom], translated by Laleh Bakhtiar and Husayn Salih, (Tehran: The Cultural Heritage Series of the Islamic Revolution n.d.) 49.

16. Eulogy by Qa'ani, quoted in *Religious Inspiration in Iranian Art* (Tehran: Negarestan Museum, 1978) n.p.

17. Quoted in Hamid Algar, *The Roots of the Islamic Revolution* (Toronto: The Open Press, 1984) 117.

18. Lecture by professor Michael Chelkowski, McGill University, Montréal, April, 1993.

19. Shariati, *Shahadat* 76.

20. Yann Richard, *L'Islam chi'ite: Croyances et idéologies* (Paris: Fayard, 1991) 28.

21. David Morgan, *Medieval Persia: 1040-1797* (London: Longman, 1988) 141-42.

22. Ibid. 121.

23. Said Amir Arjomad, *The Shadow of God and the Hidden Imam: Religion, Political Order and Societal Change in Shi'ite Iran from the Beginning to 1890* (Chicago: University of Chicago Press, 1984) 219.

24. Ibid. 161.

25. Ibid. 34-36.

26. Hamid Algar, *The Roots of the Islamic Revolution* (London: The Open Press, 1983) 15.

27. Quoted in Morgan, *Medieval Persia* 147.

28. Ali Shariati, *Red Shi'ism*, reprinted in *Payame Haajar* (Tehran: 1992).

29. Abel Pinçon, "The Journey into Persia" in *Sir Anthony Sherley and his Persian Adventure* (London: George Routledge, 1933) 160.

30. Arthur Upham Pope, *Introducing Persian Architecture* (Tehran: Soroush Press, 1969) 10-25.

31. Quoted in Bill, *Eagle and the Lion* 184.

32. Ghanoonparvar, *Prophets* 36.

33. Quoted in Ali Rahnema and Farhad Nomani, *The Secular Miracle: Religion, Politics and Economic Policy in Iran* (London: Zed Books) 227-28.

34. Ibid. 229.

35. Algar, *Roots* 19.

36. Said Amir Arjomand, see "Ideological Revolution in Shi'ism" in *Authority and Political Culture in Shi'ism* (Albany: State University of New York Press, 1988) 193-203.

37. Rahnema, *Secular Miracle* 361.

38. Ahmad Salamatian, "La révolution iranienne broyée par ses contradictions," in *Le Monde Diplomatique* juin 1993: 20.

39. Richard, *L'Islam chi'ite* 247.

40. Interview with Bernard Hourcade, Tehran, 24 January 1993.

41. Farida Adelkhah, *La révolution sous le voile: femmes islamique d'Iran* (Paris: Éditions Karthala, 1988) 58-60; 15.

42. Ibid. 12.

43. See Hentsch, *Imagining the Middle East*.

44. Adelkhah, *La révolution sous le voile* 35-36.

45. Ibid. 54.

46. "Images of Women in the Words of Imam Khomeini" (Tehran: 1987), quoted in *Stories by Iranian Women since the Revolution*, translated from the Persian by Soraya

Paknazar Sullivan; introduction by Farzaneh Milani. Modern Middle East Literatures in Translation Series (University of Texas at Austin: Center for Middle Eastern Studies, 1991) 4.

47. Adelkhah, *La révolution sous le voile* 240.

48. Mortada Motahhari, *The Rights of Women in Islam* (Tehran: World Organization for Islamic Services, 1981) 175; 236.

49. Ali Shariati, *Fatima is Fatima* (Tehran: The Shariati Foundation, n.d.).

50. Richard N. Frye, *The Golden Age of Persia: Arabs in the East* (London: Weidenfeld and Nicholson, 1975) 2-3.

51. Ibid. 100.

52. Rypka, *History of Iranian Literature* 131.

53. Ghanoonparvar, *Prophets* 19.

54. Rypka, *History of Iranian Literature* 156-57.

55. Jalal Al-e Ahmad, *Occidentosis: A Plague From the West*, translated by Robert Campbell; introduction by Hamid Algar (Berkeley: Mizan Press, 1984) 13.

56. Ibid. 92.

57. Ibid. 53

58. Nikos Kazantzakis, *Zorba the Greek* (London: Faber and Faber, 1961) 14.

59. Oleg Grabar, *The Formation of Islamic Art* (New Haven: Yale UP, 1973) 92.

60. Terry Allen, *Five Essays on Islamic Art* (Solipsis Press) 19.

61. Ibid. 36.

62. Ibid. 34.

63. S.A. Melikian-Chirvani, "The Aesthetics of Islam" in *Treasures of Islam* (Genève/London: Sotheby's/Philip Wilson Publishers, 1985) 22.

64. *A Decade with Painters of the Islamic Revolution: 1979-1989* (Tehran: Islamic Propagation Organization, 1989) 5.

65. Ibid. 5.

66. Interview with Bernard Hourcade, Tehran, December 1990.

67. Murtada Motahhari, "Sociology of the Quran," *Al Tawhid* vol. 1 no. 3 (Apr. 1984): 139. Quoted in *Secular Miracle* 26.

68. Algar, *Roots* 49.

69. *The Observer* January, 1980

70. *Secular Miracle* 346.

71. *Secular Miracle* 333.

72. *Secular Miracle* 348.

73. *Kayhan International*, 11 Dec. 1986.

74. Hojjatoleslam Ansari, quoted in *Kayhan*, 13 Apr. 1989. Ansari, then information minister, noted that Montazeri had adopted widely varying positions on such issues as land reform, the free market economy and the Tehran subway project. But, he continued, Montazeri had always defended Hashemi as a pious man. Then he quoted a letter from Hashemi to the Ayatollah: "The system has nothing against me; I am not their target. You will see later that they will hammer your image in my name...."

75. *Secular Miracle* 355.

76. Beheshti and Bahonar, *The Philosophy of Islam* (Accra: The Islamic Seminary, 1982) 567.

77. The *Jihad* has since been restored to full ministry status, and now occupies a former hotel on Taleqani Avenue. But, like the building which houses it, the organization is only a shell of its former revolutionary self, kept alive by pressure from the weakening "radical" faction.

78. Ali Shariati, *Yea, Brother! That's the Way It Is* (Tehran: The Shariati Foundation, 1979).

79. *A Selection from Nahj al-Balaghah* (Tehran: n.d.).

80. *Secular Miracle* 100.

81. Beheshti, *Philosophy of Islam* 422.

82. Bill, *Eagle and the Lion* 98-99; 209-10.

83. Ibid. 262.

84. See Hentsch, *Imagining the Middle East*.